D1625626

030371

KNITTING IN
VOGUE

PHOTOGRAPHS BY ANTHONY CRICKMAY

KNITTING IN VOGUE

Christina Probert

DAVID & CHARLES
Newton Abbot London

F96
6MT
762.64
PRO

To my godmother Elizabeth

British Library Cataloguing in Publication Data
Probert, Christina
  Knitting in Vogue
  patterns from the '30s to
  the '80s to knit now.
  1. Knitting–Patterns
  746.9'2 TT820

ISBN 0-7153-8208-X

© The Condé Nast Publications Ltd 1982

All rights reserved. No part of this
publication may be reproduced, stored in
a retrieval system, or transmitted, in any
form or by any means, electronic,
mechanical, photocopying, recording or
otherwise, without the prior permission of
David & Charles (Publishers) Limited

Printed in The Netherlands
by Royal Smeets Offset Weert
for David & Charles (Publishers) Limited
Brunel House   Newton Abbot   Devon

Acknowledgements

I am indebted to all Vogue's knitting editors, past and present, who first commissioned the designs in this book, and to all the knitting yarn companies who were so co-operative in revising and reknitting the patterns, namely Art Needlework Industries, Chat Botte, Emu Wools, Hayfield Textiles Ltd, Jaeger Handknitting, Laines Anny Blatt, Laines Plassard, Laines Tiber, Lister-Lee (George Lee & Sons Ltd), Patons and Baldwins Ltd, Pingouin Yarns (French Wools Ltd), Richard Poppleton & Sons Ltd, Robin Wools, Sirdar Ltd, Sunbeam Yarns (Richard Ingham & Co Ltd), James Templeton & Son Ltd, 3 Suisses, H G Twilley Ltd, Wendy International. I would like to pay particular tribute to Alex Kroll, who guided the book through all its stages, to Anne Matthews whose generous help with pattern checking was invaluable, to Liz Prior for the book's design and her support throughout the project, to Anna Houghton for her patience with me and the innumerable editorial chores which arose, to Lucy Dickens for all her help in styling and organising the photographic sessions.

Colour photographs by Anthony Crickmay Colour details by Dudley Mountney Black and white photographs: Casanova 139; Donovan 71, 111; Duffy 40, 46, 107; Ferri 82; Forland 133; Himmel 77, 99; Hispard 55; Honeyman 123; Hoyningen-Huené 18, 158; Kazan 122; McCabe 90; Miles 96; Montgomery 31; Peden 58; Reinhardt 93, 150; Scavullo 101; Schiavone 128; Sieff 11; Silverstein 12; Swannell 78, 141; Vernier 38, 52. Drawings by Barbara Firth and Marion Appleton.

Hair and make-up on pages 10, 26, 52, 78, 80, 90, 97, 102, 105, 110, 117, 118, 126, 132, 144 by Pascal, on pages 12, 15, 16, 19, 22, 24, 28/9, 37, 39, 41, 42, 44, 49, 54, 57, 59, 63, 67, 73, 75, 76, 85, 87, 88, 92, 95, 98, 100, 108/109, 112, 121, 124/5, 129, 130, 135, 136, 138, 140, 143, 151, 153, 155, 156/7, 160 by Pat Lewis for Vidal Sassoon and Teresa Fairminer respectively, on pages 21, 32/3, 34, 47, 51, 60, 64, 68/9, 148/9 by Trevor at Colombe and Arianne respectively.

Clothes and accessories by Giorgio Armani, Laura Ashley, Charles Batten, Benetton, Browns, Butler and Wilson, Chevy, Lawrence Corner, Corocraft, Elle, Fenwicks, Fenn Wright & Manson, Maud Frizon, Margaret Howell, Herbert Johnson, Joseph, Calvin Klein, Ralph Lauren, John Marks, Mulberry, Andre Peters, Mary Quant, Ritva Westenius, Russell and Bromley, Sacha, Scotch House, Sunarama, Tatters, Charles de Temple, Walkers. Sequins on page 63 courtesy of Ells and Farrier. International Textile Care Labelling Code courtesy of the Home Laundering Consultative Council.

Contents

Introduction

The popularity of handknitting has waxed and waned during the twentieth century. Knitting moved into high fashion in the late twenties as designers like Elsa Schiaparelli produced exciting new knitwear in keeping with the lively, sportswear-orientated fashion atmosphere. Vogue began to publish knitting patterns and in 1932 launched Vogue's Knitting Book, the first of a series which became renowned for its high fashion designs, and for the reliability of its pattern instructions.

Even in wartime, Vogue continued to produce fashionable knitting ideas, albeit more economical than they had once been. The shortsleeved sweater, for example, was rendered fashionable by necessity. Vogue even instructed readers in the art of unravelling old sweaters and cardigans ready to reknit the yarn into the current shapes. When handknitting yarns were brought under coupon control, Vogue published patterns which used 'standard' weight yarns, to allow greatest flexibility to the reader. But luxury did return: the fifties brought a spate of thick mohair cardigans and sweaters, sloppy joes, chunky windcheaters, Arans. In direct contrast to wartime knits, everything was generously cut, designed with little regard for economy.

Handknitting began to lose popularity as the mood, and the look, of fashion in the sixties became streamlined, space-age. Vogue produced sculptured, clean-cut knitting designs in fine yarns, many with lacy, intricate patterns, and, in another vein, ultra-bulky shapes in the new light Bri-Nylon yarns. The latter shapes were a passing phase, the former were gradually replaced by machine knits — the practical skill needed to knit them having become unfashionable. The Vogue Knitting Book stopped at this time, too, and it was not until the late seventies and the return of the back-to-nature, homespun look, that handknits moved back into fashion.

Now handknitting is again as popular as it was in the twenties. The extensive, colourful range of yarns available and the current trend towards all the creative crafts have re-established knitting's fashionable image. The newest knitting patterns reflect fashion's current blend of modern design with nostalgia for past fashions.

This book contains a selection of Vogue originals, a wide variety of knitting patterns which Vogue has published since 1935. They are categorised both according to type and to difficulty: patterns marked * are suitable for beginners, ** for knitters with some previous experience, and *** for experienced knitters. There is a knitting know-how section at the end of the book to help complete beginners, and to refresh the memories of those who have already learnt to knit.

Each pattern is illustrated by two photographs: the original version in black and white, and the same design in colour, fashionably accessorised and reknitted in the modern yarn quality. Some designs have an additional colour stitch detail. All the pattern instructions have been checked and updated, to ensure that you can achieve complete success with each, for the style of knitting instructions as well as the yarn qualities have changed considerably. The designs themselves, however, remain unchanged.

The yarns used have been chosen to correspond as closely as possible in weight and character to the originals. The manufacturers of the yarns recommended in the patterns cannot take any responsibility for the success of the designs unless you knit to the tension specified, with the yarn given in the pattern. If you are an experienced knitter, and want to adapt a pattern to another yarn, or if the yarn suggested is not available, you must test your tension until you achieve that given in the tension section of the pattern, as knitting patterns are designed on the basis of a fixed tension. If the tension is not correct, the garment sizing will not be as specified in the pattern, and the proportions of any patterned stitches will alter.

Unless a pattern is designed in one size only, sizes are given in increasing order, both in the measurement section and throughout the pattern. Where only one instruction is given, in a multi-size pattern, it applies to all sizes. In many patterns, too, the sleeve seam measurement is identical for all sizes, thus only one measurement is given. Unless otherwise stated, all back measurements are taken from centre back neck to hem. Underlining all the instructions for the size you are knitting, in pencil, before you begin to knit helps to prevent mistakes, and it is a good idea, too, to read through the pattern instructions and the note, where this occurs, as these contain the details which you will need to know about the pattern.

Alterations to patterns can be undertaken with caution, but care must be taken not to distort the proportions of the garment. Sleeve lengths are simplest to alter: this should be done after the increasing, just before casting off stitches for the armhole. Length alterations to the body of the garment can usually be carried out after the side increases, before the armhole. Where the garment is worked in pattern, ensure that you end at the underarm on the same pattern row as that given in the unaltered pattern. Mark each part of the garment affected by alterations, so that you remember to alter each. Do not attempt to alter any garment in a complicated pattern, or any tailored patterns unless you are very experienced, and remember that alterations which increase length may also increase the yarn requirement.

The demand for knitting patterns is again as great as when the Vogue Knitting Book began. As Vogue said of that first Knitting Book, this book 'should keep the quickest worker occupied for some time.'!

Aran-style polo neck sweater 1976. Instructions on page 80.

Thick Tri-colour Windjammer

Hip-length, very warm sweater, worked in three-coloured pattern, with set-in sleeves and wide, patterned, doubled-over collar

★★★ Suitable for experienced knitters only

MATERIALS

Yarn
Laines Plassard Harmonieuse
5 × 75g. skeins Col. A (Sansas 38)
4 × 75g. skeins Col. B (Tuba 12)
4 × 75g. skeins Col. C (Hautbois 14)

Needles
1 pair 6½mm.

MEASUREMENTS

Bust
82(87:92:97) cm.
32(34:36:38) in.

Length
60(61:61:62) cm.
23½(24:24:24¼) in.

Sleeve Seam
46 cm.
18 in.

TENSION

9 sts. and 15 rows = 10 cm. (4 in.) square over stocking stitch on 6½mm. needles. If your tension square does not correspond to these measurements see page 166 for adjustment instructions.

ABBREVIATIONS

k. = knit; p. = purl; st(s). = stitch(es); inc. = increas(ing) (see page 166); dec. = decreas-(ing) (see page 167); beg. = begin(ning); rem. = remain(ing); rep. = repeat; alt. = alternate; tog. = together; sl. = slip stitch (transfer one stitch from left needle, knitwise unless otherwise stated, to right hand needle.); cont. = continue; patt. = pattern; foll. = following; folls. = follows; mm. = millimetres; cm. = centimetre(s); in. = inch(es); y.fwd. = yarn forward; y.bk. = yarn back; y.r.n. = yarn round needle: bring yarn over needle from front to back and then under needle; Col. = colour.

BACK

Cast on 38(40:42:44) sts. with A, using thumb method (see page 164).
Work one row in k.1, p.1 rib.
Next row: with C, k.1, * y.fwd., sl.1 purlwise, k.1, rep. from * to last st., k.1.
NB. *y.fwd. makes a crossed loop over the sl.st.*
Now work in patt. as folls.:
1st row: with B, p.1 * y.bk., sl.1, y.fwd., p.tog. the made st. and the sl.st., rep. from * to last st., p.1.

2nd row: with A, k.1, * y.fwd., sl. the B st., k. the C st., rep. from * to last st., k.1.
3rd row: with C, p.1, * sl. the A st., y.r.n., p. tog. the B and A sts., rep. from * to last st., p.1.
4th row: with B, k.1, * y.fwd., sl. the C st., y.bk., k. tog. the A and C sts., rep. from * to last st., k.1.
5th row: with A, p.1, * sl. the B st., y.r.n., p. the C st., rep. from * to last st., p.1.
6th row: with C, k.1, * y.fwd., sl. the A st., k. tog. the A and B sts., rep. from * to last st., k.1.
These 6 rows form the patt.
Cont. in patt. for another 5 rows.
** Inc. 1 st. each end of next row.
Cont. in patt. for 11 rows, but starting and ending each row with p.2, k.2 alternately.
Inc. 1 st. at each end of next row.
Next row: p.1, y.bk., sl.1, y.fwd., p.1, * y.bk., sl.1, y.fwd., p. tog. the made st. and the sl.st. Rep. from * to last 3 sts., y.bk., sl.l., y.fwd., p.2.
Cont. in patt. for 10 rows.
Inc. 1 st. each end of next row. **
Rep. from ** to ** until there are 46(48:50:52) sts.
Work until back measures 40 cm. (15¾ in.).

Shape Armholes
Cast off 2(2:3:3) sts. at beg. of next 2 rows.
Dec. 1 st. at each end of every alt. row until 36(36:38:38) sts. rem.
Work until armholes measure 18(18:19:20) cm. (7(7:7½:7¾)in.) on the straight.

Shape Shoulders
Cast off 2 sts. at beg. of next 8 rows, then 2(2:3:3) sts. at beg. of foll. 2 rows.
Cast off rem. 16 sts. *loosely.*

FRONT

Work as for back until armholes measure 13(13:14:14) cm. (5(5:5½:5½) in.) on the straight.

Shape Upper Armhole and Neck
Inc. 1 st. each end of next and foll. 4th row.
Work 1 row.
Next row: work 17(17:18:18) sts., cast off 6 sts., work to end. Finish this side first.
1st and alt. rows: patt.
2nd row: cast off 2 sts., patt. to last st., work twice into it.
4th row: cast off 2 sts., patt. to end.
6th row: work 2 tog., work to last st., work twice into last st.
8th row: work 2 tog., work to end.
9th row: work to end.
Rep. 8th and 9th rows once more [12(12:13:13) sts.]

Work 3 rows. Cast off *loosely.*
Join wool to neck edge of rem. sts. and complete in same way.

SLEEVES

Cast on 20(20:22:22) sts. with A.
Work 1 row in k.1, p.1 rib.
Now work in patt. as for back, working rows 1 to 6, and then from ** to **.
Rep. from ** to ** until there are 30(32:34:34) sts.
Work until sleeve measures 46 cm. (18 in.)

Shape Top
Cast off 2(2:3:3) sts. at beg. of next 2 rows.
Dec. 1 st. at each end of every 3rd row until 22 sts. rem., then every 4th row until 16 sts. rem.
Dec. 1 st. each end of next 3 rows.
Cast off *loosely.*

COLLAR

Cast on 54(54:56:56) sts. loosely with A.
Work 16 cm. (6¼ in.) in patt. (rows 1 to 6 inclusive of back).
Cast off *loosely.*

MAKING UP

Sew straight cast off edges of front shoulders to sloped edges of upper back.
Set in sleeves, ensuring that shoulder seam slopes slightly to back.
Sew side and sleeve seams.
Join collar to form circle, pin to neck with right side of collar to wrong side of jumper, and collar seam at centre back. Oversew seam, fold collar in half and slipstitch to seam just made, outside. Take care not to stretch neck, and to sew seam and slipstitching loosely. DO NOT PRESS.

Garter-stitch Round-neck Sweater 1981

Simple sweater in garter stitch with wide round neck, set-in sleeves and ribbed welts, knitted in velour

★ Suitable for beginners

MATERIALS

Yarn
Laines Tiber Coton Velours
9(10:11) × 50g. balls

Needles
1 pair 3¾mm.
1 pair 5mm.
2 stitch holders

MEASUREMENTS

Bust
78–80(82–87:92–97) cm.
30–31(32–34:36–38) in.

Length
58(59.5:62) cm.
22¾(23¼:24¼) in.

Sleeve Seam
43(44.5:44.5) cm.
16¾(17½:17½) in.

TENSION

16 sts. and 36 rows = 10 cm. (4 in.) square over pattern on 5mm. needles. If your tension square does not correspond to these measurements see page 166 for adjustment instructions.

ABBREVIATIONS

k. = knit; p. = purl; st(s). = stitch(es); inc. = increas(ing) (see page 166); dec. = decreas-(ing) (see page 167); beg. = begin(ning); rem. = remain(ing); rep. = repeat; alt. = alternate; tog. = together; sl. = slip stitch (transfer one stitch from left needle, knit-wise unless otherwise stated, to right hand needle.); cont. = continue; patt. = pattern; foll. = following; folls. = follows; mm. = millimetres; cm. = centimetre(s); in. = inch(es); g.st. = garter stitch (every row k.).

BACK

Cast on 69(77:85) sts. with 3¾mm. needles.
1st row (right side): k.1, * p.1., k.1, rep. from * to end.
2nd row: p.1, * k.1, p.1, rep. from * to end.
Rep. these 2 rows for 7.5 cm. (3 in.), ending with a 2nd row.

Change to 5mm. needles and work in g.st. until work measures 39(40:42) cm. (15¼(15¾:16½) in.) from beg. or desired length to underarm.

Shape Armholes
Cast off 4(4:5) sts. at beg. of next 2 rows. Dec. 1 st. at each edge on every alt. row 3(4:4) times. [55(61:67) sts.]
Work straight until armholes measure 16.5(17:18) cm. (6¼ (6½:7) in.), ending on wrong side.

Shape Neck
Next row (right side): k.11(13:15) sts., place next 33(35:37) sts. on holder, join another ball of yarn and k. to end. Working both sets of stitches on same needles, and working 1 row on each alternately, dec. 1 st. at each neck edge every other row twice. [9(11:13) sts. each side.] Work sides evenly until 19(19.5:20) cm. (7½(7½:7¾) above marked row.

Shape Shoulder
Cast off rem. 9(11:13) sts. on each side.

FRONT

Work same as for back until armholes measure 9(9.5:10) cm. (3½(3¾:4) in.) ending on wrong side.

Shape Neck
Next row (right side): k.16(18:20) sts., place next 23(25:27) sts. on holder, join another ball of yarn and k. to end. Working both sets of sts. on same needles, as before, dec. 1 st. at each neck edge on every alt. row 7 times. [9(11:13) sts. each side.]
Work sides evenly until armholes measure 19(19.5:20) cm. (7½(7½:7¾) in.) above marked row.

Shape Shoulder
Cast off rem. 9(11:13) sts. on each side.

SLEEVES

Cast on 31(35:39) sts. with 3¾mm. needles. Work in ribbing as for back for 6 cm. (2¼ in). Change to 5mm. needles and work in g.st, inc. 1 st. at each edge every 2.5 cm. (1 in.) 12 times, incorporating sts. in g.st. [55(59:63) sts.]
Work straight until sleeve measures 43(44.5:44.5) cm. (16¾(17½:17½ in.) from beg. or desired length to underarm, ending on wrong side.

Shape Top
Cast off 4(4:5) sts. at beg. of next 2 rows. Dec. 1 st. at each edge every 4th row 3 times, then every other row 14(16:17) times. Cast off rem. 13 sts.

NECKBAND

Sew right shoulder seam.
With right side facing, starting at front right, with 3¾mm. needle, pick up 98(102:106) sts. around neck edge including sts. on holders.
Work in k.1, p.1 rib for 3 cm. (1¼ in.).
Cast off loosely, ribwise.

MAKING UP

Sew up left shoulder seam.
Sew in sleeves using backstitch matching 4 cast off sts. at beg. of sleeve and armhole shaping.
Sew up side and sleeve seams.

Simply Cabled Fine Wool Sweater

Just below waist-length sweater with set-in sleeves, round neck with doubled-over welt, in cable pattern throughout

★★ Suitable for knitters with some previous experience

MATERIALS

Yarn
Lister-Lee Machine Washable Motoravia 4 ply
8(9) × 50g. balls

Needles
1 pair 2¾mm.
1 pair 3¼mm.
1 cable needle

MEASUREMENTS

Bust
82–87(92–97) cm.
32–34(36–38) in.

Length (from shoulder)
61(62) cm.
24(24¼) in.

Sleeve Seam
43(46) cm.
16¾(18) in.

TENSION

16 sts. and 18 rows = 5 cm. (2 in.) square over pattern on 3¼mm. needles. If your tension square does not correspond to these measurements, see page 166 for adjustment instructions.

ABBREVIATIONS

k. = knit; p. = purl; st(s). = stitch(es); inc. = increas(ing) (see page 166); dec. = decreas-(ing) (see page 167); beg. = begin(ning); rem. = remain(ing); rep. = repeat; alt. = alternate; tog. = together; sl. = slip stitch (transfer one stitch from left needle, knit-wise unless otherwise stated, to right hand needle.); cont. = continue; patt. = pattern; foll. = following; folls. = follows; mm. = millimetres; cm. = centimetre(s); in. = inch(es); C8 = cable 8: slip next 4 sts. onto cable needle and leave at front of work, k.4, then k.4 from cable needle.

BACK

Cast on 144(160) sts. with 2¾mm. needles.
1st row: * k.1, p.2, k.1, rep. from * to end.
2nd row: * p.1, k.2, p.1, rep. from * to end.
These 2 rows form rib. Cont. until work measures 8 cm. (3 in.), inc. 2 sts. during last row for first size only. [144(160) sts.]
Change to 3¼mm. needles.
1st row: * p.2, k.2, p.2, k.8, rep. from * to last 6 sts., p.2, k.2, p.2.
2nd row: * k.2, p.2, k.2, p.8, rep. from * to last 6 sts., k.2, p.2, k.2.
Rep. 1st and 2nd rows once.
5th row: * p.2, k.2, p.2, C8, rep. from * to last 6 sts., p.2, k.2, p.2.
6th row: as 2nd row.
Rep. 1st and 2nd rows twice more.
These 10 rows form the patt. Cont. until work measures 41 cm. (16 in.)

Shape Armholes

Cast off 5 sts. at beg. of next 2 rows. Dec. 1 st. at each end of every row until 112(126) sts. rem. ** Now cont. in patt. until work measures 61(62) cm. (24(24¼) in.).

Shape Shoulders

Cast off 8(9) sts. at beg. of next two rows.
Cast off 8(10) sts. at beg. of next 6 rows.
Leave rem. 48 sts. on spare needle or stitch holder for neckband.

FRONT

Work as back to **.
Cont. in patt. until work measures 56(58) cm. (22(22¾) in.).

Shape Neck

Patt. 43(50) sts., leave next 26 sts. on spare needle or holder for neckband and rem. 43(50) sts. on another holder or needle for other side.
Cont. in patt. on first set of sts., dec. 1 st. at neck edge on every row until 32(39) sts. rem.
Cont. without shaping until work meas-

ures same as back to shoulder, ending with a wrong side row.

Shape Shoulder

Cast off 8(9) sts. at beg. of next row.
Work 1 row.
Cast off 8(10) sts. at beg of next and foll. alt. rows.
Rejoin yarn to sts. left for other side and cont. in patt., dec. 1 st. at neck edge on every row until 32(39) sts. rem. Cont. without shaping until work measures same as left side to shoulder, ending with a right side row.
Shape shoulder as for left front.

SLEEVES

Cast on 68(72) sts. with 2¾mm. needles and work 8 cm. (3 in.) in k.2, p.2 rib, inc. 4 sts. evenly across last row. [72(76) sts.]
Change to 3¼mm. needles.
1st row: p.0(2), k.2, p.2, k.8, * p.2, k.2, p.2, k.8, rep. from * to last 4(6) sts., p.2, k.2, p.0(2).
2nd row: k.0(2), p.2, k.2, p.8, * k.2, p.2, k.2, p.8, rep. from * to last 4(6) sts., k.2, p.2, k.0(2).
Cont. in patt. as for back, inc. 1 st. each end of every 6th row until there are 102(112) sts., incorporating extra sts. into patt.
Cont. straight until work measures 43(46) cm. (16¾(18) in.).

Shape Sleeve Top

Cast off 5 sts. at beg. of next 2 rows. Dec. 1 st. at each end of every right side row until 48(52) sts. rem.
Dec. 1 st. at each end of every row until 22(24) sts. rem.
Cast off.

NECKBAND

Sew up right shoulder seam.
With 2¾mm. needles, pick up and knit 21 sts. down left side of front, knit the 26 sts. on spare needle or holder, pick up and knit 21 sts. up right side of front and knit across 48 sts. of back on holder or spare needle. [116 sts.]
Work 8 cm. (3 in.) in k.2, p.2 rib, starting with a 2nd row.
Cast off loosely in rib.

MAKING UP

Sew right shoulder and neckband seam.
Fold neckband in half onto wrong side and slipstitch neatly in position along picked up stitch seam.
Sew up side and sleeve seams.
Set in sleeves.
Press as instructions on ball band.

Diagonal Pattern Shirt Blouse

1933

Fine wool, yoked shirt blouse with buttoned front placket and collar, reaching just below the waist, worked in diagonal rib pattern

★★ Suitable for knitters with some previous experience

MATERIALS

Yarn
Wendy Shetland 4 ply
11(11:12) × 25g. balls

Needles
1 pair 2¾mm. 1 pair 3¼mm.
1 set of 4 3¼mm. (pointed each end)

Buttons
2

MEASUREMENTS

Bust
87(92:97) cm.
34(36:38) in.

Length
49(52:54) cm.
19¼(20½:21¼) in.

Sleeve Seam
49.5 cm.
19½ in.

TENSION

27 sts. and 36 rows = 10 cm. (4 in.) square over diagonal rib on 3¼mm. needles. If your tension square does not correspond to these measurements, see page 166 for adjustment instructions.

ABBREVIATIONS

k. = knit; p. = purl; st(s). = stitch(es); inc. = increas(ing) (see page 166); dec. = decreas-(ing) (see page 167); beg. = begin(ning); rem. = remain(ing); rep. = repeat; alt. = alternate; tog. = together; sl. = slip stitch (transfer one stitch from left needle, knit-wise unless otherwise stated, to right hand needle.); cont. = continue; patt. =

pattern; foll. = following; folls. = follows; mm. = millimetres; cm. = centimetre(s); in. = inch(es); g.st = garter stitch.

BACK

Cast on 128(136:144) sts. using 2¾mm. needles.
Work in k.3, p.1 rib as folls. for 5 cm. (2 in.).
1st row: * k.3, p.1, rep. from * to end.
2nd row: * k.1, p.3, rep. from * to end.
Change to 3¼mm. needles and diagonal rib as folls.:
1st row: * k.3, p.1, rep. from * to end.
2nd row: * k.1, p.3, rep. from * to end.
3rd row: * k.2, p.1, k.1, rep. from * to end.
4th row: * p.1, k.1, p.2, rep. from * to end.
5th row: * k.1, p.1, k.2, rep. from * to end.
6th row: * p.2, k.1, p.1, rep. from * to end.
7th row: * p.1, k.3, rep. from * to end.
8th row: * p.3, k.1, rep. from * to end.
These 8 rows form the patt.
Cont. straight until work measures 27 cm. (10½ in.), ending with a wrong side row.

Shape Armholes
Cast off 9 sts. at beg. of next 2 rows, then dec. 1 st. at beg. of foll. 8 rows [102(110:118) sts.]
Leave sts. on a spare needle.

FRONT

Work as given for back until work measures 23 cm. (9 in.), ending with a wrong side row.
Divide for front opening:
Patt. 64(68:72) sts., turn. Leave rem. sts. on a spare needle.
Complete left side as folls.:
Cast on 2 sts., k.2, patt. to end.
Cont. straight, working the 2 cast on sts. in g.st. and rest in patt., until work measures 27 cm. (10½ in.), ending with a wrong side row.

Shape Armhole
Cast off 9 sts. at beg. of next row, then dec. 1 st. at beg. of foll. 4 alt. rows, [53(57:61) sts.]
Patt. 1 row and leave sts. on a spare needle.
Cast on 2 sts., patt. across sts. left on spare needle, beg. at centre front, to end.
Complete to match left side reversing shaping and omitting last row.

SLEEVES

Cast on 47(47:51) sts. using 2¾mm. needles and work 11 cm.(4¼ in.) in k.3, p.1 rib, arranging sts. as folls.:
1st row: * k.3, p.1, rep. from * to last 3 sts. k.3.

2nd row: * p.3, k.1, rep. from * to last 3 sts., p.3.
Change to 3¼mm. needles and diagonal rib, inc. 1 st. each end of every 6th row until there are 87(87:95) sts.
Cont. straight until work measures 49.5 cm. (19½ in.), ending with a wrong side row.

Shape Top
Cast off 19 sts. at beg. of next 2 rows.
Leave rem. 49(49:57) sts. on spare needle.
Work second sleeve in same way.

YOKE

With four 3¼mm. needles and right side facing, rejoin yarn to right side of front, k.2, work in k.3, p.1 rib across the sts. of right front, sleeve, back, left sleeve and left front to last 2 sts., k.2. [306(322:354) sts.]
Next row: k.2, k.2 tog., rib 71(75:83) sts., p.2 tog., k.1, p.2 tog., rib 146(154:170) sts., p.2 tog., k.1, p.2 tog., rib to last 4 sts., k.2 tog., k.2.
Next row: k.2, rib to last 2 sts., k.2.
Next row: k.2, k.2 tog., rib (69:73:81) sts., p.2 tog., k.1, p.2 tog., rib 144(152:168) sts., p.2 tog., k.1, p.2 tog., rib to last 4 sts., k.2 tog., k.2.
Next row: k.2, rib to last 2 sts., k.2.
Keeping rib correct, cont. to dec. 6 sts. on alt. rows in this way until 222(232:258) sts. rem., ending with a wrong side row.

Shape Shoulders and Neck
Work 51(53:59) sts., turn.
Leave rem. 171(179:199) sts. on spare needle.
Complete right front as folls.:
1st row: cast off 2 sts., rib to last 4 sts., k.2 tog., k.2.
2nd row: patt. to end.
Rep. these 2 rows until 12(14:20) sts. rem.
Cont. casting off 2 sts. at shoulder edge on

every alt. row until 2 sts. rem. Cast off.
With right side facing, rejoin yarn to sts. left on spare needle. Cast off 2 sts., rib 117(123:137) sts., turn.
Leave rem. 51(53:59) sts. on a spare needle.
Complete back as folls.:
Cast off 2 sts. at beg. of every row until 44(44:48) sts. rem.
Next row: * k.2, k.2 tog., rep. from * to end.
Cast off.
With right side facing, rejoin yarn to sts. left on spare needle.
Cast off 2 sts., rib to last 2 sts., k.2.
Complete to match right front, reversing shapings.

COLLAR

Cast on 14 sts. using 2¾mm. needles.
Working in g.st. throughout, cont. straight until work measures 3 cm. (1¼ in.).
Work buttonhole: k.6, cast off 2 sts., k. to end.
Next row: cast on 2 sts. over those cast off in previous row.
When work measures 7 cm. (2¾ in.), work second buttonhole, repeating two buttonhole rows above.
Next row: k.6, inc. in next st., k. to end.
Inc. 1 st. in the centre of work every 6(7:7.5) cm. (2¼(2¾:3) in.) until 18 sts. are obtained. Work 23(24:24) cm. (9(9½:9½) in.) straight, then dec. 1 st. in the centre of work on next row and every foll. 6(7:7.5) cm. (2¼(2¾:3) in.), until 14 sts. rem. Cast off.

MAKING UP

Sew up shoulder seams. Sew up sleeve under-arm.
Sew up sleeve and side seams.
Attach collar (left side of collar will end at neck slit), with neat slipstitch on right side, so that seam will be hidden by collar.
Sew on buttons.

Crossover, Waist-length Blouse   1932

Lacy, cotton blouse worked in two yarn thicknesses, with short sleeves, crossover bands at waist, yoke worked on circular needle

★★ Suitable for knitters with some previous experience

MATERIALS

Yarn
Pingouin Coton Naturel 4 ply
2(3:3) × 50g. balls
Pingouin Coton Naturel 8 fils
4(5:5) × 50g. balls

Needles
1 pair long double-ended 7mm.
1 circular 7mm.
1 3mm. crochet hook

MEASUREMENTS

Bust
87(92:97) cm.
34(36:38) in.

Length
44(45:46) cm.
17¼(17¾:18) in.

Sleeve Seam
15 cm. (5¾) in.

TENSION

13 stitches and 18 rows = 10 cm. (4 in.) square over pattern on 7mm. needles. If your tension square does not correspond to these measurements, see page 166 for adjustment instructions.

ABBREVIATIONS

k. = knit; p. = purl; st(s). = stitch(es); inc. = increas(ing) (see page 166); dec. = decreas-(ing) (see page 167); beg. = begin(ning); rem. = remain(ing); rep. = repeat; alt. = alternate; tog. = together; sl. = slip stitch (transfer one stitch from left needle, knit-wise unless otherwise stated, to right hand needle.); cont. = continue; patt. = pattern; foll. = following; folls. = follows; mm. = millimetres; cm. = centimetre(s); in. = inch(es); m.st. = moss stitch.

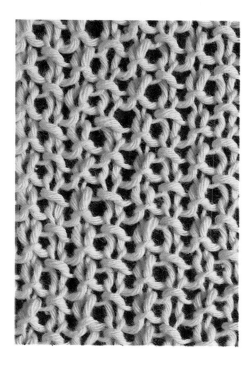

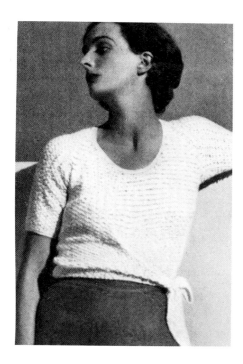

BACK

Cast on 59(63:67) sts. with the two needles and thick yarn and work in m.st. patt., working 1 row in thin yarn and 1 row in thick yarn, as folls.:

1st row (right side): using thin yarn k.1, * p.1, k.1, rep. from * to end. Return to other end of needle where the thick yarn is hanging.

2nd row (right side): with thick yarn p.1, * k.1, p.1, rep. from * to end.

3rd row (wrong side): with thin yarn p.1, * k.1, p.1, rep. from * to end. Return to other end of needle.

4th row (wrong side): with thick yarn k.1, * p.1, k.1, rep. from * to end. These 4 rows form one patt.

Cont. until you have worked 48 rows in patt. thus ending with a 4th patt. row. Cut yarns and leave these sts.

RIGHT FRONT & BELT

Cast on 87(89:91) sts. using thick yarn. Work in patt. as on back for 8 rows.

9th row (right side): with thin yarn cast off 58 sts. loosely, m.st. to end.

Cont. in patt. on rem. 29(31:33) sts., rejoining thick yarn, until you have worked 24 rows from beg., thus ending at the edge where belt sts. were cast off. Cut yarns.

LEFT FRONT & BELT

Cast on 133(135:137) sts. using thick yarn and work in patt. for 8 rows.

9th row: with thin yarn m.st. 29(31:33) then cast off rem. 104 sts. loosely and fasten off.

Return to other end of needle for 10th row and cont. in patt., rejoining thin yarn, until you have worked 24 rows in patt. from beg.

25th row: With thin yarn patt. 29(31:33) sts., turn, cast on 1 st., turn, then patt. 29(31:33) sts. of right front.

Cont. in patt. on these 59(63:67) sts. for a further 22 rows.

Shape Neck

48th row (wrong side): m.st. the 27(29:31) sts. of right front, cast off 5 sts., m.st. to end. Place the 2 groups of 27(29:31) sts. on separate holders.

SLEEVES

Cast on 35(39:41) sts. with the 2 needles and thick yarn and work in patt. as on back, but inc. 1 st. at both ends of every 6th row four times, working sts. into patt. [43(47:49) sts.]

Cont. until 28 rows have been worked in patt. Cut yarns and leave sts.

YOKE

With right side of all parts facing, circular needle and thin yarn, work as folls.:

1st row: join yarn to neck edge of right front sts., m.st. 26(28:30), k. rem. st. tog. with 1st st. of one sleeve, m.st. 41(45:47), k. rem. st. tog. with 1st st. of back, m.st. 57(61:65), k. rem. st. tog. with 1st st. of second sleeve, m.st. 41(45:47), k. rem. st. tog. with 1st st. of left front, m.st. 26(28:30). [195(211:223) sts.]

Return to other end of needle, join in thick yarn and rep. 2nd patt. row. Turn at end of row.

3rd row (wrong side): with thin yarn m.st. 23(25:27), k.2 tog., m.st. 3, k.2 tog., m.st. 35(39:41), k.2 tog., m.st. 3, k.2 tog., m.st. 51(55:59), k.2 tog., m.st. 3, k.2 tog., m.st. 35(39:41), k.2 tog., m.st. 3, k.2 tog., m.st. 23(25:27).

4th row (wrong side): m.st. with thick yarn working p.1 over each dec.

5th row (right side): with thin yarn p.2 tog., m.st. 20(22:24), k.2 tog., m.st. 3, k.2 tog., m.st. 33(37:39), k.2 tog., m.st. 3, k.2 tog., m.st. 49(53:57), k.2 tog., m.st. 3, k.2 tog., m.st. 33(37:39), k.2 tog., m.st. 3, k.2 tog., m.st. 20(22:24), p.2 tog.

6th row (right side): with thick yarn work in m.st.

Rep. 3rd row to 6th rows 6(7:7) times more, then 3rd and 4th rows again for the small and large sizes only, N.B. Work 2 sts. fewer between decs. on sleeves and back each time, dec. at front edge every 2nd dec. row so as to keep the sleeve and back decs. above each other to form a raglan line.

Cast off rem. 61(67:71) sts. using thick yarn.

MAKING UP

Join side and sleeve seams. With the crochet hook work 4 rounds of double crochet around neck and sleeve edges, using the thin yarn.

Fine Wool T-shirt Sweater

Long, slim sweater in stocking stitch, with ribbed welts, collar and buttoned neck placket, and set-in sleeves

★ Suitable for beginners

MATERIALS

Yarn
Jaeger Botany wool 3 ply
9(9:10:11) × 25g. balls

Needles
1 pair 2¼mm.
1 pair 3mm.

Buttons
3

MEASUREMENTS

Bust
82(87:92:97) cm.
32(34:36:38) in.

Length
60(61:62:63) cm.
23½(24:24¼:24¾) in.

Sleeve
44(44:45:45) cm.
17¼(17¼:17¾:17¾) in.

TENSION

16 sts. and 20 rows = 5 cm. (2 in.) square over stocking stitch on 3mm. needles. If your tension square does not correspond to these measurements, see page 166 for adjustment instructions.

ABBREVIATIONS

k. = knit; p. = purl; st(s). = stitch(es); inc. = increas(ing) (see page 166); dec. = decreas-(ing) (see page 167); beg. = begin(ning); rem. = remain(ing); rep. = repeat; alt. = alternate; tog. = together; sl. = slip stitch (transfer one stitch from left needle, knit-wise unless otherwise stated, to right hand needle.); cont. = continue; patt. = pattern; foll. = following; folls. = follows; mm. = millimetres; cm. = centimetre(s); in. = inch(es); p.s.s.o. = pass the slipped stitch over; t.b.l. = through back of loops; st.st. = stocking stitch; sl.1k. = slip one stitch knitwise.

BACK

**Cast on 139(147:155:163) sts. with 2¼ mm. needles.
1st row: k.2, * p.1, k.1, rep. from * to the last st., k.1.

2nd row: * k.1, p.1, rep. from * to the last st., k.1.
Rep. 1st and 2nd rows for 8 cm. (3¼ in.), ending with 2nd row.
Change to 3mm. needles and st.st. Work until back measures 39(41:41:42) cm. (15¼(16:16:16½) in.) from beg., ending with a p. row. **

Shape Armholes

Cast off 2(4:5:7) sts. at beg. of next 2 rows.
3rd row: k.3, sl.1k., k.1, p.s.s.o., k. to last 5 sts., k.2 tog., k.3. Work 3 rows.
Cont. to dec. in this way at each end of next row, and then every 4th row until 109(113:117:121) sts. rem. Work 21(21:21:23) rows.

Shape Shoulders

Cast off at beg. of next and foll. rows, 6(7:8:7) sts. twice, 7(7:7:8) sts. 6 times, and 7(8:8:8) sts. twice.
Cast off 41(41:43:43) rem. sts. for back of neck.

FRONT

Follow instructions for back from ** to **.

Shape Armholes

Cast off 2(4:5:7) sts. at beg. of next 2 rows.
3rd row: k.3, sl.1k., k.1, p.s.s.o., k. to last 5 sts., k.2 tog., k.3.
4th to 6th rows: Work in st.st.
7th row: As 3rd row.

Shape Front Opening

Next row: p.63(65:68:70) sts., cast off 5 sts., p. to end. Cont. on last set of sts. Work 2 rows.
Next row: k.3, sl.1k., k.1, p.s.s.o., k. to end. Cont. to dec. in this way at beg. of every 4th row until 52(54:56:58) sts. rem. Work 5(5:3:5) rows.

Shape Neck

Next row: k. to last 5 sts., cast off these sts. Break yarn. Turn and rejoin yarn at neck edge. Dec. 1 st. at neck edge on the next 7 rows, and then the 4(4:5:5) foll. alt. rows, ending at armhole edge.

Shape Shoulder

Dec. at neck edge of foll. alt. rows twice more, and at the same time cast off 6(7:8:7) sts. at beg. of next row, and 7(7:7:8) sts. at beg. of 3 foll. alt. rows. Work 1 row. Cast off 7(8:8:8) rem. sts.
Rejoin yarn to rem. sts. at opening edge. Work 2 rows.
Next row: k. to last 5 sts., k.2 tog., k.3. Cont. to dec. in this way at end of every 4th row until 52(54:56:58) sts. rem. Work 5(5:3:5) rows.

Shape Neck

Next row: cast off 5 sts., k. to end.
Now complete to match first side, working 1 row more before shaping shoulder.

SLEEVES

Cast on 63(65:67:69) sts. with 2¼mm. needles and work 8 cm. (3¼ in.) in rib as for back.
Change to 3mm. needles and st.st. Work 4 rows.
Inc. 1 st. at each end of next row, and then every 6th row until there are 77(81:91:95) sts., and then every 8th row until there are 97(101:105:109) sts. Work until sleeve measures 44(44:45:45) cm. (17¼(17¼:17¾:17¾) in.) from beg., ending with a p. row.

Shape Top

Cast off 2(4:5:7) sts. at beg. of next 2 rows.
3rd row: k.3, sl.1k., k.1, p.s.s.o., k. to last 5 sts., k.2 tog., k.3.
4th row: p.3, p.2 tog., p. to last 5 sts., p.2 tog. t.b.l., p.3. Rep. 3rd and 4th rows 5(5:4:4) times more.
Next row: as 3rd row.
Next row: p. Rep. last 2 rows until 37 sts. rem., ending with dec. row.

Cont. as folls.:
1st row: p.2 tog., p. to last 2 sts., p.2 tog.
2nd row: k.2 tog., k. to last 2 sts., k.2 tog.
Rep. 1st and 2nd rows once more, and then 1st row once.
Cast off rem. sts.

RIGHT FRONT BAND

With 2¾mm. needles and right side of work facing, knit up 45 sts. down left front opening edge. (9 sts. for 10 rows).
1st row: * k.1, p.1, rep. from * to the last st., k.1.
2nd row: k.2, * p.1, k.1, rep. from * to the last st., k.1. Rep. 1st and 2nd rows 4 times more. Cast off in rib.

LEFT FRONT BAND

With 2¾mm. needles and starting at cast off sts., knit up sts. as left side. Work in rib as left side. Work 4 rows.
Make buttonholes:
Next row: rib 4 sts., cast off 3 sts., (rib 12 sts. including st. on needle, cast off 3 sts.) twice, rib to end.
Next row: rib to end, casting on 3 sts. over those cast off. Work 4 more rows in rib. Cast off in rib.

COLLAR

Cast on 139(139:145:145) sts. with 2¾mm. needles.
1st row: k.2, * p.1, k.1, rep. from * to the last st., k.1.
2nd row: * k.1, p.1, rep. from * to the last st., k.1. These 2 rows form rib.
3rd row: rib 5 sts., (k.1, p.1, k.1) into next st., rib to last 6 sts., (k.1, p.1, k.1) into next st., rib 5 sts.
Cont. to inc. in this way at each end of every 6th row until there are 163(163:169:169) sts. Work 3 rows. Cast off in rib.

MAKING UP

Press each piece lightly with warm iron and damp cloth. Sew up shoulder, side and sleeve seams.
Sew sleeves into armholes. Sew lower edge of underwrap at back of overwrap.
Sew cast on edge of collar to neck edge with edges of collar matching centre of borders.
Press seams lightly. Sew on buttons.

Soft, Ribbed Ski Sweater

1958

Skinny-rib sweater, just below waist-length, with welts and neckband in alternated rib, and set-in, three-quarter length sleeves

★ Suitable for beginners

MATERIALS

Yarn
Poppleton Bijou Chunky
7(8:8) × 50g. balls.

Needles
1 pair 4½mm.
1 pair 5½mm.

MEASUREMENTS

Bust
87(92:97) cm.
34(36:38) in.

Length
49(50:51) cm.
19¼(19½:20) in.

Sleeve Seam
44(45:46) cm.
17¼(17¾:18) in.

TENSION

8 sts. and 10½ rows = 5 cm. (2 in.) square over unpressed rib when slightly stretched widthwise, on 5½mm. needles. If your tension square does not correspond to these measurements see page 166 for adjustment instructions.

ABBREVIATIONS

k. = knit; p. = purl; st(s). = stitch(es); inc. = increas(ing) (see page 166); dec. = decreas-(ing) (see page 167); beg. = begin(ning); rem. = remain(ing); rep. = repeat; alt. = alternate; tog. = together; sl. = slip stitch (transfer one stitch from left needle, knitwise unless otherwise stated, to right hand needle.); cont. = continue; patt. = pattern; foll. = following; folls. = follows; mm. = millimetres; cm. = centimetre(s); in. = inch(es).

BACK

Cast on 68(72:76) sts. using 4½mm. needles.
1st row: * k.1, p.1, rep. from * to last 2 sts., k.2, rep. this row until work measures 8 cm. (3¼ in.) ending on wrong side and inc. 1 st. at end of last row. [69(73:77) sts.]
Using 5½mm. needles, proceed as folls.:
1st row: k.1, * p.1, k.1, rep. from * to end.
2nd row: k.1, * k.1, p.1, rep. from * to last 2 sts. k.2.
Rep. last 2 rows until work measures 30 cm. (11¾in.) from beg., ending with a 2nd row.

Shape Armhole
Cast off 5(6:7) sts. at beg. of next 2 rows. [59(61:63) sts.] Cont. without further shaping until work measures 48(49:50) cm. (18¾(19¼:19½) in.) from beg. ending with a right side row.

Shape Shoulders
Cast off 3(4:5) sts. at beg. of next 2 rows. Cast off 4 sts. at beg. of foll. 6 rows, ending on right side. [29 sts.]

Shape Neckband
Change to 4½mm. needles. Now alternate rib (i.e. all sts. which would have been k. are p. and vice versa, thus moving rib patt. along 1 st.) as folls.:
1st row (wrong side): k.1, * p.1, k.1, rep. from * to end.
Work 8 rows more in rib.
Cast off very loosely in rib.

FRONT

Work as for back until armhole measures 10 rows less than back to shoulder shaping, ending with a wrong side row. [59(61:63) sts.]

Shape Neck
Rib 21(22:23) sts. and leave on a holder for left side, rib 17 sts. and place on a holder for neckband, rib 21(22:23) sts. for right side.
** Dec. 1 st. at neck edge on next 4 rows then on foll. 2 alt. rows. [15(16:17) sts.]
Work 2 rows.

Shape Shoulder
Cast off 3(4:5) sts. at beg. of next row.
Cast off 4 sts. at beg. of foll. 3 alt. rows.
Break off yarn. **
Rejoin yarn to armhole edge sts. left on a holder for left side, work from ** to **.
Do not break off yarn.

Shape Neckband
Using size 4½mm. needles, pick up and knit, alternating rib as for front neckband, 14 sts. down left side of neck, 17 sts. from holder for neckband, 14 sts. up right side of neck. [45 sts.]
Work 8 more rows in rib.
Cast off loosely in rib.

SLEEVES

Cast on 38(40:42) sts. using 4½mm. needles.
1st row: * k.1, p.1, rep. from * to last 2 sts., k.2. Rep. last row until work measures 4 cm. (1½ in.) ending on wrong side, inc. 1 st. at end of last row. [39(41:43) sts.]
With 5½mm. needles, cont. in rib, alternating rib on first row, and inc. 1 st. at each end of 9th and every foll. 8th row until there are 57(59:61) sts. on the needle. Cont. without further shaping until sleeve measures 44(45:46) cm. (17¼(17¾:18) in.) from beg. ending on wrong side.
Cast off loosely in rib.

MAKING UP

Sew up shoulder seams.
Sew up side and sleeve seams, leaving 6(7:8) rows at top of sleeve open.
Sew cast off edge of sleeve around armhole, sewing last few rows of sleeve to cast off sts. under arm.
Press all seams.

Twisted Rib Sweater and Scarf 1934

Round-neck twisted rib sweater with back neck zip, sleeves worked with body and seamed at upper and lower arm. Separate scarf worked in two halves

★ Suitable for beginners

MATERIALS

Yarn
Chat Botte Acrylique and Alpaga
Sweater:
8(8:9) × 40g. balls
Scarf:
1 × 40g. ball

Needles
1 pair 3¼mm.
1 pair 4mm.
1 circular 4mm. 100 cm. long.

Notions
12 cm. (4¾ in.) zip fastener

MEASUREMENTS

Bust
82(87:92) cm.
32(34:36) in.

Length
50(51:52) cm.
19½(20:20½) in.

Sleeve Seam
47 cm.
18½ in.

TENSION

26 sts. and 28 rows = 10 cm. (4 in.) square over twisted rib on 4mm. needles. If your tension square does not correspond to these measurements see page 166 for adjustment instructions.

ABBREVIATIONS

k. = knit; p. = purl; st(s). = stitch(es); inc. = increas(ing) (see page 166); dec. = decreas-(ing) (see page 167); beg. = begin(ning); rem. = remain(ing); rep. = repeat; alt. = alternate; tog. = together; sl. = slip stitch (transfer one stitch from left needle, knit-wise unless otherwise stated, to right hand needle.); cont. = continue; patt. = pattern; foll. = following; folls. = follows; mm. = millimetres; cm. = centimetre(s); in. = inch(es); st.st. = stocking stitch; k.1b. = k. into back of st; g.st. = garter stitch.

BACK

Cast on 103(109:115) sts. with 3¼mm. needles.
1st row: k.1, * p.1, k.1, rep. from * to end.
2nd row: p.1, * k.1, p.1, rep. from * to end.
Rep. these 2 rows for 7 cm. (2¾ in.), ending with a 2nd row.
Change to 4mm. needles and cont. in twisted rib as folls.:

1st row: k.1, * p.1, k.1b., rep. from * to last 2 sts., p.1, k.1.
2nd row: p.1, * k.1b., p.1, rep. from * to end.
Cont. in rib, inc. 1 st. at each end of next and every foll. 8th row until there are 119(125:131) sts.
Now cont. without shaping until work measures 30 cm. (11¾ in.) from beg., ending with a wrong side row.

Shape Sleeves
Cast on 105 sts. at beg. of next 2 rows, change to circular needle. [329(335:341) sts.] **
Cont. without shaping until work measures 7(8:9) cm. (2¼(3¼:3½) in.) from beg. of sleeve, ending with a wrong side row.

Divide for Back Neck
Next row: rib 162(165:168) sts., k.2, turn and leave rem. sts. on spare needle.
Next row: k.2, rib to end.
Cont. on these sts. until sleeve edge measures 11(12:13) cm. (4¼(4¾:5) in.), ending with a wrong side row.

Shape Top of Sleeve and Shoulder
Cast off 12 sts. at beg. of next row and foll. 7 alt. rows, ending with a wrong side row. [68(71:74) sts.]

Shape Neck
Next row: cast off 12 sts., rib 42(44:46) sts., turn and leave rem. 13(14:15) sts. on holder.
Next row: cast off 3 sts., rib to end.
Next row: cast off 11(12:13) sts., rib to end.
Rep. the last 2 rows once more, then the first of them again.
Cast off rem. 12 sts.
Return to the sts. on spare needle. With right side facing rejoin yarn, k.2 tog., k.1, rib to end.
Next row: rib to last 2 sts., k.2.
Work to match first side.

FRONT

Work as given for back to **.
Cont. without shaping until sleeve edge measures 11(12:13) cm. (4¼(4¾:5) in.), ending with a wrong side row.

Shape top of Sleeve, Shoulder and Neck
Next row: cast off 12 sts., rib 143(145:147) sts., turn and leave rem. 173(177:181) sts. on spare needle.
Next row: cast off 2 sts., rib to end.
Next row: cast off 12 sts., rib to end.
Rep. the last 2 rows 6 times more, then work 1 row.
Cast off 12 sts. at beg. of next row, then 11(12:13) sts. at beg. of foll. 2 alt. rows.
Work 1 row, then cast off rem. 12 sts.
Return to the sts. on spare needle.
Slip first 17(19:21) sts. onto holder for neck, rejoin yarn and rib to end.
Work to match first side.

NECKBAND

Sew up shoulder seams and top of sleeves.
With 3¼mm. needles work across sts. of left back neck as set, i.e.: k.2, rib 11(12:13) sts., pick up and k.9 sts. up left back neck and 25 sts. down left front neck, rib 17(19:21) front neck sts. from holder, pick up and k.25 sts. up right front neck and 9 sts. down right back neck, then work across rem. 13(14:15) sts. of right back neck. [111(115:119) sts.]
Keeping 2 sts. at each end in g.st., cont. in k.1, p.1 rib as on welt for 5 cm. (2 in.).
Cast off in rib.

CUFFS

With 3¼mm. needles and right side facing, pick up and k.51(57:63) sts. along sleeve edge and work in rib as at beg. of back for 7 cm. (2¾ in.).
Cast off loosely in rib.

SCARF (make 2 pieces)

Cast on 15 sts. with 4mm. needles and work in twisted rib as on main part for 5 cm. (2 in.).
Cont. in rib, inc. 1 st. at each end of next row and every foll. 8th row until there are 41 sts., then cont. without shaping until work measures 42 cm. (16½ in.).
Cast off loosely in rib.

MAKING UP

Do not press.
Sew up side and underarm seams. Sew in zip to come halfway up neckband. Fold neckband in half to inside and slipstitch. Sew up cast on edges of scarf.

Shetland, Honeycomb Pattern Sweater *1952*

Just below waist-length sweater in two-tone honeycomb pattern, with set-in sleeves, ribbed welts and round neck

★★ Suitable for knitters with some previous experience

MATERIALS

Yarn
Templeton's H & O Shetland Fleece
8(8:9:10) × 25g. balls (Main Colour)
2(3:3:3) × 25g. balls (Contrast Colour)

Needles
1 pair 2¾mm.
1 pair 3¾mm.
1 set of four 2¾mm.

MEASUREMENTS

Bust
82(87:92:97) cm.
32(34:36:38) in.

Length
49(51:51½:53) cm.
19¼(20:20¼:20¾) in.

Sleeve Seam
47 cm.
18½ in.

TENSION

24 sts. and 36 rows = 7 cm. (2¾ in.) square over unstretched pattern on 3¾mm. needles. If your tension square does not correspond to these measurements see page 166 for adjustment instructions.

ABBREVIATIONS

k. = knit; p. = purl; st(s). = stitch(es); inc. = increas(ing) (see page 166); dec. = decreas-(ing) (see page 167); beg. = begin(ning); rem. = remain(ing); rep. = repeat; alt. = alternate; tog. = together; sl. = slip stitch (transfer one stitch from left needle, knit-wise unless otherwise stated, to right hand needle.); cont. = continue; patt. = pattern; foll. = following; folls. = follows; mm. = millimetres; cm. = centimetre(s); in. = inch(es); M = main colour; C = contrast colour.

BACK

Cast on 96(102:108:114) sts., with 2¾mm. needles, using M.
Work 9 cm. (3½ in.) in k.1, p.1 rib.
Next row (wrong side): p.7(10:10:13), * p. twice into next st., p.9(9:10:10), rep. from * to last 9(12:10:13) sts., p. twice into next st., p. to end. [105(111:117:123) sts.]
Change to size 3¾mm. needles and honeycomb patt., carrying wools loosely up sides of work when not in use.
1st row: with C, k.
2nd row: with C, p.
3rd row: with M, k.
4th row: with M, p.
5th and 7th rows: as 3rd row.
6th and 8th rows: as 4th row.
9th row: with C, k.4, * drop next st. down to last C row, insert needle into the C stitch and under the 6M. loops, k. stitch and loops tog., k.5, rep. from * to last 5 sts., drop and k. up next st. in same way, k.4.
10th row: with C, p.
11th to 16th rows: as 3rd to 8th rows.
17th row: with C, k.1, * drop and k. up next st. as for 9th row, k.5, rep. from * to last 2 sts., drop and k. up next st., k.1.
18th row: with C, p.
Now rep. 3rd to 18th rows inclusive.
Work until back measures 30(32:32:33) cm. (11¾(12½:12½:13) in.).

Shape Armholes
Cast off 5(6:7:8) sts. at beg. of next 2 rows.
Dec. 1 st. each end of every alt. row until 83(87:91:95) sts. rem.
Work until armholes are 18(19:19:20) cm. (7(7½:7½:7¾) in.) measured on the straight ending with 4th or 12th patt. row.

Shape Shoulders
Cast off at beg. of next and foll. rows 9(10:9:10) sts. twice and 9(9:10:10) sts. 4 times. Leave rem. 29(31:33:35) sts. on holder for neckband.

FRONT

Work as for back until armholes measure 15(16½:16½:17) cm. (5¾(6¼:6¼:6½) in.), ending with a C row.

Shape Neck
Next row: work 31(32:33:34) sts., turn. Finish this side first.
** Dec. 1 st. at neck edge every k. row until 27(28:29:30) sts. rem.
Work until armhole measures same as those of back.

Shape Shoulder
Cast off at armhole edge 9(10:9:10) sts. once and 9(9:10:10) sts. twice. ** Slip centre 21(23:25:27) sts. onto holder. Join wool to neck edge of rem. sts. and work from ** to **.

SLEEVES

Cast on 48(50:52:52) sts. with size 2¾mm. needles, using M. Work 7½ cm. (3 in.) in k.1., p.1., rib.
Next row (wrong side): p.3(6:1:1) sts., * p. twice into next st., p.4(2:2:2) sts., rep. from * to last 5(8:3:3) sts., p. twice into next st., p. to end. [57(63:69:69) sts.]
Change to size 3¾mm. needles and patt.
Work 18 rows.
Inc. 1 st. each end of next and every 12th row until there are 69(75:81:85) sts.
Work until sleeve measures 47 cm. (18½ in.) or desired seam length, ending with same patt. row as at armhole.

Shape Top
Cast off 4(5:6:7) sts. at beg. of next 2 rows.
Dec. 1 st. each end of every k. row 5 times, then every 4th row until 41(43:45:47) sts. rem., then every k. row until 31 sts. rem.
Cast off 3 sts. at beg. of next 6 rows.
Cast off rem. 13 sts.

NECKBAND

Sew shoulder seams. With double pointed needles size 2¾mm., k. up sts. round neck as folls.:
1st needle: 29(31:33:35) sts. from holder at back,
2nd needle: 22(23:24:25) sts. down left side and 10(11:12:13) sts. from holder at front,
3rd needle: 11(12:13:14) rem. sts. from holder and 22(23:24:25) sts. up right side.
Work 3 cm. (1¼ in.) in rib.
Cast off loosely in rib.

MAKING UP

Set in sleeves. Sew up side and sleeve seams. Press.

Round-neck Stripy Sweater

Two-tone sweater with three-quarter length set-in sleeves, garter stitch welts and round neck with ribbed border

★ Suitable for adventurous beginners

MATERIALS

Yarn
Sirdar Country Style 4 ply
3(3:3:4) × 50g. balls (Main Colour)
3(3:3:3) × 50g. balls (Contrast Colour)

Needles
1 pair 2¾mm.
1 pair 3¼mm.
2 stitch holders

MEASUREMENTS

Bust
82(87:92:97) cm.
32(34:36:38) in.

Length
55(56:57:58) cm.
22(22½:22¾:23¼) in.

Sleeve Seam
33 cm. (approx)
13¼ in. (approx.)

TENSION

14 sts. and 20 rows = 5 cm. (2 in.) square over stocking stitch on 3¼mm. needles. If your tension square does not correspond to these measurements see page 166 for adjustment instructions.

ABBREVIATIONS

k. = knit; p. = purl; st(s). = stitch(es); inc. = increas(ing) (see page 166); dec. = decreas-(ing) (see page 167); beg. = begin(ning); rem. = remain(ing); rep. = repeat; alt. = alternate; tog. = together; sl. = slip stitch (transfer one stitch from left needle, knit-wise unless otherwise stated, to right hand needle.); cont. = continue; patt. = pattern; foll. = following; folls. = follows; mm. = millimetres; cm. = centimetre(s); in. = inch(es); st.st. = stocking st; g.st. = garter st; M = main colour; C = contrast colour.

BACK

Cast on 104(112:120:128) sts. using M, with 2¾mm. needles. Work 6 rows in g.st. Change to 3¼mm. needles and patt. of 6 rows st.st. in C, 6 rows st.st. in M. Cont. until work measures 18 cm. (7 in.). Inc. at both ends of next and every foll. 6th row until there are 118(126:134:142) sts. Cont. until work measures 37 cm. (14½ in.), ending after a p.row.

Shape Armholes
Cast off 4 sts. at beg. of next 2 rows, then dec. 1 st. at both ends of every row until 90(94:98:102) sts. rem.
Cont. until work measures 17(18:19:20) cm. (6½(7:7½:7¾) in.) from beg. of arm-holes, ending after a k. row.

Shape Neck and Shoulders
Next row: p.55(57:59:61) sts., place the last 20 sts. worked on a holder, p. to end. Cont. on last set of sts. worked for right side. Cast off 7(7:8:8) sts. at beg. of next side edge row and 3 sts. at beg. of next neck edge row. Rep. these 2 rows twice more. Cast off rem. 5(7:6:8) sts. **
Join yarn to inner edge of rem. sts. and work to end. Work from ** to **.

FRONT

Work as back until work measures 12(13:14:15) cm. (4¾(5:5½:5¾) in.) from beg. of armholes, finishing after a k. row.

Shape Neck
Next row: p.52(54:56:58) sts., place the last 14 sts. worked on a holder, p. to end. Cont. on last set of sts. worked for left side.
*** Dec. at neck edge on every row until 26(28:30:32) sts. rem. Cont. until work matches back to outer shoulder.

Shape Shoulders
Cast off 7(7:8:8) sts. at beg. of next 3 side edge rows. Work to side edge. Cast off rem. 5(7:6:8) sts. ***
Join yarn to outer edge of rem. sts. Work from *** to ***.

SLEEVES

Cast on 52(56:60:64) sts. using M, with 2¾mm. needles. Work 6 rows in g.st. Change to 3¼mm. needles and patt. as for main part. Inc. 1 st. at both ends of next and every foll. 6th row until there are 88(92:96:100) sts. Cont. until work measures approx. 33 cm. (13 in.), finish-ing after the same row of patt. as back and front before beg. armhole shaping.

Shape Top
Cast off 4 sts. at beg. of next 2 rows. Dec. at both ends of next and every alt. row until 44 sts. rem.; p.1 row.
Dec. at both ends of every row until 28 sts. rem. Cast off 3 sts. at beg. of next 4 rows. Cast off rem. 16 sts.

NECKBAND

With right side of work facing, using C and 2¾mm. needles, k. up 10 sts. along 1st side of back neck, k. central 20 sts., k. up 10 sts. along 2nd side. Work 6 rows in k.1, p.1 rib. Change to M. Work a further 6 rows in k.1, p.1 rib. Cast off in rib.
With right side of work facing, using C and 2¾mm. needles, k. up 30 sts. along 1st side of front neck, k. central 14 sts., and k. up 30 sts. along 2nd side. Complete as back neckband.

MAKING UP

Press work on the wrong side under a damp cloth, omitting g.st. and ribbing. Sew up side, shoulder, neckband and sleeve seams. Set sleeves into armholes. Press seams.

Belted Crochet-look Sweater

Hip-length, fine sweater with belt, set-in sleeves, in broken rib pattern with doubled-over stocking stitch welts and round neck with shaped, edged collar

★★ Suitable for knitters with some previous experience

MATERIALS

Yarn
Twilleys Lyscordet
14(15:16:17:18:19) × 25g. balls

Needles
1 pair 3mm.
1 pair 3¾mm.

MEASUREMENTS

Bust
82(87:92:97:102:107) cm.
32(34:36:38:40:42) in.

Length
63(64:64:65:65:66) cm.
24¾(25:25:25½:25½:26) in.

Sleeve Seam
47 cm.
18½ in.

TENSION

21 sts. and 27 rows = 9 cm. (3½ in.) square over pattern on 3¾mm. needles. If your tension square does not correspond to these measurements, see page 166 for adjustment instructions.

ABBREVIATIONS

k. = knit; p. = purl; st(s). = stitch(es); inc. = increas(ing) (see page 166); dec. = decreas-(ing) (see page 167); beg. = begin(ning); rem. = remain(ing); rep. = repeat; alt. = alternate; tog. = together; sl. = slip stitch (transfer one stitch from left needle, knit-wise unless otherwise stated, to right hand needle.); cont. = continue; patt. = pattern; foll. = following; folls. = follows; mm. = millimetres; cm. = centimetre(s); in. = inch(es); y.fwd. = yarn forward; y.bk. = yarn back; st.st. = stocking stitch; t.b.l. = through back of loops; m.1 = pick up thread lying between sts. and k.

BACK

Cast on 119(127:135:143:151:159) sts. with 3mm. needles. Beg. with a k. row work 7 rows st.st.
Next row: k. all sts. t.b.l. to form hemline.
Change to 3¾mm. needles and work in patt. thus:
1st row: *k.1, p.1, rep. from * to last st., k.1.
2nd row: *p.1, k.1, rep. from * to last st., p.1.
3rd row: as 2nd row.

4th row: as 1st row.
These 4 rows form patt. and are rep. throughout. Cont. in patt. until work measures 43 cm. (16¾ in.) from hemline (or length required to underarm) ending with a wrong side row. **

Shape Armholes

Cast off 4(5:6:7:8:9) sts. at beg. of next 2 rows. Dec. 1 st. each end of next 5 rows, then each end of every alt. row until 95(99:103:107:111:115) sts. rem. Cont. without shaping until armholes measure 16(17:18:18:19:20) cm. (6¼(6½:7:7:7½: 7¾) in.) ending with a wrong side row.

Shape Shoulders and Back Neck

Next row: cast off 10(10:10:10:11:11) sts., patt. across 22(22:24:24:24:24) sts., turn. Complete this side first.
Next row: **** dec. 1 st., patt. to end.
Next row: cast off 10(10:11:11:11:11) sts., patt. to end. Rep. last 2 rows once more. ****.
With right side of work facing rejoin yarn to rem. sts., cast off 31(35:35: 39:41:45) sts., patt. to end. Cast off 10 (10:11:11:11:11) sts., patt. to end. Work from **** to ****.

Back Neckband

With right side of back facing and 3mm. needles, pick up and k.40(44:44:48:50:54) sts. round back neck. Beg. with a p. row work 6 rows in st.st.
Next row: k. all sts. t.b.l. to form foldline. Beg. with a k. row work 6 rows in st.st. Cast off.

FRONT

Work as given for back to **.

Shape Armholes and Centre Front

Next row: cast off 4(5:6:7:8:9) sts., patt. across 53(56:59:62:65:68) sts., work 2 tog., turn.
Complete left front first:
*** Dec. 1 st. at neck edge on every foll. 3rd row, *at the same time* dec. 1 st. at armhole edge on next 5 rows, then every alt. row 3(4:5:6:7:8) times.
Keeping armhole edge straight, cont. to dec. 1 st. at neck edge on every 3rd row until 30(30:32:32:33:33) sts. rem.
Cont. without shaping until armhole measures same as back to shoulder, ending at armhole edge.

Shape Shoulder

Next row: cast off 10(10:10:10:11:11) sts. patt. to end.

Work 1 row.
Next row: cast off 10(10:11:11:11:11) sts. patt. to end.
Work 1 row.
Cast off rem. 10(10:11:11:11:11) sts.
With right side of work facing slip centre st. onto holder, rejoin yarn to rem. sts., work 2 sts. tog., patt. to end.
Next row: cast off 4(5:6:7:8:9) sts., patt. to end.
Complete to match first side, working from **.

Front Neck Band

With right side of front facing and 3mm. needles, pick up and k.62(62:66:68:70:72) sts. down left side of neck, k. centre st. from holder, pick up and k.62(62:66:68: 70:72) sts. up right side of neck.
1st row: p.60(62:64:66:68:70) sts., p.2 tog., p.1, p.2 tog. t.b.l., p. to end.
2nd row: k.59(61:63:65:67:69) sts., k.2 tog. t.b.l., k.1, k.2 tog., k. to end.
Work 4 more rows in st.st., dec. in same way at each side of centre st.
Next row: k.55(57:59:61:63:65) sts., k.3 tog. t.b.l., k. to end. Beg. with a k. row work 6 rows in st.st., inc. 1 st. at each side of centre st. Cast off.

SLEEVES

Cast on 51(51:51:55:55:55) sts. with 3mm. needles. Beg. with a k. row work 7 rows in st.st.
Next row: k. all sts. t.b.l. to form hemline. Change to 3¾mm. needles and work in patt. as given for back, inc. 1 st. at each end of next and every foll. 7th(6th:6th:

Belted Crochet-look Sweater

6th:5th:5th) row until there are 89(93:97:101:105:109) sts.
Cont. without shaping until sleeve measures 47 cm. (18½ in.) from hemline ending with a wrong side row.

Shape Top
Cast off 4(5:6:7:8:9) sts. at beg. of next 2 rows. Dec. 1 st. at each end of next 5 rows, then every alt. row until 45 sts. rem. Dec. 1 st. at each end of next 3 rows. Cast off 4 sts. at beg. of next 6 rows. Cast off rem. sts.

COLLAR

Cast on 101(103:105:107:109:111) sts. with 3¾ mm. needles.
Work in patt. as given for back, inc. 1 st. at each end of 5th and every foll. 4th row until there are 115(117:119:121:123:125) sts. Work 3 rows in patt. Cut yarn.

Border
With right side of collar facing and 3mm. needles, k. up 30 sts. along short side of collar, k. across sts. on pin and k. up 30 sts. along other side of collar.
1st row: p.
2nd row: k.30 sts., inc. 1, k. to last 30 sts., m.1, k.30 sts.
3rd row: p.
4th row: k.30 sts., m.1, k.1, m.1, k. to last 31 sts., m.1, k.1, m.1, k.30 sts.
5th row: p.
6th row: k.31 sts., m.1, k.1, m.1, k. to last 32 sts., m.1, k.1, m.1, k.31 sts.
7th row: k. all sts. t.b.l. to form foldline.
8th row: k.30 sts., k.2 tog. t.b.l., k.1, k.2 tog., k. to last 35 sts., k.2 tog. t.b.l., k.1, k.2 tog., k.30 sts.
9th row: p.
10th row: k.29 sts., k.2 tog. t.b.l., k.1, k.2 tog., k. to last 34 sts., k.2 tog. t.b.l., k.1, k.2 tog., k.29 sts.
11th row: p.
12th row: k.30 sts., k.2 tog. t.b.l., k. to last 32 sts., k.2 tog., k.30 sts.
13th row: p. Cast off.

BELT

Cast on 7 sts. with 3mm. needles.
1st row: p.
2nd row: p. twice into each st. [14 sts.].
3rd row: k.1 t.b.l., * y.fwd., sl.1 purlwise, y.bk., k.1, rep. from * to last st., y.fwd., sl.1 purlwise, y.bk.
Rep. last row until belt measures 117(122:127:132:137:143) cm. (45¾ (47¾: 49¾:51¾:53¾:56) in.).
Next row: * k.2 tog. t.b.l., rep. from * to end. Cast off.

MAKING UP

Sew up shoulder and neck border seams, side and sleeve seams using backstitch. Set in sleeves. Fold borders at hemline of lower edge, neck and sleeves to wrong side and slipstitch.
Fold collar border to wrong side and slipstitch. Attach collar to neck edge at slipstitch seam and fold over.

Fairisle Cardigan and Sweater

Long-sleeved sweater with fairisle band around lower part of set-in sleeves and yoke. Cardigan with bands around waist and sleeves, and separate button bands

★★ Suitable for knitters with some previous experience

MATERIALS

Yarn
Templeton's H & O Shetland Fleece
Cardigan:
7(7:8:8:9) × 25g. balls (Main Col., M.)
1 × 25g. ball in each of 3 contrasting cols., A, B, C
Sweater:
6(7:7:8:8) × 25g. balls (Main Col., M)
1 × 25g. ball in each of 3 contrasting cols., A, B, C

Needles
1 pair 2¼mm.
1 pair 3¾mm.
2 stitch holders

Buttons
6

MEASUREMENTS

Bust
77(82:87:92:97) cm.
30(32:34:36:38) in.

Length (cardigan)
45(48.5:50:52:54.5) cm.
17¾(19:19½:20½:21¼) in.

Length (sweater)
42(45:47:49:51) cm.
16½(17¾:18½:19¼:20) in.

Sleeve Seams (both)
42(43:44.5:46:46) cm.
16½(16¾:17½:18:18) in.

TENSION

24 sts. and 33 rows = 10 cm. (4 in.) square over stocking stitch on 3¾mm. needles. If your tension square does not correspond to these measurements, see page 166 for adjustment instructions.

ABBREVIATIONS

k. = knit; p. = purl; st(s). = stitch(es); inc. = increas(ing) (see page 166); dec. = decreas-(ing) (see page 167); beg. = begin(ning); rem. = remain(ing); rep. = repeat; alt. = alternate; tog. = together; sl. = slip stitch (transfer one stitch from left needle, knit-wise unless otherwise stated, to right hand needle.); cont. = continue; patt. = pattern; foll. = following; folls. = follows; mm. = millimetres; cm. = centimetre(s); in. = inch(es); col(s). = colour(s); st.st. = stocking stitch.

CARDIGAN BACK

Cast on 96(96:108:108:120) sts. using 2¼mm. needles and M.
Work 36 rows in k.2, p.2 rib.
Change to 3¾mm. needles and st.st.
Work 1 complete patt. from chart, work-ing within 12 st. patt. repeat section, working from right to left on knit rows, and left to right on purl rows.
On last row of patt. inc. 1 st. at end of row.
Now, working in M, inc. 1 st. at each end of next and every 4th row until there are 99(105:113:119:127) sts.
Work until back measures 28(30.5:32:33:34) cm. (11(12:12½:13:13¼) in.).

Shape Armholes
Cast off 4(5:6:7:8) sts. at beg. of next 2 rows.
Dec. 1 st. at each end of every k. row until 87(91:95:99:103) sts. rem.
Work until armholes measure 17(18:18.5:19:20) cm. (6½(7:7¼:7½:7¾) in.) on the straight.

Shape Shoulders
Cast off at beg. of next and foll. rows 10(10:11:11:11) sts. 4 times and 10(11:10:11:12) sts. twice.
Cast off rem. 27(29:31:33:35) sts. for neck.

CARDIGAN LEFT FRONT

Cast on 50(54:54:58:62) sts. using 2¼mm. needles and M.
1st row: *k.2, p.2, rep. from * to last 2 sts., k.2.
2nd row: *p.2, k.2, rep. from * to last 2 sts., p.2.
Rep. last 2 rows 17 times more.
Change to 3¾mm. needles and work 1 complete patt. in st.st. from chart as folls.:
1st row (right side): work in patt. as for 12 st. patt. repeat, to last 14(18:18:10:14) sts., work next 6(10:10:2:6) sts. to point given for size at side of chart, slip last 8 sts. onto a holder for centre front band. Work all p. rows starting from point marked for size, and then left to right across the 12 st. patt. repeat section, i.e. exactly opposite manner to k. rows.
Now cont. in M.
Inc. 1 st. at side edge of next and every 4th row until there are 52(56:56:60:64) sts.
Work until front measures same as back to armholes, ending at side edge.

Shape Armhole
Cast off 5(6:7:8:9) sts. at beg. of next row.
Dec. 1 st. at same edge every row until 40(43:45:48:50) sts. rem.

Shape Neck
Dec. 1 st. at centre front edge of next and every 4th row until 30(31:32:33:34) sts. rem. Work until armhole measures same as those of back.

Shape Shoulder
Cast off in next and foll. rows at armhole edge 10(10:11:11:11) sts. twice, and 10(11:10:11:12) sts. once.

CARDIGAN RIGHT FRONT

Work as for left front, reversing the patt. and shapings, and working the first but-tonhole at centre front in 9th and 10th rows as folls:
1st row: work 2 sts., cast off 4 sts., work to end.
2nd row: work in st.st., casting on 4 sts. over the sts. cast off in previous row. Work 2nd buttonhole in 31st and 32nd rows.

CARDIGAN SLEEVES

Cast on 48(48:60:60:60) sts. with 2¼mm. needles and M.
Work 36 rows in k.2, p.2 rib.
Change to 3¾mm. needles and work 1 complete patt. in st.st. from chart, work-ing the 12 st. patt. rep. section, and inc. 1 st. at end of last row of patt.
Now cont. in M, inc. 1 st. each end of next and every 8th(6th:8th:6th:6th) row until there are 71(77:83:89:95) sts.
Work until sleeve measures 42(43:44.5:

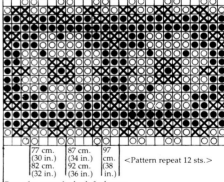

77 cm. (30 in.)	87 cm. (34 in.)	97 cm.	
82 cm. (32 in.)	92 cm. (36 in.)	(38 in.)	<Pattern repeat 12 sts.>

'Beg. of p. rows for back & sleeves

☐ M   ☒ A   ⬤ B   ◎ C

46:46) cm. (16½(16¾:17½:18:18) in.) or desired seam length.

Shape Top

Cast off 4(5:6:7:8) sts. at beg. of next 2 rows.

Dec. 1 st. at each end of every k. row until 37(39:41:43:45) sts. rem.

Cast off 3 sts. at beg. of next 6 rows.

Cast off rem. 19(21:23:25:27) sts.

CARDIGAN FRONT BANDS

Sew up shoulder seams. With 2¼mm. needles and M, pick up sts. from holder at right front and work in k.2, p.2 rib.

** Work until strip measures 5(5:6:6:7) cm. (2(2:2¼:2¼:2¾) in.) from last buttonhole. Make another buttonhole in next 2 rows. Rep. from ** 3 times more, then work until strip is long enough, when slightly stretched, to fit up neck edge of cardigan to centre back of neck.

Cast off.

Work another side in same way, omitting buttonholes.

MAKING UP

Sew on front bands, joining them at back of neck.

Sew up side and sleeve seams and set in sleeves.

Press through damp cloth.

Sew on buttons.

SWEATER BACK

Cast on 88(92:100:108:112) sts. with 2¼mm. needles and M.

Work 7 cm. (2¾ in.) in k.2, p.2 rib.

Change to 3¾mm. needles and st.st. Work 4 rows.

Inc. 1 st. each end of next and every 4th row until there are 98(106:112:120:126) sts.

Work until back measures 25.5(28:29:30.5:32) cm. (10(11:11¼:11¾:12½) in.).

Shape Armholes

Cast off 4(5:6:7:8) sts. at beg. of next 2 rows.

Dec. 1 st. at each end of every k. row until 86(90:94:98:102) sts. rem.

Work until armholes are 9(10:11.5:11.5:12) cm. (3½(4:4½:4½:4¾) in.) measured on the straight ending with a p. row.

Shape Neck

*Next row: k.30(31:32:33:34) sts., cast off 26(28:30:32:34) sts. for neck, k. to end.

Finish this side first.

Work 1 row. Cast off 5 sts. at beg. of next and foll. 2 alt. rows, then dec. 1 st. at same edge every k. row until 7(8:9:10:11) sts. rem. **. Cast off.

Rejoin yarn to armhole edge of rem. sts. and finish other side in same way.

SWEATER FRONT

Work as for back until armholes measure 6(7.5:8.5:9:9.5) cm. (2¼(3:3¼:3½:3¾)

in.) measured on the straight.

Now work from * to **.

Work until armhole measures same as those of back. Cast off.

Finish other side in same way.

SWEATER SLEEVES

Work as cardigan sleeves.

SWEATER BACK NECKBAND

With right side of work facing, using 3¾mm. needles and M, knit up 84(96:96:108:108) sts. round back neck edge; p.1 row.

Now work 1 complete patt. from chart, working across the 12 st. patt. rep. section, dec. 1 st. each end of every row and keeping patt. correct.

Change to 2¼mm. needles and k.2, p.2 rib.

Work 1 cm. (½ in.) without shaping.

Cast off.

SWEATER FRONT NECKBAND

Work as for sweater back neckband, knitting up 96(108:108:120:120) sts.

MAKING UP

Sew up shoulder seams.

Set in sleeves.

Sew up side and sleeve seams. Press.

Velvety Chessboard-check Sweater 1963

Long, raglan-sleeved, sparkly, stocking stitch sweater with two-colour allover checks, mohair welts and round, doubled, stocking stitch, neck borders

★ Suitable for beginners

MATERIALS

Yarn

Laines Tiber Psyche

5(5) × 50g. balls Col. A (Grey)

5(5) × 50g. balls Col. B (White)

Laines Tiber Le Doux Mohair, Super Kid 2(2) × 50g. balls (used *double*) to match Col. B

Needles

1 pair 5½mm.

1 pair 7mm.

MEASUREMENTS

Bust

82–88 (92–98) cm.

32–35(36–39) in.

Length

66 cm.

26 in.

Sleeve Seam

31 cm. (approx.)

12¼ in. (approx.)

TENSION

12 sts. and 12 rows = 10 cm. (4 in.) square over stocking stitch on 7mm. needles. If your tension square does not correspond to these measurements see page 166 for adjustment instructions.

ABBREVIATIONS

k. = knit; p. = purl; st(s). = stitch(es); inc. = increas(ing) (see page 166); dec. = decreas-ing) (see page 167); beg. = begin(ning);

rem. = remain(ing); rep. = repeat; alt. = alternate; tog. = together; sl. = slip stitch (transfer one stitch from left needle, knit-wise unless otherwise stated, to right hand needle.); cont. = continue; patt. = pattern; foll. = following; folls. = follows; mm. = millimetres; cm. = centimetre(s); in. = inch(es).

NOTE: Carry yarn not in use *loosely* behind work.

BACK

Cast on 64(70) sts. with size 5½mm. needles using *double* mohair.

Work 7 rows in k.1 p.1 rib.

Change to Psyche and 7mm. needles. Work check patt. as folls., dec. 4 sts. even-ly during the 1st row. [60(66) sts.]

1st row: * k.3 in A, k.3 in B, rep. from * to end.

2nd row: * p.3 in B, p.3 in A, rep. from * to end.
3rd row: * k.3 in B, k.3 in A, rep. from * to end.
4th row: * p.3 in A, p.3 in B, rep. from * to end.
These four rows form the patt. Cont. in this way until work measures 35 cm. (13¾ in.) or required length.

Shape Raglan

Cast off 3 sts. at beg. of next and foll. rows keeping check patt. correct.
Dec. 1 st. at each edge on alt. rows until 22(26) sts. rem.
Work 1 row. Leave sts. on holder.

FRONT

Work as for back until 30(32) sts. rem., ending with row 2 or 4.

Shape Neck

k.2 tog., k.8, turn, keeping check patt. correct.
Dec. 1 st. at beg. of every row until 2 sts. rem.
k.2 tog. Fasten off.
Slip the 10(14) centre sts. onto a holder.
Rejoin yarn to rem. sts., with right side facing.
k.8, k.2 tog., turn.
Dec. 1 st. at beg. of every row until 2 sts. rem.
k.2 tog. Fasten off.

SLEEVES

Cast on 30(32) sts. with 5½mm. needles, using *double* mohair.
Work 7 rows in k.1 p.1 rib. Change to

Psyche and 7mm. needles.
Cont. in checked patt. (see back), inc. 1 st. at each end of every 5th row until there are 48(50) sts.

Shape Raglan

Cast off 3 sts. at the beg. of each of the next two rows, then dec. 1 st. at each end of every alt. row until 10(12) sts. rem., keeping check patt. correct.
Leave on holder.

NECKBAND

Sew raglan seams of left sleeve to front and back using a flat seam, (see page 171), and front seam of right sleeve to front. Be careful to match checks, and use the matching yarn to sew up each square.
Join *double* mohair to neck edge of back, and using 5½mm. needles pick up and k.22(26) sts. across back, 10(12) sts. across sleeve top, 9(9) sts. down neck edge, 10(14) sts. across front edge, 9(9) sts. up neck edge and 10(12) sts. across sleeve top. [70(82) sts.]
Now work 4 rows in st.st. beg. with a p. row.
Next row: k. into the back of each st. to mark turning line for neckband.
Work 4 rows. Cast off *very loosely*.

MAKING UP

Sew up remaining raglan seam, including the neckband section at the top. Fold neckband to the wrong side, and neatly slipstitch the edge to the knitted up line. Sew side and sleeve seams.
DO NOT PRESS.

Daytime version; Check Sweater   *1963*

Long, raglan-sleeved sports sweater in stocking stitch with two-colour allover checks, and round, doubled, stocking stitch neck border

★ Suitable for beginners

MATERIALS

Yarn

Laines Plassard Harmonieuse
(5)5 × 75g. skeins Col. A (Harpe)
(5)5 × 75g. skeins Col. B (Gavotte)

Needles

1 pair 6mm.
1 pair 7½mm.

MEASUREMENTS

Bust

82–88 (92–99) cm.
32–34½ (36–39) in.

Length (with neckband, centre back)

67(69) cm.
26¼(27) in.

Sleeve Seam

45 cm.
17¾ in.

TENSION

11 sts. and 12 rows = 10 cm. (4 in.) square over stocking stitch on 7½mm. needles. If your tension square does not correspond to these measurements see page 166 for adjustment instructions.

ABBREVIATIONS

k. = knit; p. = purl; st(s). = stitch(es); inc. = increas(ing) (see page 166); dec. = decreas-

(ing) (see page 167); beg. = begin(ning); rem. = remain(ing); rep. = repeat; alt. = alternate; tog. = together; sl. = slip stitch (transfer one stitch from left needle, knitwise unless otherwise stated, to right hand needle.); cont. = continue; patt. = pattern; foll. = following; folls. = follows; mm. = millimetres; cm. = centimetre(s); in. = inch(es); col. = colour; st.st. = stocking stitch.

NOTE: Carry yarn not in use *loosely* behind work.

BACK

Cast on 54(60) sts. with 6mm. needles by thumb method (see page 164), using yarn A.

1st row: * p.1, k.1, rep. from * to last st. p.1.
2nd to 5th rows: * p.1, k.1, rep. from * to end.
Change to 7½mm. needles and join in yarn B.**
6th row: * k.3 in A, k.3 in B, rep. from * to end.
7th row: * k.3 in B, p.3 in A, rep. from * to end.
8th row: * k.3 in A, p.3 in B, rep. from * to end.
9th row: as 7th row.
10th row: * k.3 in B, k.3 in A, rep. from * to end.
11th row: * p.3 in A, k.3 in B, rep. from * to end.
12th row: * p.3 in B, k.3 in A, rep. from * to end.
13th row: * as 11th row.
Rep. rows 6 to 13 inclusive until back measures 38 cm. (15 in.), ending with 9th or 13th rows.

Shape Raglan
Cast off 2(3) sts. at beg. of next 2 rows.
Dec. 1 st. at each end of every alt. row until 20(22) sts. rem.
Work one row.
Leave sts. on holder.

FRONT

Work as for back until 28(30) sts. rem., ending with a wrong side row (odd-numbered rows).

Shape Neck
1st row: work 2 tog., work 8, turn, keeping check patt. correct.
Working on these 9 sts., dec. 1 st. at beg. of every row until 2 sts. rem.
Work 2 tog.
Fasten off.
Slip centre 8(10) sts. onto holder.
Join yarns to neck edge of rem. sts.
Dec. 1 st. at each end of every row until 2 sts. rem.
Work 2 tog.
Fasten off.

SLEEVES

Cast on 30 sts. with 6mm. needles by thumb method (see page 164), using yarn A.
Work as for back to **.
Working in checked patt. (rows 6 to 13 inclusive of back), inc. 1 st. each end of every 5th row until there are 44(48) sts.

Work until sleeve measures 45 cm. (17¾ in.), ending with 9th or 13th row of patt.

Shape Raglan
Cast off 2(3) sts. at beg. of next 2 rows.
Dec. 1 st. each end of every alt. row until 8 sts. rem.
Dec. 1 st. each end of next row.
Leave sts. on holders.

NECKBAND

Sew raglan seams of left sleeve to front and back using a flat seam (see page 171), and front seam of right sleeve to front. Be careful to match checks, and use the matching yarn to sew up each square.
Join A to neck edge of back, and using 6mm. needles pick up and knit 20(22) sts. across back, 8 sts. across left sleeve top, 6 sts. down neck edge, 8(10) sts. across front, 6 sts. up right neck edge, and 6 sts. across sleeve top. [54(58) sts.]
Now work 4 rows in st.st., beg. with a purl row.
Next row: knit into the back of each st. to mark the turning line for neckband.
Work 4 rows more in st.st. Cast off *very loosely.*

MAKING UP

Sew up rem. raglan seam, including the neckband section at the top. Fold neckband to the wrong side, and neatly slip-stitch the edge to the knitted-up line.
Sew side and sleeve seams.
DO NOT PRESS.

Soft Sweater with Patterned Yoke 1961

Soft, furry, hip-length sweater with drop shoulders, open-patterned yoke and plain round neck with doubled-over ribbed welt

★★ This pattern is suitable for new knitters who are not complete beginners

MATERIALS

Yarn
3 Suisses Barbara
6(6:7:7) × 40g. balls

Needles
1 pair 3¼mm.
1 pair 3¾mm.

MEASUREMENTS

Bust
87(92:97:102) cm.
34(36:38:40) in.

Length at Side of Shoulder
58(58:59:59) cm.
22¾(22¾:23¼:23¼) in.

Sleeve Seam
42 cm.
16½ in.

TENSION

22 sts. and 30 rows = 10 cm. (4 in.) square over stocking stitch on 3¾mm. needles. If your tension square does not correspond to these measurements see page 166 for adjustment instructions.

ABBREVIATIONS

k. = knit; p. = purl; st(s). = stitch(es); inc. = increas(ing) (see page 166); dec. = decreas-(ing) (see page 167); beg. = begin(ning); rem. = remain(ing); rep. = repeat; alt. = alternate; tog. = together; sl. = slip stitch (transfer one stitch from left needle, knit-wise unless otherwise stated, to right hand needle.); cont. = continue; patt. = pattern; foll. = following; folls. = follows; mm. = millimetres; cm. = centimetre(s); in. = inch(es); y.fwd. = yarn forward; p.s.s.o. = pass the slipped st. over.

BACK

Cast on 97(103:109:115) sts. with 3¼mm. needles.
1st row (right side): k.2, * p.1, k.1, rep. from * to last st., k.1.
2nd row: k.1, * p.1, k.1, rep. from * to end.
Rep. these 2 rows until work measures 5 cm. (2 in.), ending with a 2nd row.
Change to 3¾mm. needles and beg. with a k. row work in st.st.
Cont. without shaping until work measures 40 cm. (15¾ in.) from beg., ending with a p. row.

Cast *on* 4 sts. at beg. of next 2 rows.
Cont. on these 105(111:117:123) sts. in patt.
1st row: k.3, * y.fwd., sl.1, k.2 tog., p.s.s.o., y.fwd., k.3, rep. from * to end.
2nd row: p.
3rd row: k.1, k.2 tog., * y.fwd., k.3, y.fwd., sl.1, k.2 tog., p.s.s.o., rep. from * to last 6 sts., y.fwd., k.3, y.fwd., sl.1, k.1, p.s.s.o., k.1.
4th row: p.
These 4 rows form the patt. Cont. in patt. until work measures 58(58:59:59) cm. (22¾(22¾:23¼:23¼) in.) from beg., ending with a p. row.

Shoulder Shaping

Cast off 6 sts. at beg. of next 8 rows then 8(11:13:16) sts. at beg. of next 2 rows.
Leave rem. 41(41:43:43) sts. on a holder.

FRONT

Work as for back until you have worked 4 rows fewer than on back to start of shoulder, thus ending with a p. row.

Neck and Shoulder Shaping

Next row: patt. 46(49:51:54) sts. and leave these sts. of left front on a spare needle, cast off next 13(13:15:15) sts. loosely, patt. to end.
Cont. on 46(49:51:54) sts. now rem. on needle for right front and work 1 row straight.
** Cast off 4 sts. at beg. of next row and 2 sts. at same edge on foll. alt. row.
Now cast off for shoulder 6 sts. at beg. of next row and next 3 alt. rows, at same time cont. to dec. 1 st. at neck edge on next 8 rows.
Cast off rem. 8(11:13:15) sts. ** With wrong side facing rejoin yarn to neck edge of left front sts. Complete as for right front from ** to **, working shapings at opp. edges.

SLEEVES

Cast on 53(53:57:57) sts. with smaller needles and work in rib exactly as for back welt.
Change to 3¾mm. needles. Beg. with a k. row work in st.st. but inc. 1 st. at both ends of every 8th row until there are 79(79:83:83) sts. Cont. without shaping until work measures 42 cm. (16½ in.) from beg. Cast off rather loosely, using a size larger needle if necessary.

NECKBAND

Join right shoulder seam, backstitching this and all seams. Press all seams very

lightly on wrong side with warm iron and damp cloth using point of iron. With right side of work facing, using 3¼mm. needles, pick up and k.62(62:64:64) sts. round front neck edge then k.sts. of back neck, inc. 4 sts. evenly. Cont. on these 107(107:111:111) sts. and beg. with 2nd row work in rib for 5 cm. (2 in.). Cast off loosely ribwise.

MAKING UP

Join left shoulder seam and cont. seam along neckband leaving last 3 rows open. Fold neckband in half to wrong side and slipstitch cast off edge loosely in place, allowing the last 3 rows to lie on each side of the seam. Sew cast off edge of sleeves to sides of yoke and join entire side and sleeve seams.

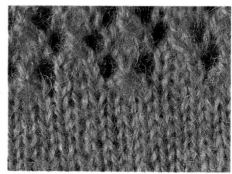

Soft, Shoulder-fastened Blouse

1935

Simple blouse in furry yarn with ribbed welts and yoke, main body in elongated garter stitch, fastened with bobbles at shoulders

★ Suitable for beginners

MATERIALS

Yarn
Jaeger Langora
9(10:11) × 20g. balls

Needles
1 pair 2¾mm.
1 pair 3¼mm.

Buttons
4

MEASUREMENTS

Bust
82(87:92) cm.
32(34:36) in.

Length
47(48:48) cm.
18½(18¾:18¾) in.

Sleeve Seam
44 cm.
17¼ in.

TENSION

20 sts. and 15 rows = 9 cm. (3½ in.) square over pattern on 3¼mm. needles. If your tension square does not correspond to these measurements see page 166 for adjustment details.

ABBREVIATIONS

k. = knit; p. = purl; st(s). = stitch(es); inc. = increas(ing) (see page 166); dec. = decreas-(ing) (see page 167); beg. = begin(ning); rem. = remain(ing); rep. = repeat; alt. = alternate; tog. = together; sl. = slip stitch (transfer one stitch from left needle, knit-wise unless otherwise stated, to right hand needle.); cont. = continue; patt. = pattern; foll. = following; folls. = follows; mm. = millimetres; cm. = centimetre(s); in. = inch(es); m.1 = pick up horizontal loop lying before next st. and work into back of it.

BACK

Cast on 97(103:109) sts. with 2¾mm. needles.
1st row: k.1, * p.1, k.1, rep. from * to end.
2nd row: p.1, * k.1, p.1, rep. from * to end.

Rep. last 2 rows until work measures 6 cm. (2¼ in.) at centre from start, ending with 2nd row and dec. 1 st. at end of last row. [96(102:108) sts.]
Change to 3¼mm. needles and patt. as folls.:
1st row: right side facing, k. into front and back of each st. all along.
2nd row: * k.1, drop next st. off needle, rep. from * to end.

These 2 rows form patt. Cont. in patt. until work measures 27 cm. (10½ in.) at centre from start, ending with 2nd row.

Shape Armholes
Cast off 4 sts. at beg. of next 2 rows, 3 sts. at beg. of next 4 rows, then dec. 1 st. at each end of every row until 72(74:76) sts. rem.
Next row: k.8(7:8) sts., m.1, * k.2, m.1, rep. from * to last 8(7:8) sts., k.8(7:8) sts. [101(105:107) sts.]
Starting with 1st row, change to k.1, p.1 rib as for welt, and shape yoke by inc. 1 st. at each end of every foll. 10th row until there are 107(111:113) sts., taking inc. sts. into rib.
Work straight in rib until work measures 44(46:46) cm. (17¼(18:18) in.) at centre from start, ending with the right side facing.

Shape Shoulders
Cast off in rib 3 sts. at beg. of next 16 rows.
Cast off rem. 59(63:65) sts. in rib.

FRONT

Work as for back.

SLEEVES

Cast on 51(55:55) sts. with 2¾mm. needles and work 6 cm. (2¼ in.) k.1, p.1 rib as for main part, ending with 1st row.
Next row: rib 3(5:5) sts., m.1, * rib 9, m.1, rep. from * to last 3(5:5) sts., rib 3(5:5) sts. [57(61:61) sts.]
Change to 3¼mm. needles.
1st row: work in patt. as for main part, shaping sides by inc. 1 st. at each end of 4th and every foll. 8th row until there are 71(75:75) sts., taking inc. sts. into patt.
Work a few rows straight until sleeve seam measures 44 cm. (17¼ in.), ending with right side facing.

Shape Top
Cast off 4 sts. at beg. of next 2 rows., 3 sts. at beg. of next 6 rows., then 2 sts. at beg. of every row until 21 sts. rem. (all sizes). Cast off.

MAKING UP

Press lightly on wrong side, omitting rib-bing and taking care not to spoil the patt. Join shoulder, side and sleeve seams; in-sert sleeves. Sew a button on each side of front and back, 2 cm. (¾ in.) from end of shoulder. Make a double loop with remaining yarn and join the 2 buttons together with it to form a shoulder fasten-ing as illustrated. Finish rem. pair of but-tons in the same way.
Press all seams.

Striped, V-neck Mohair Sweater 1978

Simple sweater in stocking stitch with three coloured mohair stripe pattern, drop shoulders, ribbed welts and neck band

★ Suitable for beginners

MATERIALS

Yarn
Lister-Lee Tahiti Mohair
9(10:11) × 25g. balls Col. A (Green)
3(3:4) × 25g. balls Col. B (White)
1(1:1) × 25g. balls Col. C (Grey)

Needles
1 pair 5mm.
1 pair 6½mm.

MEASUREMENTS

Bust
87(92:97) cm.
34(36:38) in.

Length from Shoulder
66(67:68) cm.
26(26¼:26¾) in.

Sleeve Seam
46 cm.
18 in.

TENSION

13 sts. and 18 rows = 10 cm. (4 in.) square over stocking stitch on 6½mm. needles. If your tension square does not correspond to these measurements see page 166 for adjustment instructions.

ABBREVIATIONS

k. = knit; p. = purl; st(s). = stitch(es); inc. = increas(ing) (see page 166); dec. = decreas-(ing) (see page 167); beg. = begin(ning); rem. = remain(ing); rep. = repeat; alt. = alternate; tog. = together; sl. = slip stitch (transfer one stitch from left needle, knit-wise unless otherwise stated, to right hand needle.); cont. = continue; patt. = pattern; foll. = following; folls. = follows; mm. = millimetres; cm. = centimetre(s); in. = inch(es); A = colour A (green); B = colour B (grey); C = colour C (white); k.2 tog. b. = knit 2 together through back; st.st. = stocking stitch.

BACK

Cast on 54(56:60) sts. with 5mm. needles using A.
Work in k.1, p.1, rib for 12 cm. (4¾ in.).
Next row: k.5(6:8) sts. inc. 1 st. in next st.,

* k.5., inc. 1 st. in next st., rep. from * 6 times more, k.6(7:9) sts. [62(64:68) sts.]
Change to 6½mm. needles and cont. in st.st. until work measures 20 cm. (7¾ in.) from cast on edge.
** Change to B, work 5 cm. (2 in.). Change to C, work 2 rows. Rep. from ** twice more. Cont. in A only until work measures 46 cm. (18 in.) from cast on edge. Mark each end of last row with waste yarn (armhole markers).

*** Cont. in st.st. for a further 20(21:22) cm. (7¾(8¼:8½) in.) from markers.
Next row: cast off 20(20:21) sts., k.22(24:26) sts., cast off rem. sts. Slip centre back sts. onto a spare needle.

FRONT

Work as back to ***

Divide for Neck
Next row: k.31(32:34) sts., leave these sts. on a spare needle for left front, k. to end on rem. 31(32:34) sts.

Work in st.st. for 3 rows ending at neck edge.

Shape Neck
1st row: k.1, k.2 tog., k. to end.
2nd row: p.
3rd row: k.
4th row: p. to last 3 sts., p.2 tog., p.1.
Cont. to dec. 1 st. at neck edge on every foll. 3rd row until 20(21:22) sts. rem.
Cont. straight until work measures the same as back from markers (ending with a p. row). Cast off.
Rejoin yarn at front neck, work to match right front reversing all shapings.

SLEEVES

Cast on 30(32:34) sts. with 5mm. needles using A, and work in k.1, p.1 rib for 10 cm. (4 in.).
Next row: k.1(2:3) sts., inc. 1 st. in next st., * k.2., inc. 1 st. in next st., rep. from * 8 times more, k.1(2:3). [40(42:44) sts.].
Change to 6½mm. needles, cont. in st.st.
Change to B, work 5 cm. (2 in.) *at the same time* inc. 1 st. on the 5th and every foll. 7th row until there are 58(60:62) sts.
Change to C, work 2 rows. Change to B, work 5 cm. (2 in.).
Change to C, work 2 rows.
Cont. in A only until work measures 46 cm. (18 in.) from cast on edge (or required length). Cast off.

NECKBAND

Sew up right shoulder seam.
With right side facing and 5mm. needles using B, pick up and k. 31(33:35) sts. down left front, 31(33:35) sts. up right front neck, then k. across sts. left on spare needle of centre back.
Next row: rib to within 2 sts. of centre front, p.2., rib to end.
Next row: rib to within 2 sts. of centre front, k.2 tog., k.2 tog. b., rib to end.
Rep. last two rows twice more. Cast off in rib.

MAKING UP

Sew up left shoulder seam. Sew up side seams to markers.
Sew up sleeve seams, then sew cast off edge to armhole edge. Do not press. For a luxurious effect lightly brush mohair.

Mohair Sweater with Ribbed Collar 1959

Soft, hemmed, hip-length sweater with large ribbed and rolled collar and set-in sleeves, in slipped stocking stitch

★★ Suitable for knitters with some previous experience

MATERIALS

Yarn
Hayfield Aspen Mohair
25(25:26:27) × 25g. balls

Needles
1 pair 4½mm.
1 pair 5½mm.
1 pair 6½mm.

MEASUREMENTS

Bust
82(87:92:97) cm.
32(34:36:38) in.

Length
59(60:61:62) cm.
23¼(23½:24:24¼) in.

Sleeve Seam
44 cm.
17¼ in.

TENSION

20 sts. and 32 rows = 10 cm. (4 in.) square over pattern on 5½mm. needles. If your tension square does not correspond to these measurements see page 166 for adjustment instructions.

ABBREVIATIONS

k. = knit; p. = purl; st(s). = stitch(es); inc. = increas(ing) (see page 166); dec. = decreas-(ing) (see page 167); beg. = begin(ning); rem. = remain(ing); rep. = repeat; alt. = alternate; tog. = together; sl. = slip stitch (transfer one stitch from left needle, knit-wise unless otherwise stated, to right hand needle.); cont. = continue; patt. = pattern; foll. = following; folls. = follows; mm. = millimetres; cm. = centimetre(s); in. = inch(es); st.st. = stocking stitch.

BACK

Cast on 87(91:97:101) sts. with 4½mm. needles and beg. with a k. row, work 10 rows in st.st.
Change to 5½mm. needles and cont. in patt. as folls.:
1st row: k. to end.
2nd row: p.1, * sl.1 purlwise, p.1, rep. from * to end.
These 2 rows form the patt. and are rep. throughout.
Cont. in patt., inc. 1 st. at each end of next

and every foll. 12th row until there are 97(101:107:111) sts., then cont. without shaping until work measures 42 cm. (16½ in.) from beg., ending with a p. row.

Shape Armholes

Still working in patt., cast off 3(4:5:6) sts. at beg. of next 2 rows, then dec. 1 st. at each end of next 3 rows and every alt. row until 73(75:77:79) sts. rem.
Cont. straight until armholes measure 17(18:19:20) cm. (6½(7:7½:7¾) in.).

Shape Shoulders

Cast off 5(6:6:7) sts. at beg. of next 4 rows, then 6(5:6:5) sts. at beg. of next 2 rows.
Cast of rem. 41 sts. loosely.

FRONT

Work as given for back until armholes measure 8 rows less than on back, ending with a p. row.

Shape Neck

Next row: k.28(29:30:31), cast off 17 sts., k. to end.
Cont. on last set of sts.
Dec. 1 st. at neck edge on every row until 20(21:22:23) sts. rem., ending at armhole edge.

Shape Shoulder

Next row: cast off (5:6:6:7) sts., patt. to last 2 sts., p.2 tog.
Next row: k.2 tog., k. to end.
Rep. the last 2 rows once more, then cast off rem. 6(5:6:5) sts.
Return to the other set of sts. and work to match, reversing shaping.

SLEEVES

Cast on 51(53:55:57) sts. with 4½mm. needles.
1st row: k.1, * p.1, k.1, rep. from * to end.
2nd row: p.1, * k.1, p.1, rep. from * to end.
Rep. these 2 rows for 7 cm. (2¾ in.), ending with a 2nd row.
Change to 5½mm. needles and cont. in patt. as on back, inc. 1 st. at each end of 11th and every foll. 6th row until there are 69(73:77:81) sts., then cont. without shaping until sleeve seam measures 44 cm. (17¼ in.) from beg., or length required, ending with a p. row.

Shape Top

Cast off 4(5:6:7) sts. at beg. of next 2 rows.
Dec. 1 st. at each end of next and every alt. row until 41 sts. rem., then at each end of every row until 17 sts. rem.
Cast off.

COLLAR

Cast on 18 sts. with 6½mm. needles and 2 strands of yarn, and p. 1 row.
Next row: * k.1, k. into loop below next st. and sl. the st. off needle, rep. from * to end. This row forms the patt. and is rep. throughout.
Work 3 more rows.
** *Next row:* patt. to last 4 sts., turn and patt. to end.
Work 2 complete rows.
Next row: patt. to last 6 sts., turn and patt. to end.
Work 2 complete rows. **
Rep. from ** to ** until shorter edge measures 60 cm. (23½ in.). Cast off in patt.

MAKING UP

Do not press.
Sew up shoulder seams.
Sew in sleeves.
Sew up side and sleeve seams.
Turn up hem at lower edge and slipstitch.
Sew up cast on and cast off edges of collar, then sew shorter edge of collar to neck, with seam at centre back.

Ribbed Sweater with Mitred Neckline 1935

Just below waist-length, single rib sweater with set-in sleeves and simple rib neckband forming a placket at front with mitred point

★ Suitable for beginners

MATERIALS

Yarn
Sirdar Country Style DK
8(8:9) × 50g. balls

Needles
1 pair 3mm.
1 pair 3¾mm.

Buttons
2

MEASUREMENTS

Bust
87(92:97) cm.
34(36:38) in.

Length
56(57:58) cm.
22(22¼:22¾) in.

Sleeve Seam
45 cm.
17¾ in.

TENSION

12 sts. and 15 rows = 5cm. (2 in.) square over rib patt. when slightly stretched as in wear, using 3¾mm. needles. If your tension square does not correspond to these measurements see page 166 for adjustment instructions.

ABBREVIATIONS

k. = knit; p. = purl; st(s). = stitch(es); inc. = increas(ing) (see page 166); dec. = decreas-(ing) (see page 167); beg. = begin(ning); rem. = remain(ing); rep. = repeat; alt. = alternate; tog. = together; sl. = slip stitch (transfer one stitch from left needle, knit-wise unless otherwise stated, to right hand needle.); cont. = continue; patt. = pattern; foll. = following; folls. = follows; mm. = millimetres; cm. = centimetre(s); in. = inch(es).

BACK

Cast on 119(127:135) sts. with 3mm. needles.
1st row: k.2, * p.1, k.1, rep. from * to last st., k.1.
2nd row: k.1, * p.1, k.1, rep. from * to end.
Rep. these 2 rows for 8 cm. (3¼ in.). Change to 3¾mm. needles. Cont. in rib until work measures 37 cm. (14½ in.), finishing after a wrong side row.

Shape Armholes
Cast off 4 sts. at beg. of next 2 rows, then dec. at both ends of every row until 95(99:103) sts. rem.
Cont. until work is 18(19:20) cm. (7(7½:7¾) in.) from beg. of armhole shaping, measured on the straight, finishing after a wrong side row.

Shape Shoulders
Cast off 9(10:11) sts. at beg. of next 4 rows and 9 sts. at beg. of foll. 2 rows. Cast off rem. 41 sts.

FRONT

Work as back to armholes.

Shape Armholes and Divide for Neck
Cast off 4 sts. at beg. of next 2 rows.
Next row: k.2 tog., work to end.
Next row: k.2 tog., work 50(54:58) sts. more, cast off central 7 sts., work to end.
Proceed on 1st set of 51(55:59) sts. for left side. Working neck edge straight, dec. 1st. at side edge every row until 44(46:48) sts. rem.
Cont. until work measures 12(13:14) cm. (4¾(5:5½)in.) from beg. of armhole.

Shape Neck
Dec. 1st. at neck edge on every row until 27(29:31) sts. rem.
Cont. until work matches back to outer shoulder.

Shape Shoulders
Cast off 9(10:11) sts. at beg. of next 2 side edge rows. Work to side edge. Cast off rem. 9 sts.
Join yarn to outer edge of rem. sts. and complete right side to correspond, reversing shapings.

SLEEVES

Cast on 55(59:63) sts. with 3mm. needles.
Work 8 cm. (3¼ in.) in k.1 p.1 rib. Change to 3¾mm. needles. Cont. in rib, inc. 1st. at both ends of next and every foll. 6th row until there are 87(91:95) sts. Cont. until work measures 45 cm. (17¾ in.), finishing after a wrong side row.

Shape Top
Cast off 4 sts. at beg. of next 2 rows. Dec. 1st. at both ends of next and every alt. row until 47(51:55) sts. rem. Work 1 row. Dec. 1st. at both ends of every row until 39 sts. rem. Cast off 3 sts. at beg. of next 6 rows. Cast off rem. 21 sts.

NECKBAND

Cast on 157(165:173) sts. with 3mm. needles. Work 8 rows in k.1 p.1 rib.
Next row: make buttonholes thus – rib 11 sts., cast off 3 sts., rib 16 sts., cast off 3 sts., rib to end. In next row cast on 3 sts. over those cast off. Rib 8 rows. Cast off loosely in rib.

MAKING UP

Sew up side, shoulder and sleeve seams. Set sleeves into armholes. Mitre end of neckband at buttonhole end i.e. form a point by turning in corners of neckband end. See photographs.
Sew neckband to neck edge, lapping right over left at base. Press seams. Sew on buttons.

Traditional Round-neck Sweater 1947

Long-sleeved, hip-length, round neck sweater in very soft wool, with ribbed welts, in stocking stitch

★ Suitable for beginners

MATERIALS

Yarn
Pingouin Pingolaine 4 ply
7(7:8:8) × 50g. balls

Needles
1 pair 3mm.
1 pair 3¼mm.

MEASUREMENTS

Bust
82(87:92:97) cm.
32(34:36:38) in.

Length
54(55:56:57) cm.
21¼(21½:22:22¼) in.

Sleeve Seam
45(45:46:46) cm.
17¾(17¾:18:18) in.

TENSION

28 sts. and 36 rows = 10 cm. (4 in.) square over stocking stitch on 3¼mm. needles. If your tension square does not correspond to these measurements, see page 166 for adjustment instructions.

ABBREVIATIONS

k. = knit; p. = purl; st(s). = stitch(es); inc. = increas(ing) (see page 166); dec. = decreas-(ing) (see page 167); beg. = begin(ning); rem. = remain(ing); rep. = repeat; alt. = alternate; tog. = together; sl. = slip stitch (transfer one stitch from left needle, knit-wise unless otherwise stated, to right hand needle.); cont. = continue; patt. = pattern; foll. = following; folls. = follows; mm. = millimetres; cm. = centimetre(s); in. = inch(es); st.st. = stocking stitch.

BACK

** Cast on 109(117:125:133) sts. with 3mm. needles.
1st row: k.2, * p.1, k.1, rep. from * to last st., k.1.
2nd row: k.1, * p.1, k.1, rep. from * to end.
Rep. these 2 rows until work measures 6 cm. (2¼ in.) ending with 2nd row.
Change to 3¼mm. needles and st.st.
Beg. with a k. row, work 8 rows in st.st.
Now dec. 1 st. at both ends of next and every foll. 6th row 5 times in all.
Cont. on rem. 99(107:115:123) sts. until work measures 19 cm. (7½ in.), including rib. Now inc. 1 st. at both ends of next and every foll. 6th row until there are 117(125:133:141) sts.

Cont. without shaping until work measures 36 cm. (14 in.) from beg., ending with p. row.

Armhole Shaping
Cast off 4 sts. at beg. of next 2 rows, 2 sts. at beg. of next 2(2:4:4) rows and 1 st. at beg. of next 4(8:6:10) rows. **
Cont. on rem. 101(105:111:115) sts. until armholes measure 18(19:20:22) cm. (7(7½:7¾:8½) in.), ending with a p. row.

Shoulder and Neck Shaping
Cast off 8(8:9:9) sts. at beg. of next 4 rows.
5th row: cast off 8(8:9:9) sts., k. until there are 17(19:18:20) sts. on right needle, cast off next 19(19:21:21) sts., k. to end. Finish this left side first. [25(27:27:29) sts.]
Cast off 8(8:9:9) sts. at beg. of next row.
Cast off 10 sts. at beg. of foll. row, k. to end. Cast off rem. 7(9:8:10) sts.
Rejoin yarn to neck edge of rem. sts., having wrong side facing.
Cast off 10 sts., p. to end.
Cast off rem. 7(9:8:10) sts.

FRONT

Work as for back from ** to **
Cont. on rem. 101(105:111:115) sts. until armholes measure 12(13:14:14) cm. (4¾(5:5½:5½) in.), ending with a p. row.

Neck Shaping
k. 42(44:46:48) sts. and leave on holder or spare needle, cast off next 17(17:19:19) sts., k. to end.
Cont. on rem. 42(44:46:48) sts. for right front.
Work 1 row straight.
* Now cast off 3 sts. at beg. of next row, 2 sts. at beg. of foll. 3 alt. rows, and 1 st. on foll. 2 alt. rows. [31(33:35:37) sts.]
Cont. straight until armhole matches back armhole in length, ending at armhole edge.

Shoulder Shaping
Cast off 8(8:9:9) sts. at beg. of next and 2 foll. alt. rows.
Work 1 row.
Cast off rem. 7(9:8:10) sts. *
With wrong side facing rejoin yarn to neck edge of left front sts.
Work as for right front from * to *.

SLEEVES

Cast on 59(61:63:65) sts. with 3mm. needles.
Work 1st and 2nd rows of back until work measures 6 cm. (2¼ in.) ending with a 2nd row.
Change to 3¼mm. needles, and work in st.st., beg. with a k. row, inc. 1 st. at both

ends of every 6th row until there are 93(97:101:105) sts.
Cont. straight until work measures 45(45:46:46) cm. (17¾(17¾:18:18) in.) from beg.

Shape Top
Cast off 4 sts. at beg. of next 2 rows, 2 sts. at beg. of next 6(8:8:10) rows, 1 st. at beg. of next 30(30:32:32) rows, 2 sts. at beg. of next 10 rows and 3 sts. at beg. of next 2 rows.
Cast off rem. 17(17:19:19) sts.

NECKBAND

Sew right shoulder seam.
With right side of work facing, using 3mm. needles pick up and knit 67(73:79:85) sts. round front neck edge and 46(46:48:48) sts. across back neck.
Beg. with 2nd row work in rib, as for back, for 11 rows.
Cast off loosely ribwise.

MAKING UP

Sew left shoulder and neckband seam.
Sew in sleeves.
Sew up side and sleeve seams.
Press st.st. fabric and seams very lightly with warm iron and damp cloth.

Thick Rib Raglan Sports Sweater

Thigh-length, chunky, raglan-sleeved sports sweater with round neck, in patterned rib for extra warmth

★★ Suitable for knitters with some previous experience

MATERIALS

Yarn
A.N.I Scottish Homespun
13(14:14:15:16) × 50g. hanks

Needles
1 pair 3¼mm.
1 pair 4½mm.
1 double-pointed set 3mm.
or
1 circular 3mm.

MEASUREMENTS

Bust
87(92:97:102:107) cm.
34(36:38:40:42) in.

Length (excluding neckband)
62(65:67½:71½:74½) cm.
24¼(25½:26½:28:29¼) in.

Sleeve Seam
47(48½:51:53½:53½) cm.
18½(19:20:21:21) in.

TENSION

16 sts. and 17 rows = 5 cm. (2 in.) square

over rib pattern with work unstretched, on 4½mm. needles. If your tension square does not correspond to these measurements, see page 166 for adjustment instructions.

ABBREVIATIONS

k. = knit; p. = purl; st(s). = stitch(es); inc. = increas(ing) (see page 166); dec. = decreas(ing) (see page 167); beg. = begin(ning); rem. = remain(ing); rep. = repeat; alt. = alternate; tog. = together; sl. = slip stitch (transfer one stitch from left needle, knitwise unless otherwise stated, to right hand needle.); cont. = continue; patt. = pattern; foll. = following; folls. = follows; mm. = millimetres; cm. = centimetre(s); in. = inch(es); y.fwd. = yarn forward; y.bk. = yarn back; p.s.s.o. = pass the slipped stitch over.
NOTE: When slipping sts. for raglan, except where st. is slipped for decreasing, always bring wool forward before slipping.

BACK

Cast on 147(153:161:169:177) sts. with 3¼mm. needles.
Work in k.1, p.1 rib for 9 cm. (3½ in.).
Change to 4½mm. needles and patt.:
1st row (right side): (k.1, p.1), rep. to last st., k.1.
2nd row: (y.fwd., sl.1 purlwise, y.bk., k.1), rep. to last st., y.fwd., sl.1.
Now work these 2 rows until back measures 39½(41:42:43:44½) cm., (15½(16:16½:16¾:17½) in.) ending with a 2nd row.

Shape Raglans
Cast off 9 sts. at beg. of next 2 rows.
Dec. 1 st. at each end of foll. 7 rows.
** *1st row* (wrong side): (sl.1, k.1), rep. to last st., sl.1.
2nd row: (k.1, p.1) twice, sl.1, k.1, p.s.s.o., (k.1, p.1), rep. to last 7 sts., k.1, k.2 tog., (p.1, k.1) twice.
3rd row: (sl.1, k.1) twice, sl.2, (k.1, sl.1), rep. to last 7 sts., k.1, sl.2, (k.1, sl.1) twice.
4th row: (k.1, p.1) twice, sl.1, k.1, p.s.s.o., (p.1, k.1), rep. to last 7 sts., p.1, k.2 tog., (p.1, k.1) twice.
Rep. these 4 rows until 47(49:51:53:55) sts. rem.
Leave sts. on holder for neck.

FRONT

Work as back until 63(65:67:69:71) sts. rem., ending with a 1st or 3rd row.

Shape Neck
Next row: work 4 sts., dec. 1 st., work 16 sts., turn.
Finish this side first.
** Now dec. 1 st. at neck edge on next and every foll. row, continuing raglan dec. on foll. and every alt. row until 5 sts. rem.
Dec. 1 st., at neck edge ONLY, until 2 sts. rem.
Work 2 tog.
Fasten off.
Slip centre 19(21:23:25:27) sts. onto holder.
Join yarn to neck edge of rem. sts.
Work to last 6 sts., k.2 tog., work to end.
Finish as other side from **.

SLEEVES

Cast on 62(64:66:68:70) sts. with 3¼mm. needles.
Work in k.1, p.1 rib for 7.5 cm. (3 in.).
Next row: p.7(4:9:7:5) sts., * p. twice into next st., p.3(3:2:2:2) sts., rep. from * to last 7(4:9:7:5) sts., p. twice into next st., p. to end. [75(79:83:87:91) sts.]
Change to 4½mm. needles and patt. (as in back), inc. 1 st. at each end of next and every foll. 7th(6th:6th:6th:6th) row until there are 113(119:127:135:143) sts.
Cont. straight until sleeve measures 47(48½:51:53½:53½) cm., (18½(19:20:21:21) in.) ending with a 2nd row.

Shape Raglan
Cast off 9 sts. at beg. of next 2 rows.
Dec. 1 st. at each end of next row.
Now follow instructions as for back from ** until 19(21:23:25:27) sts. rem.
Leave sts. on holder.

NECKBAND

Sew raglan seams of back, front and sleeves.
With right side of work facing, using circular needle or double-pointed 3mm. needles, k. up 47(49:51:53:55) sts. from back holder, 19(21:23:25:27) sts. from left sleeve, 14 sts. down side of neck, 19(21:23:25:27) sts. from front holder, 14 sts. up side of neck and 19(21:23:25:27) sts. from right sleeve. If using double-pointed needles, arrange these sts. on 3 needles, and work rounds of k.1, p.1 rib until neckband measures 4 cm. (1½ in.).
Cast off in rib.

MAKING UP

Sew up side and sleeve seams.
Press, using damp cloth and warm iron, ensuring that the sweater is not stretched.

Turtle-necked Sloppy Joe

1961

Two-tone, hip-length loose sweater, with contrast welts in difficult twisted pattern, body and turtle neck in fisherman's rib

★★★ This pattern is suitable for *very* experienced knitters only

MATERIALS

Yarn
Jaeger MatchMaker 4 ply
10(11:11:12:12) × 50g. balls (Main Colour)
3(3:3:3:3) × 50g. balls (Contrast Colour)

Needles
1 pair 2¾mm.
1 pair 3mm.

MEASUREMENTS

Bust
82(87:92:97:102) cm.
32(34:36:38:40) in.

Length (from top of shoulders)
58(60:60:61:61) cm.
22¾(23½:24:24) in.

Sleeve seam
44 cm.
17¼ in.

TENSION

15 sts. and 30 rows = 5 cm. (2 in.) square over Fisherman's Rib on 3mm. needles. If your tension square does not correspond to these measurements see page 166 for adjustment instructions.

ABBREVIATIONS

k. = knit; p. = purl; st(s). = stitch(es); inc. = increas(ing) (see page 166); dec. = decreas-(ing) (see page 167); beg. = begin(ning); rem. = remain(ing); rep. = repeat; alt. = alternate; tog. = together; sl. = slip stitch (transfer one stitch from left needle, knit-wise unless otherwise stated, to right hand needle.); cont. = continue; patt. = pattern; foll. = following; folls. = follows; mm. = millimetres; cm. = centimetre(s); in. = inch(es); tw.2 R. = k. into front of 2nd st. on left needle then k. into front of 1st. st. and slip both sts. off needle together; tw.2 L. = k. into back of 2nd st. on left needle then k. into the front of the 1st. st. and slip both sts. off needle together; k.1 D. = k. next st. but through the loop of the row below; M = main colour; C = contrast colour.

BACK

Cast on 142(150:158:166:174) sts. with 2¾mm. needles and C.
1st row (right side): k.1, * tw.2 R., rep. from * to last st., k.1.
2nd row: p.
3rd row: k.1, * tw.2 L., rep. from * to last st., k.1.
4th row: p.

The last 4 rows form border patt. Rep. them until work measures 20 cm. (7¾ in.) at centre from start, ending with 1st row and dec. 1 st. at end of last row. [141(149:157:165:173) sts.] Break C.
Join in M, change to 3mm. needles and fisherman's rib patt. as folls.:
1st row: p.1, * k.1 D., p.1, rep. from * to end.
2nd row (right side): k.1, * p.1, k.1, rep. from * to end.
These 2 rows form fisherman's rib patt. Work straight in patt. until back measures 47 cm. (18½ in.) at centre from start, ending with right side facing.

Shape Armholes

Cast off 5 sts. at beg. of next 2 rows, then dec. 1 st. at each end of next and every foll. 3rd row until 111(115:119:123:127) sts. rem., then on every foll. 4th row until 105(109:113:117:121) sts. rem. **
Work straight until back measures 66(67:67:69:69) cm. (26(26¼:26¼:27:27) in.) at centre from start, ending with right side facing.

Shape Shoulders

Cast off 3 sts. at beg. of next 4(6:8:10:12) rows, then 2 sts. at beg. of next 20(18:16:14:12) rows. Cast off rem. 53(55:57:59:61) sts.

FRONT

Work as for back from ** to **.
Work straight until front measures 63(65:65:66:66) cm. (24¾(25½:25½:26:26) in.) at centre from start, ending with right side facing.
Here divide for neck.
Next row: patt. 44(45:46:47:48), turn and leave rem. sts. on a spare needle.
Cont. on these 44(45:46:47:48) sts. for first side and work 1 row straight.
Dec. 1 st. at neck edge on next and every foll. alt. row until 37(38:39:40:41) sts. rem. Work 1 row straight.
Cont. dec. 1 st. at neck edge on alt. rows as before and at the same time shape shoulder by casting off 3 sts. at beg. of next and foll. 1(2:3:4:5) alt. rows, then 2 sts. at beg. of foll. 9(8:7:6:5) alt. rows.
Now keep neck edge straight and cont. shaping shoulder by casting off 2 sts. at beg. of foll. alt. row.
With right side facing, rejoin yarn to rem. sts., cast off centre 17(19:24:23:25) sts., patt. to end.
Finish to correspond with first side.

SLEEVES

Cast on 74(76:76:80:80) sts. with 2¾mm. needles and C., and work 15 cm. (5¾ in.) in

border patt., ending with 1st row, and inc. 1 st. at end of last row. [75(77:77:81:81) sts.] Break C.
Join in M, change to 3mm. needles.
Starting with 1st row, work in fisherman's rib patt., shaping sides by inc. 1 st. at each end of 15th(13th:13th:17th:17th) and every foll. 16th(14th:14th:12th:12th) row until there are 97(103:103:109:109) sts., taking inc. sts. into rib.
Work straight until sleeve seam measures 52 cm. (20½ in.), ending with right side facing.

Shape Top

Cast off 5 sts. at beg. of next 2 rows, then dec. 1 st. at each end of next and every foll. 4th row until 69(75:75:81:81) sts. rem.
Work 3 rows straight, then dec. 1 st. at each end of next and every alt. row until 55 sts. rem.
Work 1 row straight, then dec. 1 st. at each end of every row until 35 sts. rem.
Cast off 3 sts. at beg. of next 4 rows. Cast off rem. 23 sts.

COLLAR

Cast on 155(159:163:167:171) sts. with 3mm. needles and M.
1st row: k.1, * p.1, k.1, rep. from * to end.
2nd row: p.1, * k.1, p.1, rep. from * to end.
Rep. last 2 rows 3 times more, then 1st row again.
Change to fisherman's rib, starting with 1st row and work straight until collar measures 17 cm. (6½ in.) at centre from start, ending with 1st row.
Cast off loosely in rib.

MAKING UP

Press work lightly on wrong side, taking care not to spoil the patt.
Sew up shoulder, side and sleeve seams, insert sleeves. Fold welt and cuffs to wrong side and slipstitch lightly in position on wrong side.
Sew up short ends of collar, then pin cast on edge of collar in position round neck with seam at centre back, easing in any fullness.
Press all seams.

Sparkly, Fitted Evening Blouse

Waist-length, figure hugging blouse with low round neck at front, low V at back, set-in sleeves, in stocking stitch

★ Suitable for beginners

MATERIALS

Yarn
Twilleys Goldfingering
12(13:14) × 25g. balls

Needles
1 pair 2mm.
1 pair 2¼mm.
Medium sized crochet hook

MEASUREMENTS

Bust
82(87:92) cm.
32(34:36) in.

Length
49(52:53) cm.
19¼(20½:20¾) in.

Sleeve Seam
46(47:47) cm.
18(18½:18½) in.

TENSION

18 sts. and 22 rows = 5 cm. (2 in.) square over stocking stitch on 2mm. needles. If your tension square does not correspond to these measurements see page 166 for adjustment instructions.

ABBREVIATIONS

k. = knit; p. = purl; st(s). = stitch(es); inc. = increas(ing) (see page 166); dec. = decreas-(ing) (see page 167); beg. = begin(ning); rem. = remain(ing); rep. = repeat; alt. = alternate; tog. = together; sl. = slip stitch (transfer one stitch from left needle, knit-wise unless otherwise stated, to right hand needle.); cont. = continue; patt. = pattern; foll. = following; folls. = follows; mm. = millimetres; cm. = centimetre(s); in. = inch(es); st.st. = stocking stitch.

BACK

Cast on 126(134:142) sts. with 2mm. needles.
Work 9 cm. (3½ in.) in k.1, p.1 rib.
Change to 2¼mm. needles and work 4 rows in st.st.

Inc. 1 st. each end of next and every 4th row until there are 154(164:172) sts.
Work until back measures 30(32:33) cm. (11¾(12½:13) in.) from beg.

Shape Armholes
Cast off 7(8:9) sts. at beg. of next 2 rows.
Dec. 1 st. each end of next 3 rows, then

every k. row until 120(124:128) sts. rem., ending with a p. row *.

Shape Neck
1st row: k.60(62:64), turn.
Finish this side first. **
Dec. 1 st. at neck edge on next and every row until 40(40:40) sts. rem., then every alt. row until 19(20:21) sts. rem.
Work until armhole is 19(20:20) cm. (7½(7¾:7¾) in.).

Shape Shoulder
Cast off 7(6:7) sts. once at armhole edge and 6(7:7) sts. twice at beg. of foll. rows. **
Rejoin yarn to neck edge of rem. sts. and work from ** to **.

FRONT

Work as Back to *.

Shape Neck
Next row: k.48(50:52), cast off 24 sts., k. to end.
Finish right side first. ***
p. back to neck edge.
Cast off 2 sts. at this edge every alt. row until 24 sts. rem., then dec. 1 st. at same edge every 4th row until 19(20:21) sts. rem.
Work until armhole measures same as those of back.

Shape Shoulder
Cast off at armhole edge 7(6:7) sts. once and 6(7:7) sts. twice. ***
Rejoin yarn to rem. sts. at armhole edge, and work from *** to ***.

SLEEVES

Cast on 68(72:76) sts. with 2mm. needles.
Work 6 rows in k.1, p.1 rib.
Change to 2¼mm. needles and work 8 rows in st.st.
Inc. 1 st. each end of next and every 8th row until there are 112(116:120) sts.
Work until sleeve measures 46(47:47) cm. (18(18½:18½) in.) from beg.

Shape Top
Cast off 7(8:9) sts. at beg. of next 2 rows.
Dec. 1 st. each end of next 5 rows, then every k. row until 46 sts. rem.
Cast off 3 sts. at beg. of next 8 rows.
Cast off rem. 22 sts.

MAKING UP

Sew up shoulder seams.
Set in sleeves.
Sew up side and sleeve seams.
Work 3 rows of double crochet round neck edge, dec. 2 sts. at centre-back on every row.
Press lightly on the wrong side with a warm iron and a damp cloth.

V-neck, Soft Lacy Sweater

1978

Softly bloused, hip-length V-neck sweater with stocking stitch borders and neck edging, in an open, lacy pattern

★★ Suitable for knitters with some previous experience

MATERIALS

Yarn
Hayfield Beaulon 4 ply
13(14:15) × 25g. balls

Needles
1 pair 2¾mm.
1 pair 3¼mm.
1 pair 4mm.
1 set of four 2¾mm. needles pointed at both ends

MEASUREMENTS

Bust
82(87:92) cm.
32(34:36) in.

Length (from shoulder)
61 cm.
24 in.

Sleeve Seam
46 cm.
18 in.

TENSION

24 sts. and 28 rows = 10 cm.(4 in.) square over pattern, slightly stretched, on 4mm. needles. If your tension square does not correspond to these measurements see page 166 for adjustment instructions.

ABBREVIATIONS

k. = knit; p. = purl; st(s). = stitch(es); inc. = increas(ing) (see page 166); dec. = decreas-(ing) (see page 167); beg. = begin(ning); rem. = remain(ing); rep. = repeat; alt. = alternate; tog. = together; sl. = slip stitch (transfer one stitch from left needle, knit-wise unless otherwise stated, to right hand needle.); cont. = continue; patt. = pattern; foll. = following; folls. = follows; mm. = millimetres; cm. = centimetre(s); in. = inch(es); y.o.n. = yarn over needle; t.b.l. = through back loops; y.r.n. = yarn round needle; reqd. = required.

FRONT

Cast on 101(109:117) sts. with 2¾mm. needles.
Beg. with a k. row work 7 rows in st.st., then k.1 row to mark hemline.

Change to 3¼mm. needles and beg. with a k. row work 8 rows in st.st.
Change to 4mm. needles and cont. in patt. as folls.:
1st row: (right side): p.1, * k.3, p.1, rep. from * to end.
2nd row: k.1, * p.3, k.1, rep. from * to end.
3rd row: As 1st row.
4th row: k.1, * y.r.n., p.3 tog., y.o.n., k.1, rep. from * to end.
5th row: k.2, * p.1, k.3, rep. from * to last 3 sts., p.1, k.2.
6th row: p.2, * k.1, p.3, rep. from * to last 3 sts., k.1, p.2.
7th row: As 5th row.
8th row: p.2 tog., y.o.n., * k.1, y.r.n., p.3 tog., y.o.n., rep. from * to last 3 sts., k.1, y.r.n., p.2 tog. **
Rep. these 8 rows until work measures 39 cm. (15½ in.) from hem, ending with a 4th patt. row.

Shape Neck
1st row: patt. 50(54:58) sts. (last 4 sts. = p.1, k.3), turn and leave rem. sts. on spare needle.
2nd row: p.2 tog., p.1, work from * as on 6th row above.
3rd row: patt. as 7th row above.
4th row: p.2 tog., work as 8th row above from * to end.
5th row: * p.1, k.3, rep. from * to end.
6th row: p.2 tog., p.1, k.1, * p.3, k.1, rep. from * to end.
7th row: * p.1, k.3, rep. from * to last 3 sts., p.1, k.2.
8th row: p.2 tog., * k.1, y.r.n., p.3 tog., y.o.n., rep. from * to last st., k.1.
9th row: k.2, * p.1, k.3, rep. from * to end. [46(50:54) sts.]
*** Rep. the 2nd–9th rows 3 times more, then dec. 1 st. at neck edge on foll. 3rd row. [33(37:41) sts.]
Cont. without shaping until work measures 61 cm. (24 in.), from hem, ending with a wrong side row.

Shape Shoulder
Cast off 7(8:9) sts. at beg. of next and foll. 3 alt. rows. Work 1 row, then cast off rem. 5 sts. ***
Return to sts. on spare needle, joining yarn to centre end of row.
Sl. 1 st. onto a safety pin.
1st row: k.3, work as 5th front row from * to end.

2nd row: patt. as 6th front row to last 4 sts., k.1, p.1, p.2 tog.
3rd row: patt. as 7th front row.
4th row: patt. as 8th front row to last 3 sts., k.1, p.2 tog.
5th row: * k.3, p.1, rep. from * to end.
6th row: * k.1, p.3, rep. from * to last 4 sts., k.2, p.2 tog.
7th row: k.2, p.1, * k.3, p.1, rep. from * to end.
8th row: * k.1, y.r.n., p.3 tog., y.o.n., rep. from * to last 3 sts., k.1, p.2 tog.

9th row: *k.3, p.1, rep. from * to last 2 sts., p.2.
Now work from *** to *** as for other side of front.

BACK

Work as given for front to **.
Cont. in patt. until work measures the same as front to shoulders, ending with a wrong side row.

Shape Shoulders
Cast off 7(8:9) sts. at beg. of next 8 rows, then 5 sts. at beg. of foll. 2 rows.
Leave rem. 35 sts. on holder.

SLEEVES

Cast on 61 sts. with 2¾mm. needles and work as given for front to **, BUT using 3¼mm. needles instead of 4mm. for the patt.
Cont. in patt., work 2 more rows, then inc. 1 st. at each end of next and every foll. 8th row until work measures 13 cm. (5 in.) from hem. Change to 4mm. needles and cont. in patt., still inc. 1 st. at each end of every 8th row until there are 85 sts. Cont. without shaping until sleeve measures 46 cm. (18 in.) from hem, or length reqd.
Cast off.

NECKBAND

Sew shoulder seams. With set of four 2¾mm. needles and right side facing, k. back neck sts., pick up and k.66 sts. down left front neck, k. centre front st. from safety pin, pick up and k.66 sts. up right front neck. [168 sts.]
Next round: k. to 2 sts. before centre front st., k.2 tog., k.1, k.2 tog. t.b.l., k. to end.
Rep. this round 6 times more.
Next round: p. to end to mark turning line.
Next round: k. to centre front st., inc. 1 by picking up loop between sts. and k. into the back of it, k.1, inc. 1, k. to end.
Rep. this round 5 times more.
Cast off loosely.

MAKING UP

Do not press.
Sew in sleeves, placing centre of sleeves at shoulder seams.
Sew up side and sleeve seams.
Turn in all hems and slipstitch in place.

Fitted, Square-yoked Blouse

1934

Waist-length blouse with garter-stitch edged, buttoned yoke, Peter Pan collar, shirt-style sleeve worn with cufflinks, in twisted rib

★★ Suitable for knitters with some previous experience

MATERIALS

Yarn
Sunbeam St. Ives 3 ply
11(12:13) × 25g. balls

Needles
1 pair 2¾mm.
1 pair 3¾mm.

Buttons
2

MEASUREMENTS

Bust
87(92:97) cm.
34(36:38) in.

Length
52(52:54) cm.
20½(20½:21¼) in.

Sleeve Seam
44(44:45) cm
17¼(17¼:17¾) in.

TENSION

16 sts. and 20 rows = 5 cm. (2 in.) square over pattern on 3¾mm. needles. If your tension square does not correspond to these measurements see page 166 for adjustment instructions.

ABBREVIATIONS

k. = knit; p. = purl; st(s). = stitch(es); inc. = increas(ing) (see page 166); dec. = decreas-(ing) (see page 167); beg. = begin(ning); rem. = remain(ing); rep. = repeat; alt. = alternate; tog. = together; sl. = slip stitch (transfer one stitch from left needle, knit-wise unless otherwise stated, to right hand needle.); cont. = continue; patt. = pattern; foll. = following; folls. = follows; mm. = millimetres; cm. = centimetre(s); in. = inch(es); t.b.l. = through back of loop; y.fwd. = yarn forward; g.st. = garter stitch (every row knit).

FRONT

Cast on 124(130:136) sts. with 2¾mm. needles.
1st row: * p.1, k.2, rep. from * to the last st., p.1.
2nd row: * k.1, p.2, rep. from * to the last st., k.1.
Rep. 1st and 2nd rows for 8 cm. (3 in.), ending with 1st row.
Cont. in patt.
1st row (wrong side): with 3¾mm.

needle: * k.1 t.b.l., p.2, rep. from * to the last st., k.1 t.b.l.
2nd row: with 2¾mm. needle: * p.1, k.2 t.b.l., rep. from * to the last st., p.1.
These 2 rows form patt.
Work 9 more rows.
Now working the new sts. in patt. and taking care to keep patt. correct, inc. 1 st. at each end of next row, and then every 12th row until there are 136(142:148) sts.
Work until front measures 29(29:30) cm. (11¼(11¼:11¾) in.) from beg., ending with a wrong side row.
Now inc. 1 st. at each end of next row, and then every alt. row until there are 148(154:160) sts.
Work 1 row.
Cast off.

BACK

Work exactly as for front.

RIGHT FRONT YOKE

Beg. at opening edge.
Cast on 25(25:28) sts. with 3¾mm. needles.
Cont. in patt., starting with 2nd row.
Work 2 rows.
Inc. 1 st. at beg. of next row.
Work 1 row.

Make Buttonhole

Next row: inc. 1 in first st., patt. 2 sts., cast off 3 sts., patt.12(12:14) sts. including st. on needle, cast off 3 sts., patt. to end.
Next row: patt. to end, casting on 3 sts. over those cast off.
Now inc. 1 st. at beg. of next row, and then every alt. row until there are 36(36:39) sts., and then inc. 1 st. at this

same edge on every row until there are 51(51:54) sts., ending with a wrong side row.
Next row: cast on 4 sts., patt. to end.
Work 5(7:9) rows.

Shape Shoulder

** Dec 1 st. at beg. of next row, and then every 6th row until 45(45:48) sts. rem.
Work 3(5:7) rows.
Cast off.

Yoke Edging

With 2¾mm. needles and right side of work facing, k. up 1 st. from each st. along cast off edge, k. up 1 st. from corner st. and place a marker on this st., now k. up 75(78:81) sts. along lower edge (3 sts. for each 4 rows).
Next row: k. to marked st., (k.1, y.fwd., k.1) into marked st., k. to end.
Now work 6 rows in g.st.
Cast off knitwise.

LEFT FRONT YOKE

** Beg. at armhole edge.
Cast on 45(45:48) sts. with 3¾mm. needles.
1st row: with 2¾mm. needle * k.2 t.b.l., p.1, rep. from * to end.
2nd row: with 3¾mm. needle * k.1 t.b.l., p.2, rep. from * to end.
These 2 rows form patt.
Work 2(4:6) more rows.
Inc. 1 st. at beg. of next row, and then every 6th row until there are 55(55:58) sts. **
Work 3(5:7) rows.

Shape Neck

Next row: cast off 4 sts., patt. to end.
Now dec. 1 st. at neck edge on every row until 35(35:38) sts. rem., and then every alt. row until 25(25:28) sts. rem.
Work 1 row.
Cast off.

Edging

Starting at lower edge, work as right side.

BACK YOKE

Follow instructions for left front yoke from ** to **.
Cont. as folls.:
Work 67(71:75) rows without shaping, ending at shoulder edge.
Now follow instructions for right front yoke from ** to end.

Edging

With 2¾mm. needles and right side of work facing, k. up 1 st. from each st. along cast off edge, k. up 1 st. from corner st.

and place a marker on this st., now k. up 130(136:142) sts. evenly along lower edge, k. up 1 st. from corner st. and place a marker on this st., now k. up 1 st. from each st. along cast on edge.

Next row: k. to end, inc. at corners as for front yoke.

Now work 6 rows in g.st.

Cast off knitwise.

SLEEVES

Cast on 32 sts. with 3¾mm. needles.

1st row (wrong side): with 3¾mm. needle p.1, k.1 t.b.l., * p.2, k.1 t.b.l., rep. from * to end.

2nd row: with 2¾mm. needle * p.1, k.2 t.b.l., rep. from * to the last 2 sts. p.1, k.1 t.b.l. These 2 rows form patt.

Work 7 more rows.

Inc. 1 st. at beg. of next row, and then the 2 foll. 10th rows.

Break yarn and leave sts. on spare needle.

Now cast on 32 sts. with 3¾mm. needles.

1st row: with 3¾mm. needle *k.1 t.b.l., p.2, rep. from * to the last 2 sts., k.1 t.b.l., p.1.

2nd row: with 2¾mm. needle k.1 t.b.l.,

p.1, * k.2 t.b.l., p.1, rep. from * to end. These 2 rows form patt.

Work 7 more rows.

Inc. 1 st. at end of next row, and then the 2 foll. 10th rows.

Next row: patt. to end, and then work in patt. across sts. on spare needle.

Cont. on these 70 sts.

Work 8(8:6) rows.

Inc. 1 st. at each end of next row, and then every 10th (10th:8th) row until 96(96:100) sts. rem.

Work until sleeve measures 44(44:45) cm. (17¼(17¼:17¾) in.) from commencement, ending with a wrong side row.

Cast off.

COLLAR

Cast on 121 sts. with 3¾mm. needles.

1st row (wrong side): with 3¾mm. needle * k.1 t.b.l., p.2, rep. from * to the last st., k.1 t.b.l.

2nd row: with 2¾mm. needle * p.1, k.2 t.b.l., rep. from * to the last st., p.1.

These 2 rows form patt.

Dec. 1 st. at each end of next row, and

then every alt. row until 105 sts. rem., and then every row until 83 sts. rem.

Cast off, dec. 1 st. at each end of row.

Break yarn.

Now using 2¾mm. needles, with right side of work facing, and starting at cast on edge, k. up 30 sts. evenly along shaped edge of collar, 81 sts. from the cast off sts., and 30 sts. evenly along the other shaped edge.

Work 7 rows in g.st.

Cast off knitwise.

MAKING UP

Press each piece lightly with warm iron and damp cloth.

Join shoulder seams.

Sew straight edge of collar to neck edge.

Work buttonhole st. round buttonholes.

Sew front, back and sleeves to yoke on the wrong side along the picked up edge of yoke edging, with right side yoke overlapping left side 2.5 cm. (1 in.) at centre front.

Join side and sleeve seams.

Press seams lightly.

Sew on buttons.

Sequinned Evening Sweater   1968

Long-sleeved, sequinned, sweater with stand-up doubled collar, raglan sleeves and short back zip, for wintry evenings

★★ Suitable for knitters with some previous experience

MATERIALS

Yarn
Patons Beehive Shetland Style Chunky
10(11:12) × 50g. balls

NEEDLES

1 pair 5mm.
1 pair 6mm.
1 set of 4 5mm. (pointed both ends)

NOTIONS
Sequins
940(1010:1080)

Zip
18 cm.
7 in.

MEASUREMENTS

Bust
87(92:97) cm.
34(36:38) in.

Length (from top of shoulders)
58(60:60) cm.
22¾(23½:23½) in.

Sleeve Seam
43 cm.
16¾ in.

TENSION

15 sts. and 22 rows = 10 cm. (4 in.) square over pattern on 6mm. needles. If your tension square does not correspond to these measurements see page 166 for adjustment instructions.

ABBREVIATIONS

k. = knit; p. = purl; st(s). = stitch(es); inc. = increas(ing) (see page 166); dec. = decreas(ing) (see page 167); beg. = begin(ning); rem. = remain(ing); rep. = repeat; alt. = alternate; tog. = together; sl. = slip stitch (transfer one stitch from left needle, knitwise unless otherwise stated, to right hand needle.); cont. = continue; patt. = pattern; foll. = following; folls. = follows; mm. = millimetres; cm. = centimetre(s); in. = inch(es); m.1 = pick up horizontal loop lying before next st. and work into back of it; S.O.N. st. = yarn to back, bring a sequin up close to front of work, slip next st. purlwise, bring yarn to front: the sequin is now lying on top of the slipped

st.; t.b.l. = through back of loops; st. st. = stocking stitch.

BACK

** Thread on sequins, then cast on 63(67:71) sts. with 5mm needles.

1st row (right side): k.1, * p.1, k.1, rep. from * to end.

2nd row: p.1, * k.1, p.1, rep. from * to end.
Rep. last 2 rows twice more.
Change to 6mm. needles and patt. as folls.:
1st row: k.
2nd row: p.1, * S.O.N. st., p.3, rep. from * to last 2 sts., S.O.N. st., p.1.
3rd row: as 1st.
4th row: p.
5th and 6th rows: as 3rd and 4th.
7th row: as 1st.
8th row: p.3, * S.O.N. st., p.3, rep. from * to end.
9th–12th rows: as 3rd–6th.
These 12 rows form patt.
Cont. in patt. and work a further 12 rows straight, then shape sides by inc. 1 st. at each end of next and every foll. 12th row until there are 71(75:79) sts., taking inc. sts. into patt.
Work straight until back measures 36(36:34) cm. 14(14:13¼ in.) at centre from start, ending with right side facing.

Shape Raglans

Cast off 2 sts. at beg. of next 2 rows.
Next row: k.1, k.2 tog., k. to last 3 sts., k.2 tog t.b.l., k.1.
Cont. as folls.:
Next row (1st and 3rd sizes only): patt.
Next row (2nd size only): p.1, p.2 tog. t.b.l., patt. to last 3 sts., p.2 tog., p.1.
Next row (all sizes): k.1, k.2 tog., k to last 3 sts., k.2 tog. t.b.l., k.1.
Next row: in patt. **
Rep. last 2 rows until 41(41:43) sts. rem., ending with right side facing.
Here divide for neck:
Next row: k.1, k.2 tog., k.18(18:19), turn and leave rem. sts. on a spare needle.
Cont. on these 20(20:21) sts. for first side and work 1 row straight, then cont. dec. at raglan edge on next and every alt. row as before until 10(10:11) sts. rem., ending with right side facing. Leave sts. on a spare needle.
With right side facing, rejoin yarn to rem. 20(20:21) sts., cast on 1 st., k. to last 3 sts., k.2 tog. t.b.l., k.1.
Finish to correspond with first side.

FRONT

Work as for back from ** to **.
Rep. last 2 rows until 35(35:37) sts. rem., ending with right side facing.
Here divide for neck:
Next row: k.1, k.2 tog., k.9, turn and leave rem. sts. on a spare needle.
Cont. on these 11 sts. for first side and work 1 row straight, then cont. dec. 1 st. at raglan edge as before on next and every alt. row and *at the same time* dec. 1 st. at neck edge on next and every alt. row until 5 sts. rem.
Now keep neck edge straight and cont. dec. at raglan edge on alt. rows as before until 2 sts. rem.
Next row: p.2, turn, k.2 tog., and fasten off.
With right side facing, slip centre 11(11:13) sts. onto a safety-pin, rejoin yarn to rem. sts., k. to last 3 sts., k.2 tog. t.b.l., k.1.
Finish to correspond with first side.

SLEEVES

Thread on sequins, then cast on 31(35:35) sts. with 5mm. needles and work 6 rows k.1, p.1 rib, as for back.
Change to 6mm. needles and starting with 1st row, work in patt. as for back, shaping sides by inc. 1 st. at each end of (5th:7th:1st) and every foll. (8th:8th:8th) row until there are 49(51:55) sts., taking inc. sts. into patt.
Work straight until sleeve seam measures 43 cm. (16¾ in.), ending with right side facing.

Shape Raglans

Cast off 2 sts. at beg. of next 2 rows, cont. as folls.:
1st row: k.1, k.2 tog., k. to last 3 sts., k.2 tog. t.b.l., k.
2nd row: patt.
3rd row: k.
4th row: as 2nd.
Rep. last 4 rows 5 times more. [33(35:39) sts.] Now rep. 1st and 2nd rows until 9 sts. rem., ending with right side facing. Leave sts. on a safety-pin.

COLLAR

Sew up raglan seams.
Thread on sequins, then with right side facing and using the set of 5mm. needles, k.10(10:11) from left side of back, dec. 1 st. in centre, k.9 sleeve sts. from safety-pin, dec. 1 st. in centre, pick up and k.10 sts. down left side of neck, k.11(11:13) from centre, dec. 1 st., pick up and k.10 up right side, k.9 from right sleeve, dec. 1 st. in centre, then k.10(10:11) from back, dec. 2 sts. evenly. [63(63:67) sts.].
Starting with 2nd row, work 19 rows in patt. as for back, then cont. in st. st. without sequins until collar measures 15 cm. (5¾ in.) at centre from start, ending with right side facing.
Cast off.

MAKING UP

Do not press.
Join side and sleeve seams. Fold collar in half to wrong side and slipstitch lightly in position all round. Insert zip into back opening.

Fluffy, Dolman-sleeved Sweater   *1952*

Waist-length, stocking stitch, dolman sweater worked in two pieces, with elbow-length sleeves, ribbed welts and bands, and round neck

MATERIALS

Yarn
Pingouin Pingorina
9(10:11:12) × 20g. balls

Needles
1 pair 3mm.
1 pair 3¾mm.

MEASUREMENTS

Bust
82(87:92:97) cm.
32(34:36:38) in.

Length (to top of shoulder)
52(53:53:54) cm.
20½(20¾:20¾:21¼) in.

TENSION

24 sts. and 32 rows = 10 cm. (4 in.) square over stocking stitch on 3¾mm. needles. If your tension square does not correspond to these measurements, see page 166 for adjustment instructions.

ABBREVIATIONS

k. = knit; p. = purl; st(s). = stitch(es); inc. = increas(ing) (see page 166); dec. = decreas(ing) (see page 167); beg. = begin(ning); rem. = remain(ing); rep. = repeat; alt. = alternate; tog. = together; sl. = slip stitch (transfer one stitch from left needle, knitwise unless otherwise stated, to right hand needle.); cont. = continue; patt. = pattern; foll. = following; folls. = follows; mm. = millimetres; cm. = centimetre(s); in. = inch(es); st.st. = stocking stitch.

BACK

Cast on 80(86:92:98) sts. with 3mm. needles and work 9 cm. (3½ in.) in k.1, p.1 rib.
Change to 3¾mm. needles and st.st. Work 4 rows.

Inc. 1 st. at each end of next and every foll. 4th row until there are 104(110:116:122) sts.
Now inc. 1 st. at each end of alt. rows 4 times, then cast on 2 sts. at beg. of next 6 rows, 12 sts. at beg. of next 2 rows, and 14 sts. at beg. of next 8 rows. [260(266: 272:278) sts.]
Now cont. without shaping until sleeve edges, after the last casting on, measure 14(15:15:16) cm. (5½(5¾:5¾:6¼) in.) ending with a purl row. **

Shape Shoulder
Cast off 10 sts. at beg. of next 16 rows, 11(12:12:13) sts. at beg. of next 4 rows, and then 11(12:14:15) sts. at beg. of next 2 rows.
Cut yarn and place rem. 34(34:36:36) sts. on a holder.

FRONT

Work as for back to **.

Shape Shoulder and Neck
Cast off 10 sts. at beg. of next 6 rows.
Next row: cast off 10 sts., k. until there are 83(86:88:91) sts. on right needle. Turn, and complete this side first.
*** *1st row:* cast off 3 sts., p. to end.
2nd row: cast off 10 sts., k. to end.
3rd row: cast off 2 sts., p. to end.
4th row, 6th row and *8th row:* as 2nd row.
5th row: as 3rd row.
7th row: cast off 1 st., p. to end.
9th row: and 11th row: as 7th row.
10th row: cast off 11(12:12:13) sts., k. to end.
12th row: as 10th row.
13th row: p.
Cast off rem. 11(12:14:15) sts. ***
Now return to sts. left unworked.
Slip next 14(14:16:16) sts. onto holder.
Rejoin yarn to sts. of right front and knit to end.
Cast off 10 sts. at beg. of next row, p. to end.
Complete as for left front from *** to ***,

reversing shapings by reading p. for k., and k. for p.

NECKBAND

Sew up right shoulder and upper sleeve seam.
With right side of work facing, using 3mm. needles, pick up and k. 23 sts. down left front neck edge.
Now, working sts. from front holder, k.1(1:2:2), [inc. 1 st. in next st., k.1] 6 times, k.1 (1:2:2), then pick up and knit 23 sts. up right front neck edge, then working back neck sts., k.3 (3:4:4), [inc. 1 st. in next st., k.2] 10 times, k.1 (1:2:2). [110(110:114:114) sts.]
Work in k.1, p.1 rib for 3 cm. (1¼ in.).
Cast off loosely ribwise. (see page 169.)
Sew up shoulder and upper sleeve seam.

CUFFS

With right side of work facing, with 3mm. needles, pick up and k. 80(86:86:92) sts. along one sleeve edge.
Work in k.1, p.1 rib for 5 cm. (2 in.).
Cast off loosely ribwise.
Work other cuff similarly.

MAKING UP

Sew up side and underarm seams.
Press seams lightly on wrong side with warm iron and damp cloth.

Scarf-neck Fine Lace Blouse 1933

Just below waist-length fine wool lacy blouse with ribbed welts, scarf neck in garter stitch, and set-in sleeves

★★ Suitable for knitters with some previous experience

MATERIALS

Yarn
Jaeger Botany Wool 3 ply
11(11) × 25g. balls.

Needles
1 pair 2¼mm.
1 pair 3mm.

MEASUREMENTS

Bust
84(89) cm.
33(35) in.

Length
53 cm. (20¾ in.)

Sleeve Seam
46 cm. (18 in.)

TENSION

32 sts. and 40 rows = 10 cm. (4 in.) square over stocking stitch on 3mm. needles. If

Scarf-neck Fine Lace Blouse

your tension square does not correspond to these measurements see page 166 for adjustment instructions.

ABBREVIATIONS

k. = knit; p. = purl; st(s). = stitch(es); inc. = increas(ing) (see page 166); dec. = decreas-(ing) (see page 167); beg. = begin(ning); rem. = remain(ing); rep. = repeat; alt. = alternate; tog. = together; sl. = slip stitch (transfer one stitch from left needle, knit-wise unless otherwise stated, to right

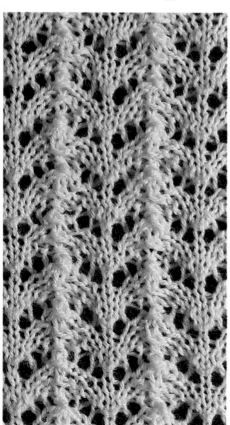

hand needle.); cont. = continue; patt. = pattern; foll. = following; folls. = follows; mm. = millimetres; cm. = centimetre(s); in. = inch(es); sl.lp. = slip stitch purlwise; y.fwd. = yarn forward; p.s.s.o. = pass slipped st. over; m.1 = make 1 st. by pick-ing up horizontal loop lying before next st. and working into back of it.

BACK

** Cast on 134(138) sts. with 2¼mm. needles, and work in rib as folls.:
1st row: (right side): k.2, * p.2, k.2, rep. from * to end.
2nd row: p.2, * k.2, p.2, rep. from * to end.
Rep. these 2 rows until back measures 8 cm. (3¼ in.), ending with a 2nd row.
Now work in k.1, p.1 rib until back measures 13 cm. (5 in.), ending with *wrong* side facing for next row.
Next row: rib 15(9), m.1, (rib 26(15), m.1) 4(8) times, rib to end. [139(147) sts.]
Change to 3mm. needles and work in patt. as folls.:
1st row (right side): sl. 1k., k.1, * y.fwd., k.2, sl. 1k., k.2 tog., p.s.s.o., k.2, y.fwd., k.1, rep. from * to last st., k.1.
2nd row: sl. 1p., p. to end.
3rd row: sl. 1k., k.2, * y.fwd., k.1, sl. 1k., k.2 tog., p.s.s.o., k.1, y.fwd., k.3, rep. from * to end.
4th row: as 2nd.
5th row: sl. 1k., k.3, * y.fwd., sl. 1k., k.2 tog., p.s.s.o., y.fwd., k.5, rep. from * to last 7 sts., y.fwd., sl. 1k., k.2 tog., p.s.s.o., y.fwd., k.4.
6th row: as 2nd.
These 6 rows form patt.
Cont. in patt. until back measures 33(34) cm. (13(13¼) in.), ending with right side facing for next row.

Shape Armholes

Cast off 8 sts. at beg. of next 2 rows, keep-ing continuity of patt.**
Dec. 1 st. at each end of next and every foll. alt. row until 109(119) sts. rem.
Work straight until back measures 53 cm. (20¾ in.), ending with right side facing for next row.

Shape Shoulders

Cast off 7(8) sts. at beg. of next 6 rows, then 8 sts. at beg. of next 2 rows.
Cast off rem. 51(55) sts.

FRONT

Work as for back from ** to **.

Divide for Neck

Next row: k.2 tog., patt. 57(61), k.2 tog., turn and leave rem. sts. on a spare needle.
Work 1 row.
Dec. 1 st. at each end of next and every foll. alt. row until 47(53) sts. rem.

Dec. 1 st. at neck edge *only* on every foll. alt. row from previous dec. until 39(44) sts. rem. Work 2 rows.
Dec. 1 st. at neck edge on next and every foll. 3rd row until 29(32) sts. rem.
Work straight until front matches back to start of shoulder shaping, ending with right side facing for next row.

Shape Shoulder

Cast off 7(8) sts. at beg. of next and foll. 2 alt. rows, keeping continuity of patt. Work 1 row, cast off rem. 8 sts.
With right side facing, rejoin yarn to rem. sts., cast off 1 st., patt. to end.
Work to match front side, reversing shap-ings.

SLEEVES

Cast on 54(58) sts. with 2¼mm. needles, and work in k.2, p.2 rib as on back for 6 cm. (2¼ in.), ending with a 1st row.
Next row: rib 3(5), m.1, (rib 4(3), m.1) 12(16) times, rib to end. [67(75) sts.]
Change to 3mm. needles and work in patt. as for back, shaping sides by inc. 1 st. at each end of 7th and every foll. 8th row until there are 103(109) sts., taking inc. sts. into patt.
Work straight until sleeve seam measures 46 cm. (18 in.), ending with right side facing for next row.

Shape Top

Cast off 6 sts. at beg. of next 2 rows, keep-ing continuity of patt.
Dec. 1 st. at each end of next and every foll. 4th row until 85(93) sts. rem. Work 1 row.
Dec. 1 st. at each end of next and every foll. alt. row until 57 sts. rem.
Work 1 row. Cast off.

MAKING UP

Omitting ribbing, press work lightly on wrong side following instructions on the ball band. Sew up shoulder, side and sleeve seams. Insert sleeves.

TIE

Cast on 3 sts. with 3mm. needles and work as folls.:
1st row (wrong side): k.1, m.1, k. to end.
2nd row: sl. 1k., k. to end.
Rep. these 2 rows until there are 25 sts.
Work straight until tie measures 100 cm. (39 in.), ending with *wrong* side facing for next row.
Next row: k.1, k.2 tog., k. to end.
Next row: sl. 1k, k. to end.
Rep. last 2 rows until 3 sts. rem. Cast off.
With right side facing and leaving 25 cm. (9¾ in.) free at each end of tie, join right side edge neatly up right side of neck, across back and down left side of neck.
Press seams.

Boat-neck Simple Silk Sweater

Just below waist-length boat-neck sweater with long or short set-in sleeves, in stocking stitch, with ribbed welts and neckline

★Suitable for beginners

MATERIALS

Yarn
Sunbeam Shantung
Long sleeved 9(9:10:11) × 25g. balls
Short sleeved 7(7:8:9) × 25g. balls

Needles
1 pair 2¾mm.
1 pair 3¼mm.

MEASUREMENTS

Bust
82(87:92:97) cm.
32(34:36:38) in.

Length
48(48:50:51) cm.
18¾(18¾:19½:20) in.

Long Sleeve Seam (with cuff turned up)
43(43:44:44) cm.
16¾(16¾:17¼:17¼) in.

Short Sleeve Seam
15(15:16:16) cm.
5¾(5¾:6¼:6¼) in.

TENSION

12½ sts. and 16 rows = 5 cm. (2 in.) square over stocking stitch on 3¼mm. needles. If your tension square does not correspond to these measurements see page 166 for adjustment instructions.

ABBREVIATIONS

k. = knit; p. = purl; st(s). = stitch(es); inc. = increas(ing) (see page 166); dec. = decreas(ing) (see page 167); beg. = begin(ning); rem. = remain(ing); rep. = repeat; alt. = alternate; tog. = together; sl. = slip stitch (transfer one stitch from left needle, knitwise unless otherwise stated, to right hand needle.); cont. = continue; patt. = pattern; foll. = following; folls. = follows; mm. = millimetres; cm. = centimetre(s); in. = inch(es); st. st. = stocking stitch.

FRONT

** Cast on 89(95:101:107) sts. with 2¾mm. needles.
1st row: k.2, * p.1, k.1, rep. from * to the last st., k.1.
2nd row: k.1, p.1, rep. from * to the last st., k.1. Rep. 1st and 2nd rows 8 times more.
Change to 3¼mm. needles and st.st.
Work 8 rows. Inc. 1 st. at each end of next row, and then every 8th row until there are 105(111:117:123) sts.
Work until front measures 29(29:30:31) cm. (11¼(11¼:11¾:12¼) in.) from beg., ending with a p. row.

Shape Armholes
Cast off 4(4:5:5) sts. at beg. of next 2 rows. Now dec. 1 st. at each end of every row until 91(93:97:99) sts. rem., and then every alt. row until 85(87:91:93) sts. rem.
** Work 26(26:28:28) rows without shaping, ending with a k. row.

Shape Neck
Next row: p.27(28:29:30) sts., cast off 31(31:33:33) sts., p. to end.
Cont. on last set of sts. Dec. 1 st. at neck edge on the next 8 rows, and then the 5 foll. alt. rows, ending at armhole edge.

Shape Shoulder
Cast off 7(8:8:8) sts. at beg. of next row. Work 1 row. Cast off 7(7:8:9) rem. sts. Rejoin yarn to rem. sts. at neck edge and complete to match first side, working 1 extra row before shaping after last dec. before shaping shoulder.

BACK

Follow instructions for front from ** to **. Work until armholes are 3 rows less than front to shoulders.

Shape Back of Neck
Next row: p.18(19:20:21) sts., cast off 49(49:51:51) sts., p. to end.
Cont. on last set of sts.
1st row: k. to last 2 sts., k.2 tog.
2nd row: p.2 tog., p. to end.

Shape Shoulders
Next row: cast off 7(8:8:8) sts. k. to last 2 sts., k.2 tog.
Next row: p.2 tog., p. to end. Cast off 7(7:8:9) rem. sts. Rejoin yarn to rem. sts. at neck edge.
1st row: k.2 tog., k. to end.
2nd row: p. to last 2 sts., p.2 tog.
3rd row: as 1st row.

4th row: cast off 7(8:8:8) sts., p. to last 2 sts., p.2 tog.
Work 1 row. Cast off 7(7:8:9) rem. sts.

LONG SLEEVES

Cast on 51(51:53:55) sts. using 2¾mm. needles and work 10 cm. (4 in.) in rib as front, ending with first row.
Change to 3¼mm. needles and st.st. Work 4 rows. Inc. 1 st. at each end of next row, and then every 8th row until there are 77(77:81:83) sts.
Work until sleeve measures 48(48:49:49) cm. (18¾(18¾:19¼:19¼) in.) from beg., ending with a p. row.

Shape Top
Cast off 4(4:5:5) sts. at beg. of next 2 rows. Now dec. 1 st. at each end of every row until 59(59:61:63) sts. rem., then every alt. row until 33(33:33:35) sts. rem., and then every row until 19(19:19:21) sts. rem. Cast off.

SHORT SLEEVES

Cast on 67(67:69:71) sts. with 2¾mm. needles and work 10 rows in rib as front.
Change to 3¼mm. needles and st.st. Work 4(4:2:2) rows.
Inc. 1 st. at each end of next row, and then every 6th row until there are 77(77:81:83) sts.
Work until sleeve measures 15(15:16:16) cm. (5¾(5¾:6¼:6¼) in.) from beg., ending with a p. row.
Shape top as long sleeve.

MAKING UP AND NECK BORDER

With wrong side facing, pin each piece out to size and shape, omitting ribbing. Press lightly with warm iron and damp cloth. Join right shoulder seam.

Neck Border
With 2¾mm. needles, and with right side of work facing, knit up 23(23:23:23) sts. down left side of front neck edge, 31(31:33:33) sts. from the cast off sts., 23(23:23:23) sts. up right side of neck, and 68(68:70:70) sts. evenly along back neck edge.
1st row: * k.1, p.1, rep. from * to the last st., k.1.
2nd row: k.2, * p.1, k.1, rep. from * to the last st., k.1.
Rep. 1st and 2nd rows 3 times more. Cast off in rib. Sew up left shoulder and neck border seam. Sew up side and sleeve seams, reversing seam on long sleeves for 8 cm. (3¼ in.) from cast on edge. Sew sleeves into armholes. Press seams lightly.

Short-sleeved Shantung Sweater   *1980*

Very simple round-neck sweater with ribbed welts, short sleeves, knitted in stocking stitch

★ Suitable for beginners

MATERIALS

Yarn
Sunbeam Shantung
7(8:9:10) × 25g. balls

Needles
1 pair 2¾mm.
1 pair 3¼mm.

MEASUREMENTS

Bust:
82(87:92:97) cm.
32(34:36:38) in.

Length
48(48:50:51) cm.
18¾(18¾:19½:20) in.

Sleeve Seam
17 cm. (6½ in.)

TENSION

12½ sts. and 16 rows = 5 cm. (2 in.) square over stocking stitch on 3¼mm. needles. If your tension square does not correspond to these measurements, see page 166 for adjustment instructions.

ABBREVIATIONS

k. = knit; p. = purl; st(s). = stitch(es); inc. = increas(ing) (see page 166); dec. = decreas-(ing) (see page 167); beg. = begin(ning); rem. = remain(ing); rep. = repeat; alt. = alternate; tog. = together; sl. = slip stitch (transfer one stitch from left needle, knit-wise unless otherwise stated, to right hand needle.); cont. = continue; patt. = pattern; foll. = following; folls. = follows; mm. = millimetres; cm. = centimetre(s); in. = inch(es); st.st. = stocking stitch.

FRONT

** Cast on 89(95:101:107) sts. with 2¾mm. needles.
1st row: k.2, *p.1, k.1, rep. from * to last st., k.1.
2nd row: * k.1, p.1, rep. from * to last st., k.1.
Rep. 1st and 2nd rows 6 times more.
Change to 3¼mm. needles and st.st. Work 8 rows. Inc. 1 st. at each end of next row, and then every 8th row until there are 105(111:117:123) sts.
Work until front measures 29(29:30:30) cm. (11¼(11¼:11¾:11¾) in.) from beg., ending with a p. row.

Shape Armholes

Cast off 4(4:5:5) sts. at beg. of next 2 rows.

Now dec. 1 st. at each end of next row, and then every alt. row until 85(87:91:93) sts. rem. ** Work until armholes measure 13(14:15:15) cm. (5(5½:5¾:5¾) in.), measured straight, ending with a p. row.

Shape Neck

Next row: k.35(36:37:38) sts., turn, leaving rem. sts. on a spare needle. Cont. on these sts., dec. 1 st. at neck edge on the next 7 rows, and then the foll. 3 alt. rows, ending at armhole edge.

Shape Shoulder

Cast off 6(7:6:7) sts. at beg. of next row, and 6(6:7:7) sts. at beg. of 2 foll. alt. rows.
Work 1 row.
Cast off rem. 7 sts.
Rejoin yarn to rem. sts. at neck edge.
Next row: cast off 15(15:17:17) sts. loosely, k. to end.
Complete to match first side, working 1 row more, to reach armhole edge, before shaping shoulder.

BACK

Work as for front from ** to **. Work until armholes measure same as front, ending with a p. row.

Shape Shoulders and Back of Neck

Cast off 6(7:6:7) sts. at beg. of next 2 rows.
Next row: cast off 6(6:7:7) sts., k.16(16:17:17) sts. including st. on needle, cast off 29(29:31:31) sts. loosely, k. to end.
Cont. on last set of sts.
1st row: cast off 6(6:7:7) sts., p. to last 2 sts., p.2 tog.
2nd row: k.2 tog., k. to end.
3rd row: as 1st row. Work 1 row.
Cast off 7 rem. sts.
Rejoin yarn to rem. sts. at neck edge.
1st row: p.2 tog., p. to end.
2nd row: cast off 6(6:7:7) sts., k. to last 2 sts., k.2 tog.
3rd row: as 1st row.
Cast off 7 rem. sts.

SLEEVES

Cast on 67(69:69:71) sts. with 2¾mm. needles.
1st row (wrong side): * k.1, p.1, rep. from * to last st., k.1.
2nd row: k.2, * p.1, k.1, rep. from * to last st., k.1.
Rep. 1st and 2nd rows 3 times more, and then 1st row once.
Change to 3¼mm. needles and st.st. Work 4 rows.
Inc. 1 st. at each end of next row, and then every 7th(7th:6th:6th) row until there are 79(81:83:85) sts. Work 8(8:7:7) rows.

Shape Top

Cast off 4(4:5:5) sts. at beg. of next 2 rows.
Now dec. 1 st. at each end of next row, then every alt. row until 65(65:67:67) sts. rem., then every 4th row until 49 sts. rem., and then every row until 39 sts. rem.
Next row: (k.2 tog.) twice, * k.1, (k.2 tog.) twice, rep. from * to end.
Cast off.

MAKING UP AND NECK BORDER

With wrong side facing, pin each piece out to size and shape, and omitting ribbing, press lightly with a warm iron and damp cloth.
Sew up right shoulder seam.

Neck Border

With right side of work facing and 2¾mm. needles, k. up 23 sts. down left side of front neck edge, 19(19:21:21) sts. evenly from the 15(15:17:17) cast off sts., 23 sts. up right side of neck and 5 sts. down right side of back neck edge, k. up 34(34:36:36) sts. evenly from the 29(29:31:31) cast off sts., and 5 sts. up left side of neck.
1st row: * k.1, p.1, rep. from * to last st., k.1.
2nd row: k.2, * p.1, k.1, rep. from * to last st., k.1.
Rep. 1st and 2nd rows 3 times more, and then 1st row once.
Cast off in rib.
Sew up left shoulder and neck border seam. Sew up side and sleeve seams.
Sew sleeves into armholes.
Press seams lightly.

Contrast-edged V-neck Sweater

Simple V-neck sweater in stocking stitch, shaped at the waistline, with hemmed cuff and lower edge and contrast-coloured V and cuffs

★ Suitable for beginners

MATERIALS

Yarn
Wendy Shetland 4 ply
12(13:13:14:14) × 25g. balls (Main)
2(2:2:2:2) × 25g. balls (Contrast)

Needles
1 pair 2¾mm.
1 pair 3¼mm.
1 set of 4 double-pointed 2¾mm.

MEASUREMENTS

Bust
87(92:97:102:107) cm.
34(36:38:40:42) in.

Length (excluding neckband and hem)
56(57:59.5:60.5:62.5) cm.
22(22¼:23¼:23¾:24½) in.

Sleeve Seam
46 cm.
18 in.

TENSION

28 sts. and 38 rows = 10 cm. (4 in.) square over stocking stitch on 3¼mm. needles. If your tension square does not correspond to these measurements see page 166 for adjustment instructions.

ABBREVIATIONS

k. = knit; p. = purl; st(s). = stitch(es); inc. = increas(ing) (see page 166); dec. = decreas-(ing) (see page 167); beg. = begin(ning); rem. = remain(ing); rep. = repeat; alt. = alternate; tog. = together; sl. = slip stitch (transfer one stitch from left needle, knit-wise unless otherwise stated, to right hand needle.); cont. = continue; patt. = pattern; foll. = following; folls. = follows; mm. = millimetres; cm. = centimetre(s); in. = inch(es); st.st. = stocking stitch; M = main colour; C = contrast colour.

BACK

Cast on 112(120:126:134:142) sts. with 2¾mm. needles using M.
Work 15 rows, ending with a k. row.
Next row: k. to mark hemline.
Change to 3¼mm. needles.
Work 14 rows.
Dec. 1 st. each end of next and every foll. 6th row until 98(106:112:120:128) sts. rem.
Work until back measures 16 cm. (6¼ in.) from hemline.
Inc. 1 st. each end of next and every foll. 4th row until there are 124(132:138:146:154) sts. *
Work until back measures 36(36:37½:37½:38½) cm. (14(14:14¾:14¾:15¼) in.) from hemline.

Shape Armholes

Cast off 5(6:7:8:9) sts. at beg. of next 2 rows. Dec. 1 st. each end of every k. row until 102(106:110:114:118) sts. rem.
Work until armholes measure 18(19:20:21:22) cm. (7(7½:7¾:8¼:8½) in.) on the straight.

Shape Shoulders

Cast off at beg. of next and foll. rows 7(8:9:7:8) sts. twice and 8(8:8:9:9) sts. 6 times. Leave rem. 40(42:44:46:48) sts. on holder for neckband.

FRONT

Follow instructions for back to *.
Work 5(5:11:11:15) rows, ending with a p. row.

Shape Neck

Next row: k. 62(66:69:73:77) sts., turn. Finish this side first.
** Dec. 1 st. at beg. of next and every foll. 4th row until 56(60:63:67:71) sts. rem., ending at a side edge.

Shape Armhole

1st row: cast off 5(6:7:8:9) sts., k. to end.

2nd row: p. Dec. 1 st. at armhole edge every k. row 6(7:7:8:9) times, at same time cont. to dec. at neck edge every 4th row until 31(32:33:34:35) sts. rem.
Work until armhole measures same as those of back.

Shape Shoulder

Cast off at armhole edge 7(8:9:7:8) sts. once, and 8(8:8:9:9) sts. 3 times.
Join yarn to neck edge of rem. sts. and work from **, reading p. for k. and k. for p.

SLEEVES

Cast on 50(54:58:62:66) sts. with 2¾mm. needles using C. Work 15 rows, ending with a k. row.
Next row: k. to mark hemline.
Work 15 rows.
Next row: p.5(0:2:4:6), * p. twice into next st., p.2(3:3:3:3), rep. from * to last 6(2:4:6:8) sts., p. twice into next st., p. to end. [64(68:72:76:80) sts.]
Change to 3¼mm. needles and M. Inc. 1 st. each end of next and every 6th row until there are 98(102:106:110:114) sts.
Work until sleeve measures 46 cm. (18 in.).

Shape Top

Cast off 5(6:7:8:9) sts. at beg. of next 2 rows. Dec. 1 st. at each end of next 5 rows, then every k. row until 46 sts. rem.
Cast off 3 sts. at beg. of next 8 rows.
Cast off.

NECKBAND

Sew up shoulder seams. With right side of work facing and 2¾mm. needles, using C, knit up sts. round neck as folls.:
1st needle: 96(98:100:102:104) sts. down left side.
2nd needle: 96(98:100:102:104) sts. up right side.
3rd needle: 40(42:44:46:48) sts. across holder at back.
1st round:
1st needle: k. to last 2 sts., k.2 tog.
2nd needle: sl. 1, k.1, p.s.s.o., k. to end.
3rd needle: k. Rep. this round 14 times more. p. next round to mark hemline.
Work 15 more rounds, inc. 2 sts. at centre front every round.
Cast off loosely.

MAKING UP

Set in sleeves. Sew side and sleeve seams. Turn in hem, cuffs and neckband at turning lines and slipstitch on wrong side. Press.

Cotton Sweater with Ribbed Yoke   *1938*

Waist-length sweater with narrow rib rollover collar, rib yoke pattern and welts, set-in sleeves, main part knitted in stocking stitch

★ Suitable for beginners

MATERIALS

Yarn
Pingouin Fil d'Ecosse No. 5
8(8:9) × 50g. balls

Needles
1 pair 2¼mm.
1 pair 2¾mm.

MEASUREMENTS

Bust
87(92:97) cm.
34(36:38) in.

Length
45(46:47) cm.
17¾(18:18½) in.

Sleeve Seam
46 cm.
18 in.

TENSION

31 sts. and 44 rows = 10 cm. (4 in.) square over stocking stitch on 2¾mm. needles. If your tension square does not correspond to these measurements, see page 166 for adjustment instructions.

ABBREVIATIONS

k. = knit; p. = purl; st(s). = stitch(es); inc. = increas(ing) (see page 166); dec. = decreas-(ing) (see page 167); beg. = begin(ning); rem. = remain(ing); rep. = repeat; alt. = alternate; tog. = together; sl. = slip stitch (transfer one stitch from left needle, knit-wise unless otherwise stated, to right hand needle.); cont. = continue; patt. = pattern; foll. = following; folls. = follows; mm. = millimetres; cm. = centimetre(s); in. = inch(es); st.st. = stocking stitch.

FRONT

Cast on 122(130:138) sts. with 2¼mm. needles and work in rib:
1st row (right side): k.2, * p.2, k.2, rep. from * to end.
2nd row: p.2, * k.2, p.2, rep. from * to end.
Rep. these 2 rows until work measures 5 cm. (2 in.), ending with a 2nd row, but inc. 1 st. in centre of last row.
Change to 2¾mm. needles and beg. with a k. row, work in st.st., inc. 1 st. at each

end of every foll. 8th row until there are 139(147:155) sts.
Cont. without shaping until work measures 24 cm. (9½ in.) from beg., end-ing with a p. row.

Shape Yoke Pattern
1st row: k.69(73:77), p.1, k.69(73:77).
2nd row: p.68(72:76), k.3, p.68(72:76).
3rd row: k.67(71:75), then for yoke k.2, p.1, k.2, then k.67(71:75).
4th row: p.66(70:74), k.1, p.1, k.3, p.1, k.1, p.66(70:74).
5th row: k.65(69:73), (p.1, k.3) twice, p.1, k.65(69:73).
6th row: p.64(68:72), (k.3, p.1) twice, k.3, p.64(68:72).
7th row: k.63(67:71), then k.2, (p.1, k.3) twice, p.1, k.2, then k.63(67:71).
8th row: p.62(66:70), k.1, (p.1, k.3) 3 times, p.1, k.1, p.62(66:70).

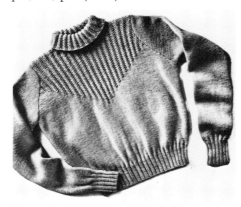

9th row: k.61(65:69), (p.1, k.3) 4 times, p.1, k.61(65:69).
10th row: p.60(64:68), (k.3, p.1) 4 times, k.3, p.60(64:68).
Cont. in this way, working 1 extra st. in patt. at each side of yoke on every row until 16 yoke rows have been worked.
NOTE: On right side rows where yoke begins and ends k.2, these sts. must be considered as part of yoke.

Shape Armholes
Cont. shaping yoke while shaping arm-hole. Cast off 3 sts. at beg. of next 8 rows, 2 sts. at beg. of next 2(4:6) rows and dec. 1 st. at both ends of every alt. row 10 times. [91(95:99) sts.]
During armhole dec., yoke patt. will reach armhole edge. Yoke patt. rows will read as folls.:
*** *1st row* (right side): k.1(3:1), * p.1, k.3,

rep. from * to last 2(4:2) sts., p.1, k.1(3:1).
2nd row: k.3(1:3), * p.1, k.3, rep. from * to last 4(2:4) sts., p.1, k.3(1:3). ***
Cont. in this patt. until work measures 39(40:41) cm. (15¼(15¾:16) in.) from beg., ending with a wrong side row.

Shape Neck and Shoulders
1st row: patt. 38(40:42) sts. and leave these sts. (left front) on spare needle; cast off next 15 sts., patt. to end. Cont. patt. on 38(40:42) sts. rem. for right front.
Work 1 row straight.
** Cast off 3 sts. at beg. of next row, 2 sts. at same edge on next 5 alt. rows and 1 st. on next 7 alt. rows, thus ending at side edge. [18(20:22) sts.]
Keeping neck edge straight, cast off 6 sts. at beg. of next and the foll. alt. row, for shoulder.
Work 1 row then cast off rem. 6(8:10) sts. **
With wrong side facing rejoin yarn to neck edge of left front sts.
Complete as for right front from ** to **.

BACK

Work as for front until side incs. are com-pleted, then cont. on 139(147:155) sts. in st.st. until work matches front to arm-holes, ending with a p. row.

Shape Armhole
Cast off 3 sts. at beg. of next 8 rows, 2 sts. at beg. of next 2(4:6) rows, and dec. 1 st. at both ends of every alt. row 10 times, ending with a p. row. [91(95:99) sts.]
Now work from *** to *** across all sts. without shaping until armholes measure same as front, ending with a wrong side row.

Shape Neck and Shoulders
1st row: cast off 6 sts., patt. until there are 22(24:26) sts. on right needle, leave on spare needle or holder for right back, cast off 35 sts., patt. to end.
Cont. on these 28(30:32) sts. for left back. Cast off 6 sts. at beg. of next row and 5 sts. at neck edge on foll. row. Rep. last 2 rows once.
Cast off rem. 6(8:10) sts.
With wrong side facing rejoin yarn to neck edge of right back sts., cast off 5 sts., patt. to end.
Cast off 6 sts. at beg. of next row and 5 sts. at neck edge on foll. row. Cast off rem. 6(8:10) sts.

Cotton Sweater with Ribbed Yoke

SLEEVES

Cast on 62(66:70) sts. with 2¼mm. needles and work in rib as for front welt for 7 cm. (2¾ in.), ending with a 2nd row. Change to 2¾mm. needles and beg. with a k. row work in st.st., inc. 1 st. at both ends of every foll. 8th row 20 times. Cont. on 102(106:110) sts. until work measures 46 cm. (18 in.) from beg.

Shape Top

Cast off 3 sts. at beg. of next 8 rows, 2 sts. at beg. of next 2(4:6) rows, 1 st. at beg. of next 20(24:28) rows, 2 sts. at beg. of next 8(6:4) rows and 4 sts. at beg. of next 2 rows.
Cast off rem. 30 sts.

COLLAR

Sew up right shoulder seam, matching patt. and backstitching this and all seams. With right side of work facing, pick up and k. 143 sts., with 2¾mm. needles, all round neck edge. Work in yoke patt., as given for small size, for 10 cm. (4 in.). Cast off loosely in patt.

MAKING UP

Sew up left shoulder seam, cont. seam along collar for 2 cm. (¾ in.) then join remainder of seam on reverse side, fold collar over.
Sew in sleeves.
Sew up side and sleeve seams.
Press all seams lightly on wrong side with warm iron and damp cloth.

Boat-neck Dolman Sweater   *1957*

Two-tone simple dolman sweater with hem, neck facing and three-quarter length sleeves worked all-in-one with body, in stocking stitch

★ Suitable for beginners

MATERIALS

Yarn
Sirdar Majestic Wool 4 ply
7(7:7:7:8) × 50g. balls (Main Colour)
2(2:2:2:3) × 50g. balls (Contrast Colour)

Needles
1 pair 2¾mm.
1 pair 3¼mm.

MEASUREMENTS

Bust
82(87:92:97:102) cm.
32(34:36:38:40) in.

Length
60(61:62:63:64) cm.
23½(24:24¼:24¾:25) in.

TENSION

14 stitches and 18 rows = 5 cm. (2 in.) square over stocking stitch on 3¼mm. needles. If your tension square does not correspond to these measurements, see page 166 for adjustment instructions.

ABBREVIATIONS

k. = knit; p. = purl; st(s). = stitch(es); inc. = increas(ing) (see page 166); dec. = decreas-(ing) (see page 167); beg. = begin(ning); rem. = remain(ing); rep. = repeat; alt. = alternate; tog. = together; sl. = slip stitch (transfer one stitch from left needle, knit-wise unless otherwise stated, to right hand needle.); cont. = continue; patt. = pattern; foll. = following; folls. = follows; mm. = millimetres; cm. = centimetre(s); in. = inch(es); st.st. = stocking stitch; M = main colour; C = contrast colour.

BACK AND FRONT (alike)

Cast on 104(112:120:128:136) sts. with M using 2¾mm. needles.
Work 9 rows in st.st.; k. 1 row on wrong side to denote hemline.
Change to 3¼mm. needles. Work 10 rows. Join in C. Work 14 rows.
Break C. With M, cont. until work measures 20 cm. (7¾ in.) from hemline, finishing after a p. row. Now inc. 1 st. at both ends of next and every foll. 6th row until there are 118(126:134:142:150) sts.
Cont. until work measures 36 cm. (14 in.) from hemline, finishing after a p. row.

Shape Sleeves
Cast on 16 sts. at beg. of next 10 rows. [278(286:294:302:310) sts.]
Begin sleeve bands:
1st row: with C, cast on 9 sts.; k. these 9 sts. with C, k. to end with M. With 2nd ball of C, cast on 9 sts.
2nd row: p., keeping colours as set and twisting yarns when changing colour to avoid leaving holes in the work.
3rd row: Join in 2nd ball of M. Cast on 14 sts. k. 14 M, k.9C, k.278(286:294:302:310) M, k.9C.
Join in 3rd ball of M.
Cast on 14 sts. [324(332:340:348:356) sts.]
Working colours as set, cont. until sleeve edge measures 12(13:14:15:16) cm. (4¾(5:5½:5¾:6¼) in.), finishing after a p. row.

Shape Upper Sleeves and Shoulders
Cast off 14 sts. with M at beg. of next 2 rows, then 9 sts. with C at beg. of foll. 2 rows.
Cast off 9 sts. with M. at beg. of next 10(10:10:12:12) rows. [188(196:204:194:202) sts.]

Work Shoulder Band
Break M. Join in C. Cast off 9 sts. at beg. of next 12 rows and 10(12:16:11:13) at beg. of foll. 2 rows. [60(64:64:64:68) sts.]
Break C. Join in M. Work 9 rows. k. 1 row on wrong side. Change to 2¾mm. needles. Work 9 rows. Cast off very loose-ly.

MAKING UP

Press on the wrong side under a damp cloth. Sew up upper sleeve, shoulder, neckband, side and underarm seams using the matching yarn for each colour section.
Press seams. Turn in and hem lower edge and neck facing. Double M edge of cuff to wrong side and hem. Press hems.

Bloused Diamond Patterned Sweater   *1978*

Hip-length bloused sweater with ribbed welts, full sleeves, round neck and drop shoulders, in lacy diamond pattern

★★ Suitable for knitters with some previous experience

MATERIALS

Yarn

Pingouin Type Shetland DK
13(13:14:14) × 50 g. balls

Needles

1 pair 3mm.
1 pair 3¼mm.
1 pair 4mm.

MEASUREMENTS

Bust
82(87:92:97) cm.
32(34:36:38) in.

Length
71(71:72:72) cm.
27¾(27¾:28¼:28¼) in.

Sleeve Seam
53 cm.
20¾ in.

TENSION

11 sts. and 15 rows = 5 cm. (2 in.) square over pattern on 4mm. needles. If your tension square does not correspond to these measurements, see page 166 for adjustment instructions.

ABBREVIATIONS

k. = knit; p. = purl; st(s). = stitch(es); inc. = increas(ing) (see page 166); dec. = decreas-(ing) (see page 167); beg. = begin(ning); rem. = remain(ing); rep. = repeat; alt. = alternate; tog. = together; sl. = slip stitch (transfer one stitch from left needle, knit-wise unless otherwise stated, to right hand needle.); cont. = continue; patt. = pattern; foll. = following; folls. = follows; mm. = millimetres; cm. = centimetre(s); in. = inch(es); m.1. = make one by pick-ing up thread lying before next stitch and knitting into the back of it; y.fwd. = yarn forward; p.s.s.o. = pass slipped stitch over; incl. = including.

BACK

Cast on 90(96:102:108) sts. using 3mm. needles and work in double rib:
1st row: k.2(3:2:3), * p.2, k.2, rep. from * ending last rep. k.2(3:2:3).
2nd row: p.2(3:2:3), * k.2, p.2, rep. from * ending last rep. p.2(3:2:3). Rep. these 2 rows until welt measures 14 cm. (5½ in.) ending after a 2nd row and inc. 3 sts.

evenly across last row. [93(99:105:111 sts.)]. Change to 4mm. needles and proceed in patt:
1st row: k.1, * y.fwd., sl.1, k.1, p.s.s.o., k.1, y.fwd., k.2 tog., k.1, rep. from * to last 2 sts., y.fwd., sl.1, k.1, p.s.s.o.
2nd and alt. rows: p.
3rd row: k.2, * y.fwd., sl.1, k.1, p.s.s.o., k.1, k.2 tog., y.fwd., k.1, rep. from * to last st., k.1.
5th row: k.3, * y.fwd., sl.1, k.2 tog., p.s.s.o., y.fwd., k.3, rep. from * to end.
7th row: k.1, * y.fwd., k.2 tog., k.1, y.fwd., sl.1, k.1, p.s.s.o., k.1, rep. from * to last 2 sts., y.fwd., k.2 tog.
9th row: k.2, * k.2 tog., y.fwd., k.1, y.fwd., sl.1, k.1, p.s.s.o., k.1, rep. from * to last st., k.1.
11th row: k.1, k.2 tog., y.fwd., * k.3, y.fwd., sl.1, k.2 tog., p.s.s.o., y.fwd., rep. from * ending last rep. k.3, y.fwd., sl.1, k.1, p.s.s.o., k.1.
12th row: as 2nd row.
These 12 rows form the patt.
Cont. in patt. until work measures 51 cm. (20 in.) ending after a wrong side row. Place a coloured thread at both ends of last row to indicate beg. of armholes.
Cont. in patt. until armhole measures 20(20:21:21) cm. (8(8:8½:8½) in.) from thread, ending after a wrong side row.

Shape Neck
Next row: patt. 34(36:38:40) sts., turn and complete this half first.
Next row: cast off 2 sts., work to end.
Next row: work to last 2 sts., k.2 tog.
Next row: work to end.

Shape Shoulder
Cast off 10(11:11:12) sts. at beg. of next row and 10(11:12:12) sts. at beg. of foll. alt. row. Work 1 row. Cast off rem. 11(11:12:13) sts. Return to rem. sts. and

slip centre 25(27:29:31) sts. onto a st. holder. Rejoin yarn to rem. sts. at neck edge and complete to correspond with first half, reversing shapings.

FRONT

Work as given for back until armhole measures 11(11:13:13) cm. (4¼(4¼:5:5) in.) from thread, ending after a wrong side row.

Shape Neck
Next row: patt. 39(41:43:45) sts., turn and complete this half first. Cont. in patt. cast-ing off 2 sts. at neck edge on next row, then dec. 1 st. at same edge on next 4 rows then on every foll. alt. row until 31(33:35:37) sts. rem.
Cont. straight until work measures the same as back to shoulder shaping, ending at armhole edge.

Shape Shoulder
Work as given for back shoulder shaping. Return to rem. sts. and slip centre 15(17:19:21) sts. onto a st. holder.
Rejoin yarn to rem. sts. at neck edge and complete to correspond with first half, reversing shapings.

SLEEVES

Cast on 54(54:58:58) sts. using 3¼mm. needles and work in k.2, p.2 rib for 7 cm. (2¾ in.) ending after a 1st row.
Next row: rib 8(8:9:9) sts., (m.1, rib 1), rep. 39(39:41:41) times, rib 7(7:8:8). [93(93:99:99) sts.]
Change to 4mm. needles and proceed in patt. as given for back until sleeve measures 53 cm. (20¾ in.) ending after a right side row. Cast off fairly loosely.

NECKBAND

Using a back stitch seam, sew up right shoulder. With right side of work facing, using 3¼mm. needles, pick up and knit 33 sts. down left side of neck, k.15(17:19:21) sts. from front stitch holder, pick up and knit 33 sts. up right side of neck and 33(35:37:39) sts. across back of neck (incl. sts. on stitch holder). [114(118:122:126) sts.] Work in k.2, p.2 rib for 6 cm. (2¼ in.) Cast off very loosely in rib.

MAKING UP

Sew up rem. shoulder and neckband. Fold neckband in half and slip stitch lightly and loosely to wrong side.
Pin sleeve tops to body, positioning each end of sleeve tops at coloured threads. Sew up side and sleeve seams.

Aran-style Polo Neck Sweater

Long polo-neck sweater in lozenge pattern, vandyke stitch, bobble stitch and astrakan stitch, with welt and polo collar in twisted flat rib

★★★ For experienced knitters only

MATERIALS

Yarn
Sirdar Majestic 4 Ply
9(10:11) × 50g. balls

Needles
1 pair 3¼mm.
1 cable needle

MEASUREMENTS

Bust
87(92:97) cm.
34(36:38) in.

Length
57(57:58) cm.
22¼(22¼:22¾) in.

Sleeve Seam
47 cm. (18½ in.).

TENSION

14 sts. and 18 rows = 5 cm. (2 in.) square over stocking stitch on 3¼mm. needles. If your tension square does not correspond to these measurements see page 166 for adjustment instructions.

ABBREVIATIONS

k. = knit; p. = purl; st(s). = stitch(es); inc. = increas(ing) (see page 166); dec. = decreas-(ing) (see page 167); beg. = begin(ning); rem. = remain(ing); rep. = repeat; alt. = alternate; tog. = together; sl. = slip stitch (transfer one stitch from left needle, knit-wise unless otherwise stated, to right hand needle.); cont. = continue; patt. = pattern; foll. = following; folls. = follows; mm. = millimetres; cm. = centimetre(s); in. = inch(es), cross 2 b. = take the needle behind the first st. on left hand needle and purl the 2nd st., then knit the 1st st., slip both sts. off the needle together; cross 2 b.p. = take the needle behind the 1st st. on the left hand needle and purl the 2nd st., then purl the 1st st., slip both sts. off the needle together; cross 2 f. = knit 2nd st. on left hand needle and then purl the 1st st., slip both sts. off the needle together ; y.fwd. = yarn forward; p.s.s.o. = pass slip st. over; to make a bobble = knit into the front, back, front, back, front of next st., making 5 sts. out of one, knit next st., turn and purl 5, turn and knit 5, turn and purl 5. Now slip 2nd, 3rd, 4th and 5th sts. over the first st. and knit into the back of the bobble st.; m.1 = increase 1 st. by picking up loop from between needles and purling into the back of it; cable 6 front = slip next 3 sts. on cable needle and hold at front of work, k. next 3 sts. and then k.3 sts. onto cable needle; cable 6 back = slip next 3 sts. onto cable needle and hold at back of work, k. next 3 sts. and then k.3 sts. on cable needle.

CENTRE PANEL (referred to as patt. 22)

1st row (wrong side): p.
2nd row: k.8, k.2 tog., y.fwd., k.2, y.fwd., sl.1, k.1, p.s.s.o., k.8.
3rd row: p.
4th row: k.7., (k.2 tog., y.fwd.) twice, sl.1, k.1, p.s.s.o, y.fwd., sl.1, k.1, p.s.s.o., k.7.
5th row: p.10, p. into front and back of next st., p.10.
6th row: k.6, (k.2 tog., y.fwd.) twice, k.2, (y.fwd., sl.1, k.1, p.s.s.o.) twice, k.6.
7th and foll. alt. rows: p.
8th row: k.5, (k.2 tog., y.fwd.) twice, k.4, (y.fwd., sl.1, k.1, p.s.s.o.) twice, k.5.
10th row: k.4, (k.2 tog., y.fwd.) twice, k.6, (y.fwd., sl.1, k.1, p.s.s.o.) twice, k.4.
12th row: k.3, (k.2 tog., y.fwd.) twice, k.3, make a bobble, k.3, (y.fwd., sl.1, k.1, p.s.s.o.) twice, k.3.
14th row: k.2, (k.2 tog., y.fwd.) twice, k.10, (y.fwd., sl.1, k.1, p.s.s.o.) twice, k.2.
16th row: k.1, (k.2 tog., y.fwd.) twice, k.12, (y.fwd., sl.1, k.1, p.s.s.o.) twice, k.1.
18th and 20th rows: k.
These 20 rows form the patt.

FRONT

** Cast on 119(126:135) sts. with 3¼mm. needles.
Next row: k.2(2:3), k.1, p.2, * k.5, p.2, rep. from * to the last 2(2:3) sts., k.2(2:3).
Cont. in welt patt.:
1st row (wrong side): p.2(2:3), k.2, p.1, * p.4, k.2, p.1, rep. from * to the last 2(2:3) sts., p.2(2:3).
2nd row: k.2(2:3), cross 2 b., p.1, * k.4, cross 2 b., p.1, rep. from * to the last 2(2:3) sts., k.2(2:3).
3rd row: p.2(2:3), k.1, p.1, k.1, * p.4, k.1, p.1, k.1, rep. from * to the last 2(2:3) sts., p.2(2:3).
4th row: k.2(2:3), p.1, cross 2 b., * k.4, p.1, cross 2 b., rep. from * to the last 2(2:3) sts., k.2(2:3).
5th row: p.2(2:3), p.1, k.2, * p.5, k.2, rep. from * to the last 2(2:3) sts., p.2(2:3).
6th row: k.2(2:3), p.1, cross 2 f., * k.4, p.1, cross 2 f., rep. from * to the last 2(2:3) sts., k.2(2:3).
7th row: p.2(2:3), k.1, p.1, k.1, * p.4, k.1, p.1, k.1, rep. from * to the last 2(2:3) sts., p.2(2:3).
8th row: k.2(2:3), cross 2 f., p.1, * k.4, cross 2 f., p.1, rep. from * to the last 2(2:3) sts., k.2(2:3).
These 8 rows form the patt.
Work 25 more rows.
Next row (1st size only): p.25, k.1, p.3, k.2, (p.4, k.2) twice, p.3, k.1, p.1, k.10, k.2 tog., k.11, p.1, k.1, p.3, k.2, (p.4, k.2) twice, p.3, k.1, p.25. [(118 sts.)]
Next row (2nd size only): p.29, k.1, p.3, k.2, (p.4, k.2) twice, p.3, k.1, p.1, k.22, p.1, k.1, p.3, k.2, (p.4, k.2) twice, p.3, k.1, p.29. [126 sts.]
Next row (3rd size only): p.33, k.1, p.3, k.2, (p.4, k.2) twice, p.3, k.1, p.1, k.10, k.2 tog., k.11, p.1, k.1, p.3, k.2, (p.4, k.2) twice, p.3, k.1, p.33. [134 sts.]
Cont. in patt. as folls.:
1st row (wrong side): (p.3 tog., (k.1, p.1, k.1) into next st.) 6(7:8) times, k.1, p.1, k.3, cross 2 b.p., (k.4, cross 2 b.p.) twice, k.3, p.1, k.1, p.22 (1st row of centre panel), k.1, p.1, k.3, cross 2 b.p., (k.4, cross 2 b.p.) twice, k.3, p.1, k.1, (p.3 tog., (k.1, p.1, k.1) into next st.) 6(7:8) times.
2nd row: p.25(29:33), k.1, p.2, (cross 2 f., cross 2 b., p.2) 3 times, k.1, p.1, patt. 22, p.1, k.1, p.2, (cross 2 f., cross 2 b., p.2) 3 times, k.1, p.25(29:33).
3rd row: ((k.1, p.1, k.1) into next st., p.3 tog.) 6(7:8) times, k.1, p.1, (k.2, p.1) 7 times, k.1, p.22, k.1, p.1, (k.2, p.1) 7 times, k.1, ((k.1, p.1, k.1) into next st., p.3 tog.) 6(7:8) times.
4th row: p.25(29:33), k.1, p.1, (cross 2 f., p.2, cross 2 b.) 3 times, p.1, k.1, p.1, patt. 22, p.1, k.1, p.1, (cross 2 f., p.2, cross 2 b.) 3 times, p.1, k.1, p.25(29:33).
These 4 rows form the patt. for side panels.
5th row: patt. 24(28:32), k.1, p.1, k.1, p.1, (k.4, cross 2 b.p.) twice, k.4, p.1, k.1, p.1, k.1, patt. 22, k.1, p.1, k.1, p.1, k.1, (k.4, cross 2 b.p.) twice, k.4, p.1, k.1, p.1, k.1, patt. to end.
6th row: p.25(29:33), k.1, p.1, cross 2 b., (p.2, cross 2 f., cross 2 b.) twice, p.2, cross 2 f., p.1, k.1, p.1, patt. 22, p.1, k.1, p.1, cross 2 b., (p.2, cross 2 f., cross 2 b.) twice,

Aran-style Polo Neck Sweater

p.2, cross 2 f., p.1, k.1, p.25(29:33).

7th row: patt. 24(28:32), k.1, p.1, (k.2, p.1) 7 times, k.1, p.22, k.1, p.1, (k.2, p.1) 7 times, k.1, patt. to end.

8th row: p.25(29:33), k.1, (p.2, cross 2 b., cross 2 f.) 3 times, p.2, k.1, p.1, patt. 22, p.1, k.1, (p.2, cross 2b., cross 2 f.) 3 times, p.2, k.1, p.25(29:33).

These 8 rows form the patt. for the panels on each side of centre panel. Rep. these 8 rows, at the same time continuing over the 22 sts. for centre panel.

Work until front measures 39.5(39.5:41) cm. (15½(15½:16) in.) from beg., ending with a wrong side row. **

Shape Armholes

Dec. 1 st. at each end of the next 4(6:8) rows. [110(114:118) sts.]

Work until armholes measure 15(15:16) cm. (5¾(5¾:6¼) in.) measured straight, ending with a right side row.

Shape Neck

Next row: work 43(45:47) sts., cast off 24 sts. work to end.

Cont. on last set of sts. as folls.:

Keeping armhole edge straight, dec. 1 st. at neck edge on the next 8 rows, and then the foll. alt. row, ending at armhole edge.

Shape Shoulder

Dec. at neck edge on alt. rows twice more, cast off 8(9:9) sts. at beg. of next row, and 8(8:9) sts. at beg. of foll. 2 alt. rows.

Work 1 row.

Cast off 8(9:9) rem. sts.

Rejoin wool to rem. sts. at neck edge and complete to match first side, working 1 row more before shaping shoulder.

BACK

Work as for front from ** to **.

Work until armholes measure same as those of front, ending with a wrong side row.

Shape Shoulders and Back of Neck

Cast off 8(8:9) sts. at beg. of next 2 rows.

Next row: cast off 8(8:9) sts., work 19(20:21) sts. including st. on needle, cast off 40 sts., work to end.

Cont. on last set of sts. as folls.:

1st row: cast off 8(8:9) sts., work to the last 2 sts., k.2 tog.

2nd row: k.2 tog., work to end.

3rd row: as 1st row.

Work 1 row.

Cast off 8(9:9) rem. sts.

Rejoin wool to rem. sts. at neck edge.

1st row: k.2 tog., work to end.

2nd row: cast off 8(8:9) sts., work to the last 2 sts., k.2 tog.

3rd row: as 1st row.

Cast off 8(9:9) rem. sts.

SLEEVES

Cast on 56 sts. with 3¼mm. needles and work 33 rows in welt patt. as for front of 1st size.

Next row: p.4, m.1, k.6, m.1, k.6, m.1, p.24, m.1., k.6, m.1, k.6, m.1, p.4. [62 sts.]

Cont. in patt.

1st row (wrong side): p.3 tog., (k.1, p.1, k.1) into next st., k.1, p.6, k.1, p.6, k.1, (p.3 tog., (k.1, p.1, k.1) into next st.) 6 times, k.1, p.6, k.1, p.6, k.1, p.3 tog., (k.1, p.1, k.1) into last st.

2nd row: p.5, k.6, p.1, k.6, p.26, k.6, p.1, k.6, p.5.

3rd row: (k.1, p.1, k.1) into first st., p.3 tog., k.1, p.6, k.1, p.6, k.1, ((k.1, p.1, k.1) into next st., p.3 tog.) 6 times, k.1, p.6, k.1, p.6, k.1, (k.1, p.1, k.1) into next st., p.3 tog.

4th row: p.5, cable 6 front, p.1, cable 6 back, p.26, cable 6 front, p.1, cable 6 back, p.5.

5th row: as 1st row.

6th row: as 2nd row.

7th row: as 3rd row.

8th row: as 2nd row.

9th row: as 1st row.

10th row: as 2nd row.

11th row: as 3rd row.

12th row: p.5, cable 6 back, p.1, cable 6 front, p.26, cable 6 back, p.1, cable 6 front, p.5.

13th row: as 1st row.

14th row: as 2nd row.

15th row: as 3rd row.

16th row: as 2nd row.

These 16 rows form the patt.

Cont. with 2 cable panels and the remainder in blackberry stitch.

Work 1 more row.

Now, keeping extra sts. in purl fabric until there are sufficient to form a complete patt., inc. 1 st. at each end of the next row, and then every 6th row until there are 68(72:80) sts. and then every 8th row until there are 86(90:94) sts.

Work until sleeve measures 47 cm. (18½ in.) from beg., ending with a wrong side row.

Shape Top

Dec. 1 st. at each end of every row until 66(66:70) sts. rem., then every alt. row until 36(36:40) sts. rem., and then every row until 22 sts. rem.

Cast off.

COLLAR

Cast on 142(142:142) sts. with 3¼mm. needles and work 49 rows in welt patt. as for front of 3rd size.

Now work 8 cm. (3¼ in.) in k.1, p.1 rib.

Cast off in rib.

MAKING UP

Press each piece lightly with warm iron and damp cloth.

Sew up shoulder, side and sleeve seams.

Sew sleeves into armholes.

Sew up side edges of collar.

Place collar seam at centre back and sew cast off edge of collar to neck edge.

Press seams lightly.

High-neck Heart Pattern Sweater

Simple, thick sweater, with four-coloured stocking stitch heart pattern, stand-up doubled collar, raglan sleeves and ribbed welts

★★ Suitable for knitters with some previous experience

MATERIALS

Yarn

Sunbeam Aran
12(12:13) × 50g. balls (Main Colour A) (Cream)
3(3:3) × 50g. balls (Contrast Colour B) (Navy)
2(3:3) × 50g. balls (Contrast Colour C) (Mid-Blue)
2(3:3) × 50g. balls (Contrast Colour D) (Grey)

Needles

1 pair 4mm.
1 pair 5mm.

MEASUREMENTS

Bust

87(92:97) cm.
34(36:38) in.

Length (from back neck)

64(66:66) cm.
25(26:26) in.

Sleeve Seam

43 cm.
16¾ in.

TENSION

10½ sts. and 10½ rows = 5 cm. (2 in.) square over pattern on 5mm. needles. If your tension square does not correspond to these measurements, see page 166 for adjustment instructions.

ABBREVIATIONS

k. = knit; p. = purl; st(s). = stitch(es); inc. = increas(ing) (see page 166); dec. = decreas-(ing) (see page 167); beg. = begin(ning); rem. = remain(ing); rep. = repeat; alt. = alternate; tog. = together; sl. = slip stitch (transfer one stitch from left needle, knit-wise unless otherwise stated, to right hand needle.); cont. = continue; patt. = pattern; foll. = following; folls. = follows; mm. = millimetres; cm. = centimetre(s); in. = inch(es); A = A colour; B = B colour; C = C colour; D = D colour; st.st. = stock-ing stitch.

BACK

Cast on 84(90:90) sts. with 4mm. needles and A.

1st row: p.1(2:2), k.2, * p.2, k.2, rep. from * to the last 1(2:2) sts., p.1(2:2).
2nd row: k.1(2:2), p.2, * k.2, p.2, rep. from * to the last 1(2:2) sts., k.1(2:2).
Rep. 1st and 2nd rows for 12 cm. (4¾ in.), ending with 1st row.
Next row: p.1(4:4), p. into front and back of next st., * p.4(4:3), p. into front and back of next st., rep. from * to the last 2(5:5) sts., p. to end. [101(107:111) sts.]
Change to 5mm. needles.
Joining in and breaking off colours as required, cont. in st.st., working in patt. from chart No. 1 for 1st size, chart No. 2 for 2nd size, or chart No. 3 for 3rd size, rep. the 10 patt. sts. 10(10:11) times across, and working odd sts. as indicated.
Work until the 22nd(24th:22nd) row of the 2nd patt. from beg. has been completed.

Shape Raglan Armholes

Dec. 1 st. at each end of next 6(6:8) rows.
1st size only:
Next row: k.2 tog., work to last 2 sts, k.2 tog.
Next row: work to end.
All sizes:
1st row: k.2 tog., work to last 2 sts., k.2 tog.
2nd row: p.2 tog., work to last 2 sts., p.2 tog.
3rd row: work to end.
4th row: as 2nd row.
5th row: as 1st row.
6th row: work to end.
Rep. 1st. to 6th rows 6(7:7) times more.
Break yarn and leave 31 rem. sts. on a stitch holder.

FRONT

Work as back.

SLEEVES

Cast on 46 sts. with 4mm. needles and A.
1st row: * p.2, k.2, rep. from * to the last 2 sts., p.2.
2nd row: * k.2, p.2, rep. from * to the last 2 sts., k.2.
Rep. 1st and 2nd rows for 12 cm. (4¾ in.), ending with 1st row.
Next row: * p.2, p. into front and back of next st., rep. from * to the last st., p.1. [61 sts.]
Change to 5mm. needles.
Cont. in st.st., working in patt. from chart No. 1 for all sizes, but starting with 31st patt. row.
Work 4(2:4) rows.
Now working the new sts. in patt., inc. 1

st. at each end of next row, and then every 6th(5th:4th) row until there are 81(87:91) sts.
Work 5(3:3) rows, ending with same row as back at underarms.

Shape top

Dec. 1 st. at each end of next 6(6:8) rows.
1st size only:
Next row: k.2 tog., work to last 2 sts., k.2 tog.
Next row: work to end.
All sizes:
1st row: k.2 tog., work to last 2 sts., k.2 tog.
2nd row: p.2 tog., work to last 2 sts., p.2 tog.
3rd row: work to end.
4th row: as 2nd row.
5th row: as 1st row.
6th row: work to end.
Rep. 1st to 6th rows 6(7:7) times more.
Break yarn and leave 11 rem. sts. on a stitch holder.

COLLAR

Press each piece lightly with warm iron and damp cloth.

High-neck Heart Pattern Sweater

With wrong side of work facing, slip sts. from stitch holders on to a 5mm. needle in the foll. order: sts. of back, sts. of right sleeve, sts. of front, and sts. of left sleeve. Patt. to last st. of left sleeve, k. last st. of sleeve tog. with first st. of front, patt. to last st. of front, k. last st. tog. with first st. of right sleeve, patt. to last st. of sleeve, k. last st. of sleeve tog. with first st. of back, patt. to end. Work 11 rows. Cont. with A.
Next row: k.
Change to 4mm. needles.
k. next row on wrong side to mark hem-line.
Now work 12 rows in st.st., starting with a k. row. Cast off.

MAKING UP

Sew up raglan and collar seams.
Fold collar to wrong side at the hemline and slipstitch in position.
Sew up side and sleeve seams.
Press seams lightly.

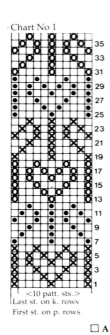

Chart No 1

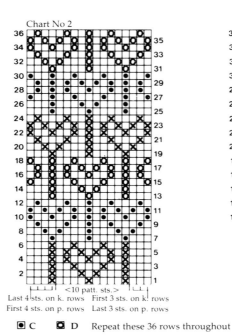

Chart No 2

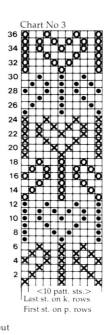

Chart No 3

□ A   ☒ B   ◉ C   ▣ D   Repeat these 36 rows throughout

Turtle-neck, Leaf Pattern Sweater   1950

Thick, just below waist-length sweater with turtle-neck and set-in sleeves, in leaf pattern on garter stitch ground

★★ This pattern is suitable for knitters with some previous experience

MATERIALS

Yarn
Patons Clansman DK
9(9:10) × 50g. balls

Needles
1 pair 3mm.
1 pair 4mm.

MEASUREMENTS

Bust
87(92:97) cm.
34(36:38) in.

Length
48(49:51) cm.
18¾(19¼:20) in.

Sleeve Seam
46 (46:47) cm.
18(18:18½) in.

TENSION

10 sts. and 16 rows = 5 cm. (2 in.) square over stocking stitch on 4mm. needles. If your tension square does not correspond to these measurements see page 166 for adjustment instructions.

ABBREVIATIONS

k. = knit; p. = purl; st(s). = stitch(es); inc. = increas(ing) (see page 166); dec. = decreas-(ing) (see page 167); beg. = begin(ning); rem. = remain(ing); rep. = repeat; alt. = alternate; tog. = together; sl. = slip stitch (transfer one stitch from left needle, purl-wise unless otherwise stated, to right hand needle.); cont. = continue; patt. = pattern; foll. = following; folls. = follows; mm. = millimetres; cm. = centimetre(s); in. = inch(es); m.1 = pick up horizontal loop lying before next stitch and work into back of it; L.1 = pick up horizontal loop lying before next stitch and knit it; p.s.s.o. = pass the slipped stitch over; 0 = no stitches; rev.st.st. = reversed stocking stitch i.e. right side purl.
NOTE: Where numbers of sts. are given, these refer to the basic number and do not include those made in the pattern.

BACK

** Cast on 83(89:95) sts. with 3mm. needles.
1st row (right side): k.1, * p.1, k.1, rep. from * to end.
2nd row: p.1, * k.1, p.1, rep. from * to end.
Rep. last 2 rows until work measures

9(10:11) cm. (3½(4:4¼) in.) at centre from start, ending with 1st row.
Next row: rib 3(6:3), m.1, * rib 7(7:8), m.1, rep. from * to last 3(6:4) sts., rib 3(6:4), [95(101:107) sts.]
Change to 4mm. needles.
Next row: p.
Next row: k.
Rep. last 2 rows once more.
Now work in patt.
1st row (right side): p.7(10:13), * L.1, k.1, L.1, p.15, rep. from * to last 8(11:14) sts. L.1, k.1, L.1, p.7(10:13).
2nd row: k.7(10:13), * p.3, k.15, rep. from * to last 10(13:16) sts., p.3, k.7(10:13).
3rd row: p.7(10:13), * L.1, k.3, L.1, p.15, rep. from * to last 10(13:16) sts., L.1, k.3, L.1, p.7(10:13).
4th row: k.7(10:13), * p.5, k.15, rep. from * to last 12(15:18) sts., p.5, k.7(10:13).
5th row: p.7(10:13), * L.1, k.1, sl.1, k.1, p.s.s.o., k.2, L.1, p.15, rep. from * to last 12(15:18) sts., L.1, k.1, sl.1, k.1, p.s.s.o., k.2, L.1, p.7(10:13).
6th row: k.7(10:13), * p.6, k.15, rep. from * to last 13(16:19) sts., p.6, k.7(10:13).
7th row: p.7(10:13), * L.1, k.2, sl.1, k.1, p.s.s.o., k.2, L.1, p.15, rep. from * to last 13(16:19) sts., L.1, k.2, sl.1, k.1, p.s.s.o., k.2, L.1, p.7(10:13).
8th row: k.7(10:13), * p.7, k.15, rep. from *

84

Turtle-neck, Leaf Pattern Sweater

to last 14(17:20) sts., p.7, k.7(10:13).

9th row: p.7(10:13), * L.1, k.3, sl.1, k.1, p.s.s.o., k.2, L.1, p.15, rep. from * to last 14(17:20) sts., L.1, k.3, sl.1, k.1, p.s.s.o., k.2, L.1, p.7(10:13).

10th row: k.7(10:13), * p.8, k.15, rep. from * to last 15(18:21) sts., p.8, k.7(10:13).

11th row: p.7(10:13), * k.4, sl.1, k.1, p.s.s.o., k.2, p.15, rep. from * to last 15(18:21) sts., k.4, sl.1, k.1, p.s.s.o., k.2, p.7(10:13).

12th row: k.7(10:13), * p.7, k.15, rep. from * to last 14(17:20) sts., p.7, k.7(10:13).

13th row: p.7(10:13), * sl.1, k.1, p.s.s.o., k.1, sl.1, k.1, p.s.s.o., k.2 tog., p.15, rep. from * to last 14(17:20) sts., sl.1, k.1, p.s.s.o., k.1, sl.1, k.1, p.s.s.o., k.2 tog., p.7(10:13).

14th row: k.7(10:13), * p.4, k.15, rep. from * to last 11(14:17) sts., p.4, k.7(10:13).

15th row: p.7(10:13), * sl.1, k.1, p.s.s.o., k.2 tog., p.15, rep. from * to last 11(14:17) sts., sl.1, k.1, p.s.s.o., k.2 tog., p.7(10:13).

16th row: k.7(10:13), * p.2 tog., k.15, rep. from * to last 9(12:15) sts., p.2 tog., k.7(10:13).

17th and 19th rows: p.

18th and 20th rows: k.

21st row: p.0(3:6), * p.15, L.1, k.1, L.1, rep. from * to last 15(18:21) sts., p.15 (18:21).

22nd row: k.0(3:6), * k.15, p.3, rep. from * to last 15(18:21) sts., k.15(18:21).

23rd row: p.0(3:6), * p.15, L.1, k.3, L.1, rep. from * to last 15(18:21) sts., p.15(18:21).

24th row: k.0(3:6), * k.15, p.5, rep. from * to last 15(18:21) sts., k.15(18:21).

25th row: p.0(3:6), * p.15, L.1, k.1, sl.1, k.1, p.s.s.o., k.2, L.1, rep. from * to last 15(18:21) sts., p.15(18:21).

26th row: k.0(3:6), * k.15, p.6, rep. from * to last 15(18:21) sts., k.15(18:21).

27th row: p.0(3:6), * p.15, L.1, k.2, sl.1, k.1, p.s.s.o., k.2, L.1, rep. from * to last 15(18:21) sts., p.15(18:21).

28th row: k.0(3:6), * k.15, p.7, rep. from * to last 15(18:21) sts., k.15(18:21).

29th row: p.0(3:6), * p.15, L.1, k.3, sl.1, k.1, p.s.s.o., k.2, L.1, rep. from * to last 15(18:21) sts., p.15(18:21).

30th row: k.0(3:6), * k.15, p.8, rep. from * to last 15(18:21) sts., k.15(18:21).

31st row: p.0(3:6), * p.15, k.4, sl.1, k.1, p.s.s.o., k.2, rep. from * to last 15(18:21) sts. k.15(18:21).

32nd row: k.0(3:6), * k.15, p.7, rep. from * to last 15(18:21) sts., k.15(18:21).

33rd row: p.0(3:6), * p.15, sl.1, k.1, p.s.s.o., k.1, sl.1, k.1, p.s.s.o., k.2 tog., rep. from * to last 15(18:21) sts., p.15(18:21).

34th row: k.0(3:6), * k.15, p.4, rep. from * to last 15(18:21) sts., k.15(18:21).

35th row: p.0(3:6), * p.15, sl.1, k.1, p.s.s.o., k.2 tog., rep. from * to last 15(18:21) sts., p.15(18:21).

36th row: k.0(3:6), * k.15, p.2 tog., rep. from * to last 15(18:21) sts., k.15(18:21).

37th–40th rows: as 17th–20th.

These 40 rows form patt.

Patt. a further 20 rows straight.

Shape Armholes

Cont. in patt., casting off 6(6:7) sts. at beg. of next 2 rows, then dec. 1 st. at each end of next and every alt. row until 75(79:83) sts. rem. **

Work a further 47(47:49) rows straight in patt.

Shape Shoulders

Cont. in rev. st.st., casting off 9(8:9) sts. at beg. of next 2 rows, then 8(9:9) sts. at beg. of next 4 rows.

Leave rem. 25(27:29) sts. on a spare needle.

FRONT

Work as for back from ** to **.

Work a further 27 rows straight, thus ending with 16th(18th:18th) row of patt.

Shape Neck

Next row: p.28(29:30) sts., turn and leave rem. sts. on a spare needle.

Cont. on these 28(29:30) sts. for first side, dec. 1 st. at neck edge on every row until 25(26:27) sts. rem.

Working leaf at armhole edge only, cont. in patt. until front matches back to start of shoulder shaping, ending with right side facing.

Shape Shoulder

Cast off 9(8:9) sts. at beg. of next row, then 8(9:9) sts. at beg. of foll. 2 alt. rows.

With right side facing, slip centre 19(21:23) sts. onto a spare needle, rejoin yarn to rem. 28(29:30) sts., p. to end.

Finish to correspond with first side.

SLEEVES

Cast on 46(48:50) sts. with 3mm. needles.

Work 9(9:10) cm. (3½(3½:4) in.) in k.1, p.1 rib, inc. 1(3:5) sts. evenly across the last row. [47(51:55) sts.]

Change to 4mm. needles and patt. as for back. The first 2 rows will read:

1st row: p.7(9:11), * L.1, k.1, L.1, p.15, rep. from * to last 8(10:12) sts., L.1, k.1, L.1, p.7(9:11).

2nd row: k.7(9:11), * p.3, k.15, rep. from * to last 10(12:14) sts., p.3, k.7(9:11).

Cont. in patt. thus, shaping sides by inc. 1 st., at each end of 5th and every foll. 6th row until there are 73(77:81) sts., taking inc. sts. into patt.

Work 23 rows straight, thus ending with 20th patt. row.

Shape Top

Cast off 4(5:6) sts. at beg. of next 2 rows, then dec. 1 st. at each end of next and every alt. row until 47(49:51) sts. rem.

Cont. in rev. st.st., dec. 1 st. at each end of every foll. alt. row until 45 sts. rem.

Knit back, then dec. 1 st. at each end of every foll. alt. row until 31 sts. rem.

Cast off. rem. 13 sts.

NECK BORDER

Sew up right shoulder seam.

With right side facing and 3mm. needles, pick up and k.26 sts. down left side of neck, k.19(21:23) from centre, pick up and k.26 up right side, then k.25(27:29) from back. [96(100:104) sts.]

Work 9 cm. (3½ in.) in k.1, p.1 rib.

Cast off loosely in rib, using a bigger needle.

MAKING UP

Press work lightly on wrong side, omitting ribbing and taking care not to spoil the patt.

Sew up left shoulder seam, then sew up neck border with a flat seam.

Sew up side and sleeve seams; set in sleeves.

Press all seams.

Star Pattern Sweater

1937

Round-neck, waist-length sweater with star pattern on front and set-in sleeves, shaped pattern on back, in stocking stitch on garter stitch ground

★★ Suitable for knitters with some previous experience

MATERIALS

Yarn
Jaeger MatchMaker 4 Ply
7 × 50g. balls

Needles
1 pair 2¾mm.
1 pair 3¼mm.

MEASUREMENTS (one size)

Bust
84 cm.
33 in.

Length (from shoulder top)
47 cm.
18½ in.

Sleeve Seam
43 cm.
17 in.

TENSION

13 sts. and 24 rows = 5 cm. (2 in.) square over garter stitch on 3¼mm. needles. If your tension square does not correspond to these measurements see page 166 for adjustments.

ABBREVIATIONS

k. = knit; p. = purl; st(s). = stitch(es); inc. = increas(ing) (see page 166); dec. = decreas-(ing) (see page 167); beg. = begin(ning); rem. = remain(ing); rep. = repeat; alt. = alternate; tog. = together; sl. = slip stitch (transfer one stitch from left needle, knit-wise unless otherwise stated, to right hand needle.); cont. = continue; patt. = pattern; foll. = following; folls. = follows; mm. = millimetres; cm. = centimetre(s); in. = inch(es); m.l = pick up horizontal loop lying before next st. and work into back of it; g.st. = garter stitch (every row k.).

FRONT

** Cast on 105 sts. with 2¾mm. needles.
1st row (right side facing): k.1, * p.1, k.1, rep. from * to end.
2nd row: p.1, * k.1, p.1, rep. from * to end.
Rep. last 2 rows until front measures 10 cm. (4 in.) at centre from start, ending with 2nd row.
Change to 3¼mm. needles and g.st., shaping sides by inc. 1 st. at each end of 17th and every foll. 20th row until there are 111 sts.
Work straight until front measures 28 cm.

(11 in.) at centre from start, ending with right side facing.
Cast off 4 sts. at beg. of next 2 rows, then dec. 1 st. at each end of next and every foll. 3rd row until 95 sts. rem. **
Work 15 rows straight.
With wrong side facing, introduce yoke as folls.:
1st row: k.47, p.1, k.47.
2nd and every alt. row: k.
3rd row: k.46, p.3, k.46.
5th row: k.45, p.5, k.45.
7th row: k.44, p.7, k.44.
Cont. working 2 sts. more in st.st. on every alt. row until 27 sts. are in st.st.
Next row: k.
Next row: k.15, p.65, k.15.
Next row: k.
Rep. last 2 rows once more.
Next row: k.16, p.63, k.16.
Next row: k.
Rep. last 2 rows once more.
Next row: k.17, p.61, k.17.
Next row: k.
Rep. last 2 rows once more. Cont. working 2 sts. less in st.st. on next and every foll. 4th row until 53 sts. are in st.st. with 21 sts. in g.st. at each end.

Divide for Neck
Next row: k.37, turn and leave rem. sts. on a spare needle. Cont. on these 37 sts. for first side as folls.:
Next row: p.2 tog., p.14, k. to end.
Next row: k. to last 2 sts., k.2 tog.
Next row: p.2 tog., p.17, k. to end.
Cont. dec. 1 st. at neck edge on every row *and at the same time* take 4 sts. more into st.st. for yoke on every foll. alt. row until 28 sts. rem.
Keeping 5 sts. at armhole edge in g.st. and remainder in st.st., work a further 2 rows, dec. 1 st. at neck edge as before. [26 sts.]
Now keep neck edge straight and shape shoulder by casting off 7 sts. at beg. of next and foll. alt. row, then 6 sts. at beg. of foll. 2 alt. rows.
With right side facing, rejoin yarn to rem. 58 sts. Cast off centre 21 sts. using bigger needles, k. to end.
Finish to correspond with first side.

BACK

Work as for front from ** to **.
Work 65 rows straight.
With wrong side facing, cont. as folls.:
Next row: k.29, p.37, k.29.
Next row: k.
Next row: k.25, p.45, k.25.
Next row: k.
Cont. thus working 4 sts. more in st.st. on next and every foll. alt. row until there

are 5 sts. in g.st. at each end.
Keeping 5 sts. at each end in g.st., work a further 2 rows, then shape shoulders by casting off 7 sts. at beg. of next 4 rows, then 6 sts. at beg. of next 4 rows.
Cast off rem. 43 sts. using bigger needles.

SLEEVES

Cast on 50 sts. with 2¾mm. needles, and work 10 rows in k.1, p.1 rib.
Next row: * rib 5, m.1, rep. from * to last 5 sts., rib 5. [59 sts.]
Change to 3¼mm. needles and work 21 rows straight in st.st., starting with a k. row.
With wrong side facing, cont. as folls.:
Next row: p.13, k.1, p.31, k.1, p.13.
Next row: k.
Next row: p.12, k.3, p.29, k.3, p.12.
Next row: k.
Cont. thus in st.st., taking 4 sts. more into g.st. on next and every alt. row until all sts. are in g.st., and *at the same time* shape sleeves by inc. 1 st. at each end of next and every foll. 10th row until there are 85 sts.
Work straight until sleeve seam measures 43 cm. (16¾ in.), ending with right side facing.

Shape Top
Cast off 4 sts. at beg. of next 2 rows, then dec. 1 st. at each end of next and every foll. 4th row until 69 sts. rem.
Work 3 rows straight, then dec. 1 st. at each end of next and every alt. row until 41 sts. rem.
Work 1 row straight, then dec. 1 st. at each end of every row until 17 sts. rem.
Cast off.

NECK BORDER

Cast on 138 sts. with 2¾mm. needles and work 4 cm. (1½ in.) in k.1, p.1 rib.
Cast off evenly in rib.

TO MAKE UP

Press work very lightly on wrong side, omitting ribbing and taking care not to spoil g.st.
Sew up shoulder, side and sleeve seams; insert sleeves.
Sew up short ends of neck border, then pin border in position round neck on top of work, with seams on left shoulder.
Sew in position.
Press all seams.

Tweedy Polo-neck Cable Sweater

1980

Chunky, hip-length polo-neck sweater in reversed stocking stitch with simple cable pattern on upper parts of body and raglan sleeves

★ Suitable for beginners

MATERIALS

Yarn
Pingouin Iceberg
19(21) × 50g. balls
or
Pingouin Pingoland
19(21) × 50g. balls

Needles
1 pair 5mm.
1 pair 6½mm.
1 cable needle
1 stitch holder

MEASUREMENTS

Bust
82–87(92–97) cm.
32–34(36–38) in.

Length
67 cm.
26¼ in.

TENSION

16 sts. and 16 rows = 10 cm. (4 in.) square over stocking stitch on 6½mm. needles. If your tension square does not correspond to these measurements see page 166 for adjustment instructions.

ABBREVIATIONS

k. = knit; p. = purl; st(s). = stitch(es); inc. = increas(ing) (see page 166); dec. = decreas-(ing) (see page 167); beg. = begin(ning); rem. = remain(ing); rep. = repeat; alt. = alternate; tog. = together; sl. = slip stitch (transfer one stitch from left needle, knit-wise unless otherwise stated, to right hand needle.); cont. = continue; patt. = pattern; foll. = following; folls. = follows; mm. = millimetres; cm. = centimetre(s); in. = inch(es); rev.st.st. = reverse stock-ing stitch, (i.e. right side purl, wrong side knit); p.s.s.o. = pass the slip stitch over; cable twist = on rows indicated, work k.6 sections: sl.3 onto cable needle, leave at front of work, k.3, k.3 from cable needle.

BACK

Cast on 82(86) sts. with 5mm. needles.

Work in k.1, p.1 rib for 13 cm. (5 in.).
Change to 6½mm. needles and rev.st.st.
NB. purl is right side of work.
Work straight for 25 cm. (9¾ in.) (total length of work 38 cm. (15 in.)).
Start cable pattern:
1st row: p.10(12), * k.6, p.8, k.6, p.8, k.6, p.8, k.6, p.8, k.6, * p.10(12).
2nd row: k.10(12), * p.6, k.8, p.6, k.8, p.6, k.8, p.6, k.8, p.6, * k.10(12).

Shape Raglan Armhole

3rd row: cast off 3(5) sts., p.6(6), work as for 1st row from * to *, p.10(12).
4th row: cast off 3(5) sts., k.6(6), work as for 2nd row from * to *, k.7(7).
5th row: p.2, sl.1, p.1, p.s.s.o., work in patt. as before to last 4 sts., p.2 tog., p.2.
6th row: as work faces you, k. all knit sts., p. all p. sts.
Continue working rows 5 and 6 to neck, with the exception of rows 7, 19, 31 and 43 where the k.6 section should be twisted for the cable, (see abbreviations).

Shape Neckline

47th row: k.6, turn, work 2 sts. tog. at neck edge on next 3 alt. rows, cast off.
Leave centre 22 sts. on stitch holder.
Rejoin yarn to shoulder edge of work. Work 1 row. Work 2 sts. tog. at beg. of next and foll. 2 alt. rows.
Cast off.

FRONT

Work as for back.

SLEEVES

Cast on 44 sts. with 5mm. needles.
Work in k.1, p.1 rib for 13 cm. (5 in.).
Change to 6½mm needles and rev.st.st.
Inc. 1 st. at beg. and end of every 10th row until there are 52 sts.
Work straight until total work length is 46 cm. (18 in.).
Start cable patt. at right side: p.9, k.6, p.8, k.6, p.8, k.6, p.9.
Next row: k.9, p.6, k.8, p.6, k.8, p.6, k.9.
Now work dec. and patt. as in rows 5 and 6 of back, working cable twist on 7th and every foll. 12th row, until 10 sts. rem.
Now dec. at beg. and end of every row 4 times.
k.2 tog., fasten off.

POLO NECK

Join right shoulder seam.
Starting at left shoulder pick up, on 5mm. needles, 7 sts. down left side of neck, 22 sts. across front, 14 sts. around right side of neck, 22 sts. across back, 7 sts. up left side of neck. [72 sts.]
Work in k.1, p.1 rib for 24 cm. (9½ in.).
Cast off loosely in rib.

MAKING UP

DO NOT PRESS.
Sew polo-neck seam.
Sew in raglan sleeves.
Sew side seams.

V-neck Dolman Velour Cardigan

Dolman-sleeved, velour, hip-length cardigan with low V-neck, and separate front bands, in stocking stitch

★ Suitable for beginners

MATERIALS

Yarn
Laines Tiber Coton Velour
9(10) × 50g. balls

Needles
1 pair 3¼mm.
1 pair 4½mm.

Buttons
4

MEASUREMENTS

Bust
84–89(94.5–99.5) cm.
33–35(37–39) in.

TENSION

16 sts. and 28 rows = 10 cm.(4 in.) square over stocking stitch on 4½mm. needles. If your tension square does not correspond to these measurements see page 166 for adjustment instructions.

ABBREVIATIONS

k. = knit; p. = purl; st(s). = stitch(es); inc. = increas(ing) (see page 166); dec. = decreas-(ing) (see page 167); beg. = begin(ning); rem. = remain(ing); rep. = repeat; alt. = alternate; tog. = together; sl. = slip stitch (transfer one stitch from left needle, knit-wise unless otherwise stated, to right hand needle.); cont. = continue; patt. = pattern; foll. = following; folls. = follows; mm. = millimetres; cm. = centimetre(s); in. = inch(es); st.st. = stocking stitch (see page 166).
NOTE: Cast on and off loosely with this cotton yarn.

BACK

Cast on 74(83) sts. with 3¼mm. needles.
Work as folls.:
1st row: * k.2, p.1, rep. from * to last 2 sts., k.2.
2nd row: k.1, p.1, * k.1, p.2, rep. from * to last 3 sts., k.1, p.1, k.1.
Rep. these 2 rows for 10 cm.(4 in.).
Change to 4½mm. needles.
Work in st.st. until work measures 28(29) cm. (11(11¼)in.). Mark bottom of armhole with a contrasting coloured thread.
Cont. until back measures 53(54) cm. (20¾(21¼) in.).

Shape Shoulders

Cast off 7 sts. at beg. of next and foll. row.

Cast off 5(6) sts. at the beg. of each of the next 6 rows.
Cast off the rem. 30(33) sts.

RIGHT FRONT

* Cast on 35(38) sts. with 3¼mm. needles.
Work 1st and 2nd rows (as in back) until work measures 10 cm. (4 in.).
Change to 4½mm. needles, working 20(21) cm. (8(8½) in.) in st.st., ending with a p. row. *

Shape Neck

Next row: k.1, dec. 1, k. to end.
Cont. in st.st., dec. as above on every 6th row 13(12) times. [22(26) sts.]. Mark bottom of armhole as for back.
Work until front measures 53(54) cm. (20¾(21¼) in.).
Cast off.

LEFT FRONT

Work as for right front from * to *.

Shape Neck

Next row: k. to last 2 sts., dec. 1, k.1.
Cont. in st.st., dec. as above on every 6th row 13(12) times. [22(26) sts.]. Mark bottom of armhole as for back.
Work until front measures 53(54) cm. (20¾(21¼) in.).
Cast off.

SLEEVES

Cast on 41(44) sts. with 3¼mm. needles.

Work 1st and 2nd rows of back until work measures 8 cm.(3¼ in.).
Change to 4½mm. needles.
Next row: working in st.st., inc. 3(2) sts. evenly across first row. [44(46) sts.]

Shape Dolman

Inc. 1 st. at each end of every 8th row 10 times. [64(66) sts.]
Now inc. 1 st. each end of every 6th row 6 times. [76(78) sts.]
Work straight until work measures 48(49) cm. (18¾(19¼) in.).
Cast off.

FRONT BAND

Cast on 6 sts. with 3¼mm. needles.
Work 5 rows in k.1, p.1 rib.
Make a buttonhole in next row by casting off the 2 central sts.
Next row: rib 2, cast on 2, rib 2.
Make 3 more buttonholes in this way, 5 cm.(2 in.) apart. Work band to match length of front edges and neck, (approx. 140 cm.(55 in.)), stretching the band slightly for best fit.
Cast off.

MAKING UP

Sew shoulder seams, sew on front band. Sew in sleeves. Sew sleeve and side seams. With a matching sewing cotton, invisibly strengthen edges of buttonholes by threading yarn around edge of button-holes close to edge. Sew on buttons.

Round-necked Cable Cardigan

1951

Hip-length cardigan with round neck and knitted-in front bands, in reversed stocking stitch with cable panels in fronts, back and sleeves

★★★ Suitable for experienced knitters only

MATERIALS

Yarn
Wendy DK wool
10(10:10) × 50g. balls.

Needles
1 pair 3¼mm.
1 pair 4mm.
1 cable needle
1 3.5 crochet hook

Buttons
11

MEASUREMENTS

Bust
87(92:97) cm.
34(36:38) in.

Length
55(56:57) cm.
21½(22:22¼) in.

Sleeve Seam
46(46:47) cm.
18(18:18½) in.

TENSION

24 sts. and 32 rows = 10 cm. (4 in.) square over stocking stitch on 4mm. needles. If your tension square does not correspond to these measurements see page 166 for adjustment instructions.

ABBREVIATIONS

k. = knit; p. = purl; st(s). = stitch(es); inc. = increas(ing) (see page 166); dec. = decreas-(ing) (see page 167); beg. = begin(ning); rem. = remain(ing); rep. = repeat; alt. = alternate; tog. = together; sl. = slip stitch (transfer one stitch from left needle, knit-wise unless otherwise stated, to right hand needle.); cont. = continue; patt. = pattern; foll. = following; folls. = follows; mm. = millimetres; cm. = centimetre(s); in. = inch(es); st.st. = stocking stitch; C6F = cable 6 front: (slip 3 sts. onto cable needle and leave at front of work, knit next 3 sts., then knit 3 sts. from cable needle.); d.c. = double crochet.

BACK

Cast on 90(94:100) sts. with 3¼mm. needles. Work 10 cm. (4 in.) in k.1, p.1. rib.
Change to 4mm. needles.
1st row (right side): p.18(20:22) sts. Set next 20 sts. for cable patt. as folls.: C6F, p.1, k.6, p.1, C6F, p.14(14:16) sts. Set next 20 sts. for cable patt. as folls.: C6F, p.1, k.6, p.1, C6F, p.18(20:22) sts.
2nd row: k.18(20:22) sts., p.6, k.1, p.6, k.1, p.6, k.14(14:16) sts., p.6, k.1, p.6, k.1, p.6, k.18(20:22) sts.
Patt. sections in other 6 rows of patt. work as folls.:
3rd row: k.6, p.1, k.6, p.1, k.6.
4th row: as 2nd.
5th row: C6F, p.1, C6F, p.1, C6F.
6th row: as 2nd.
7th row: as 3rd.
8th row: as 2nd.
Keeping patt. correct in these panels, work 2 more rows.
Inc. 1 st. each end of next and every 4th row until there are 120(126:132) sts., work-ing inc. sts. into the reversed st.st. Cont. until work measures 36(37:37) cm. (14(14½:14½) in.).

Shape Armhole
Cast off 9(10:11) sts. at beg. of next 2 rows.
Dec. 1 st. each end of every alt. row until 88(92:96) sts. rem.
Cont. straight until armhole measures 19(20:21) cm.(7½(7¾:8¼) in.).

Shape Shoulders
Cast off 9(10:10) sts. at beg. of next 4 rows.
Cast off 10(10:11) sts. at beg. of next 2 rows. Leave rem. 32(32:34) sts. on holder.

LEFT FRONT

Cast on 52(56:62) sts. with 3¼mm. needles. Work 10 cm. (4 in.) in k.1, p.1. rib. Change to 4mm. needles.
1st row (right side): p.18(20:22) sts. Set next 20 sts. for cable patt. as folls.: C6F, p.1, k.6, p.1, C6F, p.14(16:20) sts.
2nd row: k.14(16:20) sts., p.6, k.1, p.6, k.1, p.6, k.18(20:22) sts.
Keeping patt. correct in these panels, work 8 more rows.
Inc. 1 st. at beg. of next and every 4th row until there are 67(72:78) sts., working inc. sts. into the reversed st.st. Cont. straight until front measures the same as back to armhole, ending at side edge.

Shape Armhole
Cast off 9(10:11) sts. at beg. of next row.
Dec. 1 st. at same edge every row 3(3:4) times, then every alt. row until 51(53:57) sts. rem.
Work until armhole measures 17(18:19) cm. (6½(7:7½) in.) measured on the straight, ending at centre front edge.

Shape Neck
Next row: work 14(14:17) sts.

Place these sts. on holder, work to end.
Next row: patt. to end. Cast off 3 sts. at neck edge 3 times. [29(30:31) sts.]
Work straight until armhole measures same as back, ending at armhole edge.

Shape Shoulder
Cast off 9(10:10) sts. at beg. of next 2 alt. rows, then 10(10:11) sts. once.

RIGHT FRONT

Work as for left front reading 1st. row on 4mm. needle backwards as folls.: p.14(16:20) sts., C6F, p.1, k.6, p.1, C6F, p.18(20:22) sts., and reverse all shapings.

Round-necked Cable Cardigan

Work first buttonhole when welt measures 1 cm. (1½ in.) as folls.:
Rib 4 sts., cast off 3 sts., rib to end.
In next row cast on 3 sts. over cast off sts. of preceding row.
Work 9 more buttonholes at centre front 6 cm. (2¼ in.) apart, with 11th buttonhole in neckband.

SLEEVES

Cast on 52(56:60) sts. with 3¼mm. needles. Work 8 cm. (3¼ in.) in k.1, p.1 rib.
Change to 4mm. needles.
1st row: p.16(18:20) sts., C6F, p.1, k.6, p.1, C6F, p.16(18:20) sts.

Work 3 rows.
Inc. 1 st. at each end of next and every foll. 6th row until there are 76(80:84) sts., working all inc. sts. into the reversed st.st. Work straight until sleeve measures 46(46:47) cm. (18(18:18½) in.) or length required.

Shape Top

Cast off 9(10:11) sts. at beg. of next 2 rows. Dec. 1 st. each end of every alt. row until 20 sts. rem. Cast off.

NECKBAND

Sew up shoulder seams. With right side of work facing, with 3¼mm. needles

k.14(14:17) sts. from right front holder, k.18(20:20) sts. up neck edge, 32(32:34) sts. from holder at back, k. up 18(20:20) sts. down left side of neck edge, and 14(14:17) sts. from holder. [96(100:108) sts.]
Work 5 rows in k.1, p.1 rib.
Work 11th buttonhole in next 2 rows.
Rib 4 rows. Cast off in rib.

MAKING UP

Work 2 rows d.c. down centre front edges. Set in sleeves. Sew side and sleeve seams. Press carefully. Sew on buttons opposite buttonholes.

Double-breasted Sand Stitch Jacket 1935

Hip-length, figure-hugging jacket in sand stitch, with cuffed set-in sleeves and patterned collar

★ Suitable for beginners

MATERIALS

Yarn
Sirdar Sportswool
17(17:18) × 50g. balls

Needles
1 pair 4mm.

Buttons
8

MEASUREMENTS

Bust
87(92:97) cm.
34(36:38) in.

Length
59(60:61) cm.
23¼(23½:24) in.

Sleeve seam (with cuff extended)
54 cm.
21¼ in.

TENSION

9 sts. and 13½ rows = 5 cm. (2 in.) square over pattern on 4mm. needles. If your tension square does not correspond to these measurements see page 166 for adjustment instructions.

ABBREVIATIONS

k. = knit; p. = purl; st(s). = stitch(es); inc. = increas(ing) (see page 166); dec. = decreas-(ing) (see page 167); beg. = begin(ning); rem. = remain(ing); rep. = repeat; alt. = alternate; tog. = together; sl. = slip stitch (transfer one stitch from left needle, knit-wise unless otherwise stated, to right

hand needle.); cont. = continue; patt. = pattern; foll. = following; folls. = follows; mm. = millimetres; cm. = centimetre(s); in. = inch(es).

BACK

Cast on 103:(109:115) sts. Beg. patt.:
1st row: * k.1, p.1, rep. from * to last st., k.1.
2nd row: k.
These 2 rows form the patt. Proceed until work measures 8 cm. (3¼ in.). Dec. at both ends of next and every foll. 6th row until 93(99:105) sts. rem.
Cont. until work measures 23 cm. (9 in.). Inc. 1 st. at both ends of next and every foll. 8th row until there are 101(107:113) sts. Cont. until work measures 39 cm. (15¼ in.), finishing after a wrong side row.

Shape Armhole

Cast off 3 sts. at beg. of next 2 rows, then dec. 1 st. at both ends of every row until 77(79:81) sts. rem.
Cont. until work measures 19(20:21) cm. (7½(7¾:8¼) in.) from beg. of armholes, after a wrong side row.

Shape Shoulders

Cast off 8 sts. at beg. of next 4 rows and 6(7:8) sts. at beg. of foll. 2 rows. Cast off rem. 33 sts.

LEFT FRONT

Cast on 65(68:71) sts. Work 8 cm. (3¼ in.) in patt. noting that for middle size 1st row will end p.1. Dec. 1 st. at side edge on next and every foll. 6th row until 60(63:66) sts. rem. Cont. until work measures 23 cm. (9 in.). Inc. 1 st. at side edge on next and every foll. 8th row until there are 64(67:70)

sts. Cont. until work matches back to armholes, finishing at side edge.

Shape Armhole

Cast off 3 sts. at beg. of next row. Work back. Dec. at side edge on every row until 52(53:54) sts. rem. Cont. until work measures 12(13:14) cm. (4¾(5:5½) in.) from beg. of armhole, finishing at front edge.

Shape Neck

Cast off 27 sts. at beg. of next row, then dec. 1 st. at neck edge on next 3 rows. [22(23:24) sts.]
Cont. until work matches back to outer shoulder.

Shape Shoulder

Cast off 8 sts. at beg. of next 2 side edge rows. Work to side edge.
Cast off rem. 6(7:8) sts.

RIGHT FRONT

Work to correspond with left front, reversing shapings and making 4 pairs of buttonholes, 1st on 1st row of side inc., last just under neck edge, remainder evenly spaced between.
Buttonholes are worked thus, beg. at centre front edge: work 4 sts., cast off 3 sts., (1 st. now on right hand needle), work 14 sts. more, cast off 3 sts., work to end.
Next row: cast on 3 sts. over each group of cast off sts.

SLEEVES

Cast on 45(47:49) sts.
1st row: k.2, * p.1, k.1, rep. from * to last st., k.1.

2nd row: k.1, * p.1, k.1, rep. from * to end. Rep. these 2 rows for 12 cm. (4¾ in.), finishing after a 1st row of rib. Change to patt., beg. with 1st row – (this reverses right side of work). Inc. at both ends of the 7th and every foll. 6th row until there are 75(77:79) sts. Cont. until work measures 54 cm. (21¼ in.), finishing after a wrong side row.

Shape Top

Cast off 3 sts. at beg. of next 2 rows. Dec. 1 st. at both ends of next and every alt. row until 41 sts. rem. Work 1 row. Dec. 1 st. at both ends of every row until 17 sts. rem. Cast off.

COLLAR

Cast on 93 sts. Work 2 rows in k.1 p.1 rib as given for cuffs. Cont. thus:
1st row: k.2, p.2 tog., rib to last 4 sts., p.2 tog., k.2.
2nd row: k.1, p.1, k.2, rib to last 4 sts., k.2, p.1, k.1.
3rd row: k.2, p.2, rib to last 4 sts., p.2, k.2.
4th row: as 2nd.
5th row: as 1st.
6th, 7th and 8th rows: work in rib.
Rep. these 8 rows until 81 sts. rem.
Cast off in rib.

MAKING UP

Sew up side, shoulder and sleeve seams. Set sleeves into armholes. Sew cast off edge of collar to back and sides of neck, to end of dec. sts. (see photograph).
Press seams.
Sew on buttons.

Round-neck Polka Dot Cardigan

Simple stocking stitch straight cardigan with allover pattern, just below waist-length, with set-in sleeves, ribbed welts and separate front bands

★★ Suitable for knitters with some previous experience

MATERIALS

Yarn
Emu Superwash Wool 4 ply
13(13:14) × 25g. balls (Main Colour)
3(3:4) × 25g. balls (Contrast Colour)

Needles
1 pair 2¾mm.
1 pair 3¼mm.

Buttons
9

MEASUREMENTS

Bust
82(87:92) cm.
32(34:36) in.

Length
53(53:55) cm.
20¾(20¾:21½) in.

Sleeve
43(43:46) cm.
16¾(16¾:18) in .

TENSION

7 sts. and 9 rows = 2½ cm. (1 in.) square over stocking stitch on 3¼mm. needles. If your tension square does not correspond to these measurements see page 166 for adjustment instructions.

ABBREVIATIONS

k. = knit; p. = purl; st(s). = stitch(es); inc. = increas(ing) (see page 166); dec. = decreas-(ing) (see page 167); beg. = begin(ning); rem. = remain(ing); rep. = repeat; alt. = alternate; tog. = together; sl. = slip stitch (transfer one stitch from left needle, knit-wise unless otherwise stated, to right hand needle.); cont. = continue; patt. = pattern; foll. = follow(ing); folls. = follows; mm. = millimetres; cm. = centimetre(s); in. = inch(es); M = main colour; C = contrast colour; st.st. = stocking stitch.

BACK

Cast on 118(124:130) sts. with 2¾mm. needles.
Work in k.1, p.1 rib for 7 cm. (2¾ in.).
Change to 3¼mm. needles and cont. in patt. as folls., working in st.st.
1st row: k., using M.
2nd row: p., using M.
3rd row: (k.4 M, k.2 C), rep. to last 4 sts., k.4 M.
4th row: (p.4 M, p.2 C), rep. to last 4

sts., p.4 M.
5th row: as 1st row.
6th row: as 2nd row.
7th row: k.1 M, * k.2 C, k.4 M, rep. from * to last 3 sts., k.2 C, k.1 M.
8th row: p.1 M, * p.2 C, p.4 M, rep. from * to last 3 sts., p.2 C, p.1 M.
These 8 rows form patt., rep. until work measures 32(32:33) cm. (12½(12½:13) in.).

Shape Armholes

Cast off 6 sts. at beg. of next 2 rows.
Dec. 1 st. at each end of every row 6 times. [94(100:106) sts.].
Cont. straight on these sts. until work measures 52(52:54) cm. (20½(20½:21¼) in.).

Shape Shoulders

Cast off 10(11:12) sts. at beg. of next 6 rows. Sl. rem. sts. onto a stitch holder.

LEFT FRONT

Cast on 52(58:64) sts. with 2¾mm. needles and M.
Work in k.1, p.1 rib for 7 cm. (2¾ in.).
Change to 3¼mm. needles and cont. in patt. as for back until work measures 32(32:33) cm. (12½(12½:13) in.).

Shape Armhole

Cast off 6 sts. at beg. of next row, work 1 row.
Dec. 1 st. at armhole edge every row 4(6:8) times, then cont. straight on these sts. until work measures 46(46:47) cm. (18(18:18½) in.) from beg. ending at arm-hole edge.

Shape Neck

Work to last 6(8:10) sts., turn.
Dec. 1 st. at neck edge every alt. row until 30(33:36) sts. rem.
Cont. straight on these sts. until work corresponds with back to shoulders, ending at armhole edge.
Cast off 10(11:12) sts. at beg. of next 3 alt. rows.

RIGHT FRONT

Work as for left front, reversing all shap-ings.

SLEEVES

Cast on 58(58:64) sts. using 2¾mm. needles.
Work in k.1, p.1 rib for 7 cm. (2¾ in.).
Change to 3¼mm. needles. Keeping patt. correct, inc. 1 st. at each end of 7th and every foll. 6th row until there are 94(100:106) sts.

Cont. straight until work measures 43(46:46) cm. (16¾(18:18) in.).

Shape Top

Cast off 6 sts. at beg. of next 2 rows.
Dec. 1 st. at each end of next and every foll. 4th row 3 times, then at each end of every alt. row 6(10:12) times.
Cast off 4 sts. at beg. of next 8 rows, cast off rem. sts.

FRONT BANDS

Cast on 14 sts. with 2¾mm. needles and M.
Work in k.1, p.1 rib until band, when very slightly stretched, fits front edge; leave sts. on stitch holder.
Work second band as first, but working buttonholes as folls.:
1st row: work 6 sts., cast off 2 sts., work to end.
2nd row: cast on 2 sts. over those cast off in previous row.
Work buttonholes on 7th and every foll. 25th row.
Stitch bands into position. Backstitch shoulder seams.

NECKBAND

With 2¾mm. needles and right side of work facing, pick up and rib 124 sts. round neck.
Work buttonhole on 5th row, above other buttonholes in band. Cont. until 10 rows have been worked. Cast off loosely in rib.

MAKING UP

Press all pieces lightly on reverse side, sew in all ends.
Backstitch side and sleeve seams, stitch sleeves into armholes. Sew on buttons.

V-neck, Tri-colour Striped Cardigan   1959

Striped V-neck cardigan with three-quarter length sleeves, hemmed cuffs and lower edge, and doubled, separate front bands

★ Suitable for beginners

MATERIALS

Yarn
Wendy DK
3 × 50g. balls Col. A (Blue)
4(5:5:5) × 50g. balls Col. B (White)
4(4:5:5) × 50g. balls Col. C (Red)

Needles
1 pair 3¼ mm.
1 pair 4mm.

Buttons
5

MEASUREMENTS

Bust
82(87:92:97) cm.
32(34:36:38) in.

Length
57(58:60:61) cm.
22¼(22¾:23½:24) in.

Sleeve Seam
36 cm.
14 in.

TENSION

24 sts. and 32 rows = 10 cm. (4 in.) square over stocking stitch on 4mm. needles. If your tension square does not correspond to these measurements see page 166 for adjustment instructions.

ABBREVIATIONS

k. = knit; p. = purl; st(s). = stitch(es); inc. = increas(ing) (see page 166); dec. = decreas-(ing) (see page 167); beg. = begin(ning); rem. = remain(ing); rep. = repeat; alt. = alternate; tog. = together; sl. = slip stitch (transfer one stitch from left needle, knit-wise unless otherwise stated, to right hand needle.); cont. = continue; patt. = pattern; foll. = following; folls. = follows; mm. = millimetres; cm. = centimetres; in. = inch(es); st.st. = stocking stitch; A = colour A; B = colour B; C = colour C.

BACK

Cast on 102(108:114:120) sts. with 3¼ mm. needles using A and work in st.st. stripes throughout, working 9 rows for this stripe, ending with a k. row.
Next row: k. to mark hemline.
Change to 4mm. needles and work as folls.:
*10 rows A, 10 rows B, 10 rows C, 10 rows B. Rep. from * throughout. At the same time, inc. 1 st. at each end of 32nd row from beg. and foll. 12th rows until there are 108(114:120:126) sts.
Work to the end of 12th stripe when work should measure 41 cm. (16 in.).

Shape Armholes
Cast off 3 sts. at beg. of next 2 rows and dec. 1 st. at each end of foll. 3 alt. rows.
Cont. to keep stripe sequence correct and when back measures 57(58:60:61) cm. (22¼(22¾:23½:24) in.), cont. as folls.:

Shape shoulders
Cast off 10 sts. at beg. of next 6 rows and 2(4:6:8) sts. at beg. of foll. 2 rows.**
Work neckband on rem. sts. in A.
Work 10 rows, ending with a p. row.
Change to 3¼ mm. needles, p. into back of each st. on next row to mark hemline.
Work 9 rows. Cast off.

LEFT FRONT

Cast on 49(52:55:58) sts. with 3¼ mm. needles using A and work as for back, changing to 4mm. needles after hem, as for back.
Inc. 1 st. at beg. of 32nd row from beg. and every foll. 12th row until there are 52(55:58:61) sts.
Cont. to last row of 11th stripe.

Shape Neck and Armhole
k. to last 2 sts., k.2 tog. Work 3 rows in st.st.
Cont. to shape at front edge on every 4th row until there are 32(34:36:38) sts.
At same time, when front measures same as back to armholes, ending at side edge, shape armhole as for back. After shaping, cont. to keep armhole edge straight.
When front measures same as back to shoulder, end at side edge.

Shape Shoulder
Cast off 10 sts. at beg. of next and foll. 2 alt. rows. Cast off rem. 2(4:6:8) sts.

RIGHT FRONT

Work as for left front, reversing shapings.

SLEEVES

Cast on 54(56:58:60) sts. with 3¼ mm. needles using C and work in stripes as for back, changing to 4mm. needles after hemline.
Inc. 1 st. at each end of 8th row after cuff is worked (same as back hem) and at each end of foll. 8th rows until there are 76(78:80:82) sts.
Work straight until sleeve measures 36 cm. (14 in.).

Shape top
Cast off 3 sts. at beg. of next 2 rows and

dec. 1 st. at each end of foll. 3 rows.
Then dec. 1 st. at each end of every alt. row until there are 36 sts.
Now dec. 1 st. at each end of foll. rows until there are 24 sts. Cast off.

FRONT BANDS

With right side facing, beg. at top of left front and with 3¼ mm. needles using A, pick up and k. 56(58:60:62) sts. down to front shaping and 90 sts. down to hemline.
Work in st.st. for 10 rows, work hemline as before and work a further 10 rows. Cast off.
Work right band to match starting to pick up and k. sts. from hemline, and working double buttonholes as positions are reached on right front as folls.:
4th row: k.5, cast off 3 sts., * k.18, including st. already on needle, cast off 3 sts., rep. from * 3 times more.
Next row: cast on 3 sts. over those cast off in previous row. Work 5 rows, then hem-line row and a further 5 rows.
Now work a 2nd buttonhole row and foll. row similarly. Complete band.

MAKING UP

Press pieces. Sew up shoulder and neck-band seams. Fold band and hems to wrong side and catch down neatly using slipstitch.
Set in sleeves and sew up side and sleeve seams. Neaten buttonholes. Sew on but-tons and press seams.

Simple Garter Stitch Jacket 1934

Body-hugging, hip-length garter stitch jacket with four pockets, the lower body and sleeves worked sideways, edged with crochet

★★ Suitable for knitters with some previous experience

MATERIALS

Yarn
Patons Capstan
13(14:15) × 50g. balls

Needles
1 pair 4mm.
1 4mm. crochet hook
Stitch holder

Buttons
5 (large)
2 (small)

MEASUREMENTS

Bust
82(87:92) cm.
32(34:36) in.

Length (from top of shoulders)
53(54:54) cm.
20¾(21¼:21¼) in.

Sleeve Seam
51 cm.
20 in.

TENSION

9 sts. and 18 rows = 5 cm. (2 in.) square over garter stitch on 4mm. needles. If your tension square does not correspond to these measurements see page 166 for adjustment instructions.

ABBREVIATIONS

k. = knit; p. = purl; st(s). = stitch(es); inc. = increas(ing) (see page 166); dec. = decreas-(ing) (see page 167); beg. = begin(ning); rem. = remain(ing); rep. = repeat; alt. = alternate; tog. = together; sl. = slip stitch (transfer one stitch from left needle, knit-wise unless otherwise stated, to right hand needle.); cont. = continue; patt. = pattern; foll. = following; folls. = follows; mm. = millimetres; cm. = centimetre(s); in. = inch(es); y.fwd. = yarn forward; y.r.n. = yarn round needle; d.c. = double crochet; ch. = chain; sp. = space; g.st. = garter stitch (see page 166).

BACK AND FRONTS (worked sideways in one piece)

Cast on 68 sts. fairly loosely.

Work in g.st. for 19(20:21) cm. (7½(7¾:8¼) in.).

** Shape Armhole
Dec. 1 st. at beg. of next and foll. 3 alt. rows.
Work 5 rows straight.
Now inc. 1 st. at beg. of next and foll. 3 alt. rows. **
Work 38(41:43) cm. (15(16:16¾) in.) straight, then rep. from ** to **.
Work a further 19(20:21) cm. (7½(7¾:8¼) in.) straight.
Cast off knitwise.
With right side facing, pick up and k. 68(72:77) sts. across top edge of back for yoke, and work 15(17:17) cm. (5¾(6½:6½) in.) straight in g.st.
Next row: k.23(24:26), cast off 22(24:25) sts. for back neck, k. 23(24:26), including st. on needle after casting off.
Cont. on last group of 23(24:26) sts. for first side and work 8 rows straight.
Now shape front by inc. 1 st. at inside edge on next and every foll. 3rd row until there are 36(38:42) sts., taking inc. sts. into g.st.
Work straight until front measures 17(18:18) cm. (6½(7:7) in.) from neck cast-ing off.

Make Pocket Flap
Next row: k.12(13:14), turn and leave rem. sts. on a spare needle.
Cont. on these 12(13:14) sts. and k. 1 row.
Cast off. Slip next 12(12:14) sts. onto a stitch holder. Rejoin yarn to rem. 12(13:14) sts. and k. 2 rows.
Cast off.
Rejoin yarn to 12(12:14) sts. on stitch holder and work as folls.:
1st row: k.2 tog., k. to last 2 sts., k.2 tog.
2nd row: k.4(4:5), (work y.fwd. and y.r.n.), k.2 tog., k.4(4:5).
3rd row: k.5(5:6), k.1, letting extra loop (formed by y.fwd. and y.r.n.) fall, k.4(4:5).
Cont. in g.st., dec. 1 st. at each end of every row until 6 sts. rem.
Cast off.
Rejoin yarn to rem. 23(24:26) sts. and finish to correspond with first side.

SLEEVES

Cast on 90 sts., k.2 rows.

Shape Top
Inc. 1 st. at beg. of next and every foll. alt. row until there are 102(104:104) sts.

Work 1 row straight.
1st and 2nd rows: inc. in 1st st., k.20, turn and work back.
3rd and 4th rows: inc. in 1st st., k.26, turn and work back.
5th and 6th rows: inc. in 1st st., k.32, turn and work back.
Cont. inc. 1 st. at top of sleeve on next and every foll. alt. row and *at the same time* work 5 sts. more on next and every alt. row until the rows 'inc. in 1st st., k.74, turn and work back' have been worked.
Now keep top edge of sleeve straight and cont. working 5 sts. more on next and every alt. row as before until the rows 'k.104, turn and work back' have been worked.
Now work 5 sts. less on next and every alt. row until the rows 'k.74, turn and work back' have been worked.
Next 2 rows: k.2 tog., k.68, turn and work back.
Next 2 rows: k.2 tog., k.62, turn and work back.
Cont. dec. 1 st. at top edge of sleeve on next and every alt. row and *at the same time* cont. working 5 sts. less on next and every alt. row until the rows 'k.2 tog., k.20, turn and work back' have been worked.
Cont. dec. at top edge on next and every alt. row until 90 sts. rem.
Work 2 rows straight.
Cast off.

POCKET

Cast on 22 sts. and work 8 cm. (3¼ in.) in g.st.

Work buttonhole in next 2 rows as folls.:

1st buttonhole row: k.10, work y.fwd. and y.r.n., k.2 tog., k.10.

2nd buttonhole row: k. back, letting extra loop (formed by the y.fwd., and y.r.n.) fall from needle.

Work a further 2 rows in g.st. Cast off.

Make another pocket in the same manner.

LINING FOR TOP POCKET

Cast on 12(12:14) sts. and work 7 cm. (2¾ in.) in g.st. Cast off.

MAKING UP

Press work very lightly, taking care not to spoil g.st. patt.

Sew 2 pieces of yoke to fronts. Sew up sleeve and side seams.

Set in sleeves.

Pin a pocket in centre of each front, bottom of pocket to come 5 cm. (2 in.) above lower edge, sew in position.

Pin linings for the top pockets in position, then slipstitch neatly all round.

With right side facing, using 4mm. crochet hook, start at lower edge and work in d.c. up right front, all round neck and down left front.

Turn and work a further row in d.c.

Cont. in d.c., making 3 buttonholes on right front in next row, 1st to come at join of yoke and body, and 2nd and 3rd spaced at 13 cm. (5 in.) intervals, first marking position of buttons on left front with pins to ensure even spacing, then working holes as folls., to correspond:

1st buttonhole row: work to position of hole, make 4 ch., miss 3 d.c.

2nd buttonhole row: work back in d.c., working 3 d.c. into each 4 ch. space.

Work a further 2 rows in d.c. Fasten off.

Work a row of d.c. all round lower edge of jacket and round each pocket flap.

Press seams lightly. Sew on buttons.

Edge to Edge Bobble Pattern Jacket 1968

Hip-length, thick jacket in bobble pattern, with set-in sleeves, stand-up patterned collar, with garter stitch knitted-in front bands

★★ Suitable for knitters with some previous experience

MATERIALS

Yarn

Lister-Lee Machine Washable Motoravia DK

19(19:20) × 50g. balls

Needles

1 pair 3mm.

1 pair 3¾mm.

MEASUREMENTS

Bust

87(92:97) cm.

34(36:38) in.

Length

61(62:64) cm.

24(24½:25) in.

Sleeve Seam

41.5 cm.

16¼ in.

TENSION

12 sts. and 16 rows = 5 cm. (2 in.) square over pattern using 3¾mm. needles. If your tension square does not correspond to these measurements see page 166 for adjustment instructions.

ABBREVIATIONS

k. = knit; p. = purl; st(s). = stitch(es); inc. = increas(ing) (see page 166); dec. = decreas-(ing) (see page 167); beg. = begin(ning); rem. = remain(ing); rep. = repeat; alt. = alternate; tog. = together; sl. = slip stitch (transfer one stitch from left needle, knit-wise unless otherwise stated, to right hand needle); cont. = continue; patt. = pattern; foll. = following; folls. = follows; mm. = millimetres; cm. = centimetre(s); in. = inch(es); mb. = make bobble: k.5 times into next st., turn, k.5, turn, k.2 tog., k.3 tog. t.b.l., slip first st. over 2nd st.; m. 1 = where m. 1 is part of bobble patt., work as folls.: pick up loop lying between stitch on needle and following stitch and knit into back of it; t.b.l. = through back of stitch; st.st. = stocking stitch; g.st. = garter stitch.

NOTE: On 2nd and 3rd sizes, the under-arm seam is off centre.

BACK

Cast on 113(127:113) sts.

1st row: k.

2nd row: k.1, * p.13, k.1, rep. from * to end.

3rd row: p.1, * k.1, p.1 (mb., p.1) 5 times, k.1, p.1, rep. from * to end.

4th row: k.1 t.b.l., * p.1, k.1 t.b.l., rep. from * to end.

5th row: p.1, * m. 1, k.1, p.2 tog., (mb., p.1) 3 times, mb., p.2 tog., k.1, m. 1, p.1, rep. from * to end.

6th row: k.1, * p.2, (k.1 t.b.l., p.1) 5 times, p.1, k.1, rep. from * to end.

7th row: p.1, * k.1, m. 1, k.1, p.2 tog., (mb., p.1) twice, mb., p.2 tog., k.1, m. 1, k.1, p.1, rep. from * to end.

8th row: (k.1, p.1) twice, * (k.1 t.b.l., p.1) 4

Edge to Edge Bobble Pattern Jacket

times, (k.1, p.1) 3 times, rep. from * to last 11 sts., (k.1 t.b.l., p.1) 4 times, k.1, p.1, k.1.

9th row: p.1, * k.1, p.1, m. 1, k.1, p.2 tog., mb., p.1, mb., p.2 tog., k.1, m. 1, p.1, k.1, p.1, rep. from * to end.

10th row: k.1, * p.1, k.1, p.2, (k.1 t.b.l., p.1) 3 times, (p.1, k.1) twice, rep. from * to end.

11th row: p.1, * k.1, p.1, k.1, m. 1, k.1, p.2 tog., mb., p.2 tog., k.1, m. 1, (k.1, p.1) twice, rep. from * to end.

12th row: k.1 * p.1, k.1, rep. from * to end.

13th row: p.1, * k.1, p.1, rep. from * to end.

Work 7 rows in st.st. (1st row – purl). These 20 rows form the patt.

Rep. these 20 patt. rows 5 times more, then 1st to 12th rows once.

Shape Armholes

Keeping patt. correct, cast off 6(10:0) sts. at beg. of next 2 rows.

Dec. 1 st. at each end of foll. 7(8:9) alt. rows. [87(91:95) sts.] Cont. in patt. until armhole measures 18(19:20) cm. (7(7½:7¾) in.)

Shape Shoulders

Cast off 7 sts. at beg. of next 6 rows. Cast off 6(7:8) sts. at beg. of next 2 rows. Cast off 33(35:37) sts.

LEFT FRONT

Cast on 60(60:74) sts., using 3¾mm. needles.

Now work in patt. with 3 sts. in g.st. at front edge as folls.:

1st row: k.

2nd row: k.4, * p.13, k.1, rep. from * to end.

3rd row: p.1, * k.1, p.1, (mb., p.1) 5 times, k.1, p.1, rep. from * to last 3 sts., k.3.

Cont. in patt. as given for back to armhole, with g.st. border.

Shape Armhole

Cast off 6(2:12) sts. at beg. of next row. Work one row. Dec. 1 st. at armhole edge on next and foll. 6(7:8) alt. rows. [47(50:53) sts.]

Cont. in patt. until armhole measures 13(14:15) cm. (5(5½:5¾) in.), ending at neck edge.

Shape Neck

Cast off 9(11:13) sts. at beg. of next row. Work one row. Cast off 3 sts. at beg. of next row. Work one row. Dec. 1 st. at neck edge on next 4 rows. Dec. 1 st. at neck edge on next and every foll. alt. row until 27(28:29) sts. rem. Cont. in patt. until work measures same as back to shoulder, ending at armhole edge.

Shape Shoulder

Cast off 7 sts. at beg. of next and foll. 2 alt. rows. Work one row.
Cast off rem. 6(7:8) sts.

RIGHT FRONT

Work to correspond with left front, reversing all shapings and working 3 sts. in g.st. at other end of row, thus 2nd row will read: k.1, * p.13, k.1, rep. from * to last 3 sts., k.3; 3rd row will read: k.3, p.1, * k.1, p.1 (mb., p.1) 5 times, k.1, p.1, rep. from * to end.

SLEEVES

Cast on 57(57:57) sts. using 3¾mm. needles, and work in patt. as for back, inc. 1 st. at each end of 3rd (3rd;11th) row, then every foll. 12th (10th:8th) row and incorporating inc. sts. into patt., until there are 79(83:87) sts. Cont. until the 12th row of 7th patt. has been worked.

Shape Top

Cast off 6 sts. at beg. of next 2 rows.
Dec. 1 st. at each end of next and every foll. alt. row until 45 sts. rem.
Cast off 2 sts. at beg. of next 8 rows.
Cast off 3 sts. at beg. of next 4 rows.
Cast off 4 sts. at beg. of next 2 rows.
Cast off rem. 9 sts.

COLLAR

Cast on 91(91:105) sts. using 3¾mm. needles.
Keeping 3 sts. at each end in g.st., work 12 rows in patt.
Using 3mm. needles, still keeping 3 sts. at each end in g.st., work 5 cm. (2 in.) in st.st. Cast off.

MAKING UP

Press as instructions on ball band. Sew shoulder, side and sleeve seams. Sew in sleeves, remembering that on second size sleeve seam will be approx. 1 cm. (½ in.) behind side seam and on the third size the sleeve seam will be 1 cm. (½ in.) forward of side seam.
Sew on collar, placing cast on edge to neck edge.
Fold collar in half onto wrong side and slipstitch neatly into position.
Press all seams.

Hip-length, Shawl-collared Jacket 1961

Hemmed jacket in stocking stitch with set-in sleeves, large doubled collar with front sections worked as extensions of front bands

★ Suitable for beginners

MATERIALS

Yarn
Hayfield Brig DK
13(13:14:14:15) × 50g. balls

Needles
1 pair 3¼mm.
1 pair 4mm.

Buttons
6

MEASUREMENTS

Bust
82(87:92:97:102) cm.
32(34:36:38:40) in.

Length
55(56:57:58:59) cm.
21½(22:22¼:22¾:23¼) in.

Sleeve Seam
43(44:45:46:47) cm.
16¾(17¼:17¾:18:18½) in.

TENSION

22 sts. and 30 rows = 10 cm. (4 in.) square over stocking stitch on 4mm needles. If your tension square does not correspond to these measurements see page 166 for adjustment instructions.

ABBREVIATIONS

k. = knit; p. = purl; st(s). = stitch(es); inc. = increas(ing) (see page 166); dec. = decreas-(ing) (see page 167); beg. = begin(ning); rem. = remain(ing); rep. = repeat; alt. = alternate; tog. = together; sl. = slip stitch (transfer one stitch from left needle, knit-wise unless otherwise stated, to right hand needle.); cont. = continue; patt. = pattern; foll. = following; folls. = follows; mm. = millimetres; cm. = centimetre(s); in. = inch(es); p.s.s.o. = pass slipped stitch over; reqd. = required; st.st. = stocking stitch.

BACK

Cast on 97(103:109:115:121) sts. with 3¼mm needles.
Beg. with a k. row, work 9 rows in st.st. then k.1 row to mark hemline.
Change to 4mm. needles and beg. with a k. row, cont. in st.st. until work measures 37cm. (14½ in.) from hemline, ending with a p. row. **

Shape Armholes
Cast off 5(5:6:6:7) sts. at beg. of next 2 rows.
Next row: k.1, sl.1, k.1, p.s.s.o., k. to last 3 sts., k.2 tog., k.1.
Next row: p. to end.
Rep. the last 2 rows 3(4:4:5:5) times more. [79(83:87:91:95) sts.]
Cont. without shaping until armholes measure 18(19:20:21:22) cm., 7(7½:7¾: 8¼:8½) in.), ending with a p. row.

Shape Shoulders
Cast off 5(5:6:6:7) sts. at beg. of next 6 rows, then 5(6:5:6:5) sts. at beg. of next 2 rows. [39(41:41:43:43) sts.]

COLLAR

Cont. on these sts., work 14 rows.
Next row: k.2, m. 1 by picking up loop bet-ween sts. and k. into the back of it, k. to last 2 sts., m. 1, k.2.
Work 5 rows.
Rep. the last 6 rows 6 times more, then the first row again. [55(57:57:59:59) sts.]
Work 17 rows.
Next row: k.2, k.2 tog., k. to last 4 sts., sl.1, k.1, p.s.s.o., k.2.
Work 5 rows.
Rep. the last 6 rows 6 times more, then the first row again. [39(41:41:43:43) sts.]
Work 13 rows. Cast off.

LEFT FRONT

Cast on 47(50:53:56:59) sts. with 3¼mm. needles and work as for back to **.

Shape Armhole
Cast off 5(5:6:6:7) sts. at beg. of next row.
Next row: p. to end.
Next row: k.1, sl.1, k.1, p.s.s.o., k. to end.
Rep. the last 2 rows 3(4:4:5:5) times more. [38(40:42:44:46) sts.]
Cont. without shaping until armhole measures the same as back, ending with a p. row.

Shape Shoulder
Cast off 5(5:6:6:7) sts. at beg. of next row and foll. 2 alt. rows, then 5(6:5:6:5) sts. at beg. of foll. alt. row.
Cast off rem. 18(19:19:20:20) sts.

RIGHT FRONT

Work to match left front, reversing all shapings.

SLEEVES

Cast on 53(55:57:59:61) sts. with 3¼mm. needles.
1st row: k.1, * p.1, k.1, rep. from * to end.
2nd row: p.1, * k.1, p.1, rep. from * to end.
Rep. these 2 rows for 10 cm. (4 in.), ending with a 1st row.
Next row: rib 3(4:5:6:7), * m. 1, rib 12, rep. from * 3 times more, m. 1, rib to end. [58(60:62:64:66) sts.]
Change to 4mm. needles and beg. with a k. row cont. in st.st., m. 1 st. at each end of 5th and every foll. 10th(10th: 8th:8th:8th) row until there are 76(80:84:88:92) sts., then cont. without shaping until sleeve seam measures 43(44: 45:46:47) cm. 16¾(17¼:17¾:18:18½) in., ending with a p. row.

Shape Top
Cast off 5(5:6:6:7) sts. at beg. of next 2 rows.

Hip-length, Shawl-collared Jacket

Dec. as on back armholes at each end of next and every alt. row until 40(42:44:46:48) sts. rem., ending with a p. row.

Cast off 2 sts. at beg. of next 6(6:6:8:8) rows, then 3 sts. at beg. of next 4 rows.

Cast off rem. 16(18:20:18:20) sts.

LEFT FRONT BAND AND COLLAR

Cast on 27 sts. with 4mm. needles and work in st.st. for 37 cm. (14½ in.) (same length as back and fronts from hemline to armholes), ending with a p. row.

Next row: k.10, m. 1, k.7, m. 1, k.10.

Next row: p. to end.

Next row: k.11, m. 1, k.7, m. 1, k.11.

Cont. to inc. at each side of 7 centre sts. on every alt. row until there are 79 sts., then cont. without shaping until straight edge of collar measures the same as front edge to shoulder, ending with a p. row.

Cast off.

Mark position of buttons with pins as folls.:

1st pin on 5th row from beg., 2nd pin level with first row of shaping, then 4 more at equal distances between these two.

RIGHT FRONT BAND AND COLLAR

Work as given for left front band and collar, making buttonholes to correspond with position of pins as folls.:

(right side facing) k.5, cast off 3, k. to last 8 sts., cast off 3, k.5.

On next row cast on 3 sts. over each 3 cast off.

MAKING UP

Press work according to instructions on ball band.

Join shoulder seams leaving 18(19: 19:20:20) sts. at front edge free.

Sew in sleeves.

Join side and sleeve seams. Turn up hem at lower edge and slipstitch.

Sew on front bands. Sew top edge of collar and top part of front to edges of back collar. Fold front bands and collar in half to inside and slipstitch. Sew round double buttonholes. Press seams. Sew on buttons.

Classic Round-neck Cardigan

Loose-fitting, simple cardigan with knitted-in pockets, set-in sleeves, ribbed front bands and welts, in stocking stitch

★ Suitable for beginners

MATERIALS

Yarn
Poppleton Pica
11(12:13:14) × 40g. balls
or
Poppleton Emmerdale Chunky
11(12:13:14) × 50g. balls

Needles
1 pair 4½mm.
1 pair 6mm.
1 stitch holder

Buttons
7

MEASUREMENTS

Bust
82(87:92:97) cm.
32(34:36:38) in.

Length
52(53:54:55) cm.
20½(20¾:21¼:21½) in.

Sleeve Seam
43(43:44:44) cm.
16¾(16¾:17¼:17¼) in.

TENSION

7½ sts. and 9½ rows = 5 cm. (2 in.) square over stocking stitch on 6mm. needles. If your tension square does not correspond to these measurements, see page 166 for adjustment instructions.

ABBREVIATIONS

k. = knit; p. = purl; st(s). = stitch(es); inc. = increas(ing) (see page 166); dec. = decreas-(ing) (see page 167); beg. = begin(ning); rem. = remain(ing); rep. = repeat; alt. = alternate; tog. = together; sl. = slip stitch (transfer one stitch from left needle, knit-wise unless otherwise stated, to right hand needle.); cont. = continue; patt. = pattern; foll. = following; folls. = follows; mm. = millimetres; cm. = centimetre(s); in. = inch(es); st.st., = stocking stitch; m.1 = increase 1 st. by picking up loop from between needles and knitting into the back of it; y.r.n. = yarn round needle.

LEFT FRONT

**** Pocket Lining**
Cast on 17 sts. with 6mm. needles.
Work 17 rows in st.st., starting with a p. row.
Break yarn and leave sts. on spare needle or stitch holder.
Now cast on 31(33:35:37) sts. with 4½mm. needles.
1st row: k.2, *p.1, k.1, rep. from * to last st., k.1.
2nd row: *k.1, p.1, rep. from * to last st., k.1.
Rep. 1st and 2nd rows 4 times more.
Change to 6mm. needles and st.st., starting with a k. row.
Work 18 rows.

Make Pocket
Next row: k.7(8:9:10) sts., slip next 17 sts. on to a stitch holder and k. pocket lining sts. in place of these, k. to end.
Cont. until front measures 35(35:36:36) cm. (13¾(13¾:14:14) in.) from beg. ending at side edge.**

Shape Armhole
Next row: cast off 3(3:4:4) sts. k. to end.

Work 1 row.
Now dec. 1 st. at beg. of next row, and then every alt. row until 25(26:27:28) sts. rem.
Work 9(9:9:9) rows, ending with a p. row.

Shape Neck
Next row: k. to last 4 sts., cast off these sts. Break yarn.
Turn and rejoin yarn at neck edge.
Dec. 1 st. at neck edge on the next 4 rows, and the 4 foll. alt. rows.
Work 3 rows, ending at armhole edge.

Shape Shoulder
Cast off 4(5:5:5) sts. at beg. of next row, and 5(4:5:6) sts. at beg. of foll. alt. row.
Work 1 row.
Cast off 4(5:5:5) rem. sts.

Pocket Border
Slip sts. from stitch holder on to a 4½mm. needle.
1st row: k.1, * m.1, (p.1, k.1) twice, p.1, rep. from * twice more, m.1, k.1. [21 sts.]
2nd row: * k.1, p.1, rep. from * to last st., k.1.
3rd row: k.2, * p.1, k.1, rep. from * to last st., k.1.
Rep. 2nd and 3rd rows once more.
Cast off in rib.

RIGHT FRONT

Follow instructions for left from ** to **, working 1 row more to end at side edge.

Shape Armhole
Next row: cast off 3(3:4:4) sts., p. to end.
Now dec. 1 st. at end of next row, and then every alt. row until 25(26:27:28) sts. rem.
Work 9(9:9:9) rows, ending with a p. row.

Shape Neck
Next row: cast off 4 sts., k. to end.
Now complete to match left front, beg. with row starting 'Dec. 1 st.', working 1 extra row before shaping shoulder.
Work pocket border as left front.

BACK

Cast on 65(69:73:77) sts. with 4½mm. needles and work 10 rows in rib as left front.
Change to 6mm. needles and st.st.
Work until back measures same as fronts to armholes, ending with a p. row.

Shape Armholes
Cast off 3(3:4:4) sts. at beg. of next 2 rows.
Now dec. 1 st. at each end of next row, and then every alt. row until 53(55:57:59) sts. rem.
Work until armholes measure same as fronts, ending with a p. row.

Shape Shoulders and Back of Neck
Next row: cast off 4(5:5:5) sts., k.12(12:13:14) sts. including st. on needle, cast off 21 sts., k. to end.
Cont. on last set of sts.
1st row: cast off 4(5:5:5) sts., p. to last 2 sts., p.2 tog.
2nd row: k.2 tog., k. to end.
3rd row: cast off 5(4:5:6) sts., p. to last 2 sts., p.2 tog.

Classic Round-neck Cardigan

4th row: k.
Cast off 4(5:5:5) rem. sts.
Rejoin yarn to rem. sts. at neck edge.
1st row: p.2 tog. p. to end.
2nd row: cast off 5(4:5:6) sts., k. to last 2 sts., k.2 tog.
3rd row: as 1st row.
Cast off 4(5:5:5) rem. sts.

SLEEVES

Cast on 33(33:35:35) sts. with 4½mm. needles and work 10 rows in rib as left front.
Change to 6mm. needles and st.st.
Work 4 rows.
Inc. 1 st. at each end of next row, and then every 12th (10th:10th:8th) row until there are 45(47:49:51) sts.
Work until sleeve measures 43(43:44:44) cm. (16¾(16¾:17¼:17¼) in.) from beg., ending with a p. row.

Shape Top

Cast off 3(3:4:4) sts. at beg. of next 2 rows.
Now dec. 1 st. at each end of next row, and then every alt. row until 21(21:21:21) sts. rem., and then every row until 13 sts. rem.
Cast off.

NECK AND FRONT BANDS

Press each piece lightly with cool iron and dry cloth.
Join shoulder seams.

Neckband

With 4½mm. needles, and with right side of work facing, k. up 22 sts. along right front neck edge, 23 sts. evenly along back neck edge, and 22 sts. along left front neck edge.
1st row: * k.1, p.1, rep. from * to last st., k.1.
2nd row: k.2, * p.1, k.1, rep. from * to the last st., k.1.
Rep. 1st and 2nd rows once more, and then 1st row once.
Cast off in rib.

Left Front Band

Cast on 8 sts. with 4½mm. needles.
1st row: (k.1, p.1) 3 times, k.2.
2nd row: (k.1, p.1) 4 times.
These 2 rows form rib.
Work until band is long enough to fit up left front edge when slightly stretched, ending with 2nd row.
Cast off firmly in rib.
Sew band to front.

Pin the positions of 7 buttons on band, the bottom button in 5th row from cast on edge, the top button in 3rd row from cast off edge, and the rest equally spaced between.

Right front band

Cast on 8 sts. with 4½mm. needles.
1st row: k.2, (p.1, k.1) 3 times.
2nd row: (p.1, k.1) 4 times.
These 2 rows form rib.
Work 2 more rows.
Make buttonhole: k.2, p.1, y.r.n., p.2 tog., k.1, p.1, k.1.
Making buttonholes in this way to correspond with marked positions, work until border measures same as left side, ending with 2nd row.
Cast off firmly in rib.

MAKING UP

Sew right front band to front.
Sew up side and sleeve seams.
Sew sleeves into armholes.
Sew pocket linings and pocket borders in position.
Press seams lightly.
Sew on buttons.

Cardigan with Huge Rollover Collar 1960

Just below waist-length cardigan in stocking stitch, with knitted-in front bands, ribbed welts, huge rollover collar and set-in sleeves

★ Suitable for beginners

MATERIALS

Yarn
Sunbeam Aran 4 ply
7(7:8:8) × 50g. balls

Needles
1 pair 2¾mm.
1 pair 3¼mm.

Buttons
9

MEASUREMENTS

Bust
82(87:92:97) cm.
32(34:36:38) in.

Length (from shoulder)
50(50:51:51) cm.
19½(19½:20:20) in.

Sleeve Seam
35(36:36:36) cm.
13¾(14:14:14) in.

TENSION

14 sts. and 18 rows = 5 cm. (2 in.) square over stocking stitch on 3¼mm. needles. If your tension square does not correspond to these measurements, see page 166 for adjustment instructions.

ABBREVIATIONS

k. = knit; p. = purl; st(s). = stitch(es); inc. = increas(ing) (see page 166); dec. = decreas(ing) (see page 167); beg. = begin(ning); rem. = remain(ing); rep. = repeat; alt. = alternate; tog. = together; sl. = slip stitch (transfer one stitch from left needle, knitwise unless otherwise stated, to right-hand needle); cont. = continue; patt. = pattern; foll. = following; folls. = follows; mm. = millimetres; cm. = centimetre(s); in. = inch(es); st.st. = stocking stitch.

LEFT FRONT

Cast on 69(73:77:81) sts. with 2¾mm. needles.
1st row: * k.2, p.2, rep. from * to the last 13 sts., (p.1, k.1) 6 times, k.1.
2nd row: k.1, (p.1, k.1) 6 times, * p.2, k.2, rep. from * to end. Rep. 1st and 2nd rows for 7 cm. (2¾ in.), ending with 2nd row.

Cardigan with Huge Rollover Collar

Change to 3¼ mm. needles.
1st row: k. to last 13 sts., rib to end.
2nd row: rib 13 sts., p. to end.
Cont. in st.st., with 13 sts. in rib for border, (always work border sts. very firmly, or use a size finer needle for border sts. only).
Work until front measures 31(31:32:32) cm. (12¼(12¼:12½:12½) in.) from beg. ending at side edge.

Shape Armhole
Next row: cast off 5(6:7:7) sts., work to end.
Work 1 row.
Now dec. 1 st. at armhole edge on the next 3(5:5:7) rows, and then the 2(3:4:4) foll. alt. rows.
Work until armhole measures 14(14:15:15) cm. (5½(5½:5¾:5¾) in.) measured straight, ending at centre front edge.

Shape Neck
Next row: cast off 20 sts., p. to end.
Now keeping armhole edge straight, dec. 1 st. at neck edge on the next 6(6:6:6) rows, and then the 6(6:6:7) foll. alt. rows, ending at armhole edge.

Shape Shoulder
Cast off 6(6:7:8) sts. at beg. of next row, and 6(7:7:7) sts. at beg. of 2 foll. alt. rows.
Work 1 row.
Cast off 7(7:8:8) rem. sts.
Pin the positions of 7 buttons on border, the bottom button in the 5th row from cast on edge, the top button in the 5th row from neck edge, and the rest equally spaced between.

RIGHT FRONT
Cast on 69(73:77:81) sts. with 2¾ mm. needles.
1st row: k.1, (k.1, p.1) 6 times, * k.2, p.2, rep. from * to end.

2nd row: * k.2, p.2, rep. from * to the last 13 sts., (k.1, p.1) 6 times, k.1.
Rep. 1st and 2nd rows once more.
Make buttonhole:
Next row: rib 5 sts., cast off 3 sts., work to end.
Foll. row: work to end, casting on 3 sts. over those cast off.
Now making buttonholes thus, to correspond with marked positions, cont. as folls.:
Work until front measures 7 cm. (2¾ in.) from beg., ending with 2nd row.
Change to 3¼ mm. needles.
1st row: rib 13 sts., k. to end.
2nd row: p. to last 13 sts., rib to end.
Cont. until front measures same as left front to armhole, working 1 more row to end at side edge.

Shape Armhole
Next row: cast off 5(6:7:7) sts., work to end.
Now dec. 1 st. at armhole edge on the next 3(5:5:7) rows, and then the 2(3:4:4) foll. alt. rows.
Work until armhole measures same as left front to neck, ending at armhole edge.

Shape Neck
Next row: work to last 20 sts., cast off these sts. Break yarn. Turn and rejoin yarn to rem. sts. at neck edge and complete to match left front, working 1 row more, in order to end at armhole edge, before shaping shoulder.

BACK
Cast on 118(124:130:136) sts. with 2¾ mm. needles.
1st row: p.2(1:2:1), k.2, * p.2, k.2, rep. from * to the last 2(1:2:1) sts., p.2(1:2:1).
2nd row: * k.2(1:2:1), p.2, * k.2, p.2, rep. from * to the last 2(1:2:1) sts., k.2(1:2:1).
Rep. 1st and 2nd rows for 7 cm. (2¾ in.), ending with 2nd row. Change to 3¼ mm. needles and st.st.
Work until back measures same as fronts to armholes, ending with a p. row.

Shape Armholes
Cast off 5(6:7:7) sts. at beg. of next 2 rows.
Now dec. 1 st. at each end of every row until 98(102:106:112) sts. rem., and then every alt. row until 94(98:102:106) sts. rem.
Work until armholes measure same as fronts, ending with a p. row.

Shape Shoulders and Back of Neck
Cast off 6(6:7:8) sts. at beg. of next 2 rows.
Next row: cast off 6(7:7:7) sts., k.16(17:18:18) sts. (including st. on needle), cast off 38(38:38:40) sts., k. to end.
Cont. on last set of sts.
1st row: cast off 6(7:7:7) sts., p. to last 2 sts., p.2 tog.
2nd row: k.2 tog., k. to end.
3rd row: as 1st row.
Work 1 row.
Cast off 7(7:8:8) rem. sts.
Rejoin yarn to rem. sts. at neck edge.

1st row: p.2 tog., p. to end.
2nd row: cast off 6(7:7:7) sts., k. to last 2 sts., k.2 tog.
3rd row: as 1st row.
Cast off 7(7:8:8) rem. sts.

SLEEVES
Cast on 66(68:70:72) sts. with 2¾ mm. needles.
1st row: p.2(1:2:1), k.2, * p.2, k.2, rep. from * to the last 2(1:2:1) sts., p. 2(1:2:1).
2nd row: k.2(1:2:1), p.2, * k.2, p.2, rep. from * to the last 2(1:2:1) sts., k. 2(1:2:1).
Rep. 1st and 2nd rows for 7 cm. (2¾ in.), ending with 2nd row.
Change to 3¼ mm. needles and st.st.
Work 6(6:2:6) rows.
Inc. 1 st. at each end of next row, and then every 8th(8th:8th:6th) row until there are 76(78:82:80) sts., and then every 10th(10th:10th:8th) row until there are 86(88:92:96) sts.
Work until sleeve measures 35(36:36:36) cm. (13¾(14:14:14) in.) from beg., ending with a p. row.

Shape Top
Cast off 5(6:7:7) sts. at beg. of next 2 rows.
Now dec. 1 st. at each end of every row until 66(66:68:70) sts. rem., then every alt. row until 36 sts. rem., and then every row until 22 sts. rem.
Cast off.

COLLAR
Cast on 212(212:216:216) sts. with 3¼ mm. needles, *very loosely.*
1st row: k.1, p.2, * k.2, p.2, rep. from * to the last st., k.1.
2nd row: k.3, * p.2, k.2, rep. from * to the last st., k.1.
Rep. 1st and 2nd rows for 4 cm. (1½ in.), ending with 1st row.
Make buttonhole:
Next row: rib 5 sts., cast off 3 sts., rib to end.
Foll. row: rib to end, casting on 3 sts. over those cast off.
Cont. until collar measures 9 cm. (3½ in.) from beg., ending with 2nd row.
Change to 2¾ mm. needles.
Work 3 rows.
Make buttonhole in next 2 rows.
Cont. until collar measures 18 cm. (7 in.) from beg., ending with 2nd row.
Next row: k.1, p.2 tog., * k.2, p.2 tog., rep. from * to the last st., k.1.
Work 9 more rows with 1 st. less in the p. ribs.
Cast off loosely in rib.

MAKING UP
Press each piece lightly with warm iron and damp cloth.
Sew up shoulder, side and sleeve seams.
Sew sleeves into armholes.
Sew cast off edge of collar to neck edge, with buttonholes at left side.
Press seams lightly. Sew on buttons.

Tailored, Plaid Sports Cardigan

1942

Round-neck cardigan in stocking stitch, shaped at the waistline, with plaid pattern worked from chart, on fronts only, and additional swiss darning

★★★ Suitable for experienced knitters only

MATERIALS

Yarn
Lister-Lee Motoravia 4 ply
6(6:7) × 50g. balls Colour A (beige)
1 × 50g. ball Colour B (green)
1 × 50g. ball Colour C (rust)

Needles
1 pair 2¾mm.
1 pair 3mm.

MEASUREMENTS

Bust
82(87:92) cm.
32(34:36) in.

Length
56 cm.
21 in.

Sleeve Seam
46 cm.
18 in.

TENSION

14 sts. and 18 rows = 5 cm. (2 in.) square on 3mm. needles. If your tension square does not correspond to these measurements see page 166 for adjustment instructions.

ABBREVIATIONS

k. = knit; p. = purl; st(s). = stitch(es); inc. = increas(ing) (see page 166); dec. = decreas(ing) (see page 167); beg. = begin(ning); rem. = remain(ing); rep. = repeat; alt. = alternate; tog. = together; sl. = slip stitch (transfer one stitch from left needle, knitwise unless otherwise stated, to right hand needle.); cont. = continue; patt(s). = pattern(s); foll. = following; folls. = follows; mm. = millimetres; cm. = centimetre(s); in. = inch(es); st.st. = stocking stitch.

LEFT FRONT

Cast on 65(69:73) sts. using 2¾ mm. needles.
1st row: * k.1, p.2, k.1, rep. from * to last 9 sts., k.9.
2nd row: p.9, * p.1, k.2, p.1, rep. from * to end.
Rep. 1st and 2nd rows 4 times more.
Using 3mm. needles, beg. patt. and side shaping, working in st.st.:
1st row: k.2 tog., k.14(16:18) work 1st row of graph over next 39 sts., knit to end.

Keeping edge sts. in Colour A, cont. to work the 39 sts., from chart (39 rows) until 5 complete patts. have been worked, noting that each alt. rep. will beg. on a purl row (i.e. 1st patt. starts on a knit row, 2nd patt. starts on a purl row), then work remainder of front all in Colour A, at the same time, work shapings as follows: dec. 1 st. at side edge on every 3rd row until 52(56:60) sts. rem.
Cont. without shaping until work measures 18 cm. (7 in.). Now inc. one st. at side edge on next and every foll. 5th row until there are 65(69:73) sts.
Cont. without shaping until work measures 38 cm. (15 in.), ending at inc. edge.

Shape Armhole
Cast off 4(5:6) sts. at beg. of next row.
Work one row.
Cast off 3(4:5) sts. at beg. of next row.
Work one row.
Cast off 3 sts. at beg. of next row.
Work one row.
Cast off 2 sts. at beg. of next row.
Dec. 1 st. at armhole edge on next 2 rows. [51(53:55) sts.] Cont. in patt. until armhole measures 15½ cm. (6 in.), ending at armhole edge.

Shape Neck
1st row: patt. to last 8 sts., leave these 8 sts. on a thread for neckband.
Cast off 4 sts. at beg. of next row. Work one row.
(Cast off 3 sts. at beg. of next row. Work one row) twice.
Cast off 1(2:3) sts. at beg. of next row. Work one row.
Cast off 1 st. at beg. of next and foll. alt. row. [30(31:32) sts.]

Shape Shoulder
Cast off 5(6:7) sts. at beg. of next row. Work one row.
Cast off 5 sts. at beg. of next and foll. 4 alt. rows.
Work embroidered stitches from chart.

RIGHT FRONT

Work to correspond with left front, reversing all shapings and working 5 buttonholes as folls.:
1st buttonhole row (9th row of rib): k.2, cast off 4 sts., k.2, rib to end.
Next row: cast on 4 sts. over cast off sts.
Work 2nd buttonhole on 39th row of 1st patt., thus – purl to last 6 sts., cast off 4 sts., p.2. Cast on 4 sts. over cast off sts. on next row.

Work 3rd buttonhole on 39th row of 2nd patt., 4th buttonhole on 39th row of 3rd patt. and 5th buttonhole on 39th row of 4th patt.

BACK

Worked in Colour A throughout.
Cast on 116(124:132) sts. using 2¾mm. needles.

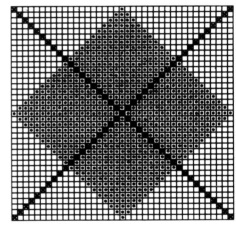

☐ A ◉ B ☒ C: worked in swiss darning.

115

Tailored, Plaid Sports Cardigan

1st row: * k.1, p.2, k.1, rep. from * to end.
2nd row: * p.1, k.2, p.1, rep. from * to end.
Rep. 1st and 2nd rows 4 times more.
Using 3mm. needles, cont. in st.st., dec.
1 st. at each end of first and every foll. 3rd
row until 90(98:106) sts. rem. Cont. in st.
st. until work measures 18 cm. (7 in.). Inc.
1 st. at each end of next and every following 5th row until there are 116(124:132)
sts. Cont. without shaping until work
measures same as left front to armhole.

Shape Armholes
Cast off 3(4:5) sts. at beg. of next 2 rows.
Cast off 3 sts. at beg. of next 2 rows.
Cast off 1(2:3) sts. at beg. of next 2 rows.
Dec. 1 st. at each end of next 4 rows.
[94(98:102)sts.] Cont. without shaping
until work measures same as left front to
shoulder.

Shape Shoulders
Cast off 5(6:7) sts. at beg. of next 2 rows.
Cast off 5 sts. at beg. of next 10 rows.
Leave rem. 34(36:38) sts. on a thread for
neckband.

SLEEVES
Worked in Colour A throughout.
Cast on 58(60:62) sts. using 2¾mm.
needles and work 7 cm. (2¾ in.) in k.2, p.2
rib as given for back.
Using 3mm. needles, cont. in st.st., inc. 1
st. at each end of first and every foll. 8th
row until there are 96(98:100) sts.
Cont. without shaping until work
measures 46 cm. (18 in.) or desired length
of sleeve seam, ending with a wrong side
row.

Shape Head
Cast off 4 sts. at beg. of next 2 rows.
Cast off 3 sts. at beg. of next 2 rows.
Cast off 2 sts. at beg. of next 2 rows. Dec.
1 st. at beg. of next and every foll. row
until 58 sts. rem.
Dec. 1 st. at each end of every foll. 4th row
until 50 sts. rem.
Cast off 4 sts. at beg. of next 4 rows.
Cast off 5 sts. at beg. of next 2 rows.
Cast off rem. 22(24:26) sts.

NECKBAND
Sew shoulder seams. Using 2¾mm.
needles and Colour A, slip the 8 sts. from
right front onto needles, pick up and knit
28(29:30) sts. to shoulder seam, knit
across 34(36:38) sts. of back, pick up and
knit 28(29:30) sts. down left front, knit
across 8 sts. on thread. [106(110:114) sts.]
1st row: p.8, * k.2, p.2, rep. from * to last 10
sts., k.2, p.8. Work 4 more rows in k.2, p.2
rib with end 8 sts. in st.st. Work a buttonhole on next 2 rows. Work 4 more rows
and cast off.

MAKING UP
Press as instructions on ball band. Sew up
side and sleeve seams. Sew in sleeves.
Work one row double crochet in Colour A
around edges of front bands. Face with
ribbon if required (make buttonholes in
ribbon to correspond with knitted buttonholes, and buttonhole st. both together).
Sew on buttons to correspond with buttonholes.

Butterfly and Moss Stitch Jacket 1936

Tailored jacket in butterfly and moss stitches, reaching hip-level.
Double-breasted, with collar and revers, it buttons only down to the waist
to give a peplum effect over the hips when belted

★★★ Suitable for experienced knitters
only

MATERIALS

Yarn
Sirdar Majestic 4 ply
11(11:12) × 50g. balls

Needles
1 pair 3mm.
1 pair 3¾mm.

Buttons
8

MEASUREMENTS

Bust
82(89:97) cm.
32(35:38) in.

Length
60(61:62) cm.
23½(24:24¼) in.

Sleeve Seam
44 cm.
17½ in.

TENSION

10 sts. and 16 rows (one repeat of the pattern) = 4 cm. (1½ in.) square over pattern
on 4¾mm. needles. If your tension
square does not correspond to these
measurements see page 166 for adjustment instructions.

ABBREVIATIONS

k. = knit; p. = purl; st(s). = stitch(es); inc. =
increas(ing) (see page 166); dec. = decreas-
(ing) (see page 167); beg. = begin(ning);
rem. = remain(ing); rep. = repeat; alt. =
alternate; tog. = together; sl. = slip stitch
(transfer one stitch from left needle, knit-
wise unless otherwise stated, to right
hand needle.); cont. = continue; patt. =
pattern; foll. = following; folls. = follows;
mm. = millimetres; cm. = centimetre(s);
in. = inch(es); m.st. = moss stitch; y.r.n.
= yarn round needle.

BACK

Cast on 107(117:127) sts. with 3¾mm.
needles. Work 6 rows in m.st. Change to
patt:
1st row: k.6, * pass yarn round needle, sl.
5 sts. carrying yarn across right side of
work, pass yarn back, k.5, rep. from * to
last st., k.1.
2nd row: p., dropping the extra loops
made in previous row. Rep. these 2 rows
twice more, then work 1st row again.
8th row: p.8, * lift the 4 threads which lie
across right side of work and place them
on left hand needle, then p. them tog.
with next st., p.9, rep. from * to end, but
finishing last rep. p.8.
9th row: k.1, then rep. from * as 1st row,
but finishing last rep. k.1.

Butterfly and Moss Stitch Jacket

10th row: p., dropping extra loops made in previous row.

Rep. these 2 rows twice more, then work 9th row again.

16th row: p.3, rep. from * as on 8th row, but finishing last rep. p.3.

These 16 rows form the patt. When shaping, threads should be linked up as necessary, as on the 8th and 16th rows.

Proceed until work measures 15 cm. (5¾ in.).

Change to 3mm needles. Work 10 cm. (4 in.).

Change back to 3¾mm. needles. Con. until work measures 41 cm. (16 in.) finishing after a wrong side row.

Shape Armholes

Cast off 5 sts. at beg. of next 2 rows, then dec. at both ends of every row until 83(89:95) sts. rem.

Proceed until work measures 18(19:20) cm. (7(7½:7¾) in.) from beg. of armholes, finishing after a wrong side row.

Shape Shoulders

Cast off 8(9:10) sts. at beg. of next 6 rows. Cast off rem. 35 sts.

LEFT FRONT

Cast on 57(62:67) sts. with 3¾mm. needles.

Work 6 rows in m.st.

Start pattern as for 1st row of back, ending row with k.1, m.st. 5.

Next row: m.st. 5, patt. to end.

Cont. working 5 sts. at front edge in m.st. and remainder in patt. until work measures 15 cm. (5¾ in.).

Change to 3mm. needles.

Cont. until work measures 20 cm. (7¾ in.).

Work to front edge.

Cast on 15 sts. [72(77:82) sts.]

Next row: m.st. 35 sts., patt. 37(42:47) sts.

Cont. with 35 sts. at front edge in m.st. and remainder in patt.

Work a further 5 cm. (2 in.) then cont. on 3¾mm. needles. Work until front matches back to armholes, finishing at side edge.

Shape Armhole

Cast off 5 sts. at beg. of next row.

Work 1 row.

Now dec. 1 st. at armhole edge on every row until 60(63:66) sts. rem.

Proceed until work measures 13 cm. (5 in.) from beg. of armhole, finishing at front edge.

Shape top of Rever

Cast off 15 sts. at beg. of next row, then dec. 1 st. at this edge on every row until 24(27:30) sts. rem.

Cont. until work matches back length to outer shoulder.

Shape Shoulder

Cast off 8(9:10) sts. at beg. of next 3 side edge rows.

RIGHT FRONT

Work to correspond with left front, reversing shapings.

At the same time make 4 pairs of buttonholes on right side rows, the 1st on 5th row after casting on the 15 sts. at front edge, the 2nd when work measures 27 cm. (10½ in.), the 3rd when work measures 33 cm. (13 in.), the last when work measures 39 cm. (15¼ in.)

Buttonholes are worked thus: m.st. 4 sts., cast off 3 sts., (there is now 1 st. on right hand needle) m.st. 21 sts., cast off 3 sts., work to end. In next row cast on 3 sts. over each buttonhole.

SLEEVES

Cast on 53(57:61) sts. with 3mm. needles.

Work 6 rows in m.st. Change to 3¾mm. needles and patt., beg. 1st patt. row k.4(6:3), and working subsequent rows to correspond.

Inc. at both ends of 9th row and every foll. 10th row until there are 83(87:91) sts.

Proceed until work measures 44 cm. (17¼ in.) finishing after a wrong side row.

Shape Top

Cast off 5 sts. at beg. of next 2 rows. Dec. 1 st. at both ends of next and every alt. row until 27 sts. rem.

Work 1 row.

Dec. 1 st. at both ends of every row until 19 sts. rem.

Cast off.

COLLAR

Cast on 75 sts. with 3¾mm. needles. Work 5 cm. (2 in.) in m.st. Cast off 4 sts. at beg. of next 10 rows. Cast off rem. 35 sts.

MAKING UP

Press on the wrong side under a damp cloth.

Join side, shoulder and sleeve seams. Set sleeves into armholes.

Sew cast off edge of collar to back of neck and shaped edges of revers. Press seams. Sew on buttons.

Mohair Cardigan with Rounded Collar *1960*

Long, stocking stitch, mohair cardigan with two large pockets at hip-level, raglan sleeves, and huge, rounded, twisted rib collar

★★ Suitable for knitters with some previous experience

MATERIALS

Yarn
Jaeger Mohair-Spun
15(16:17:18:19) × 25g. balls.

Needles
1 pair 4½mm.
1 pair 5½mm.

Buttons
5

MEASUREMENTS

Bust
82(87·92:97:102) cm.
32(34:36:38:40) in.

Length (from top of shoulders)
60(61:61:62:62) cm.
23½(24:24:24¼:24¼) in.

Sleeve Seam
36 cm.
14 in.

TENSION

16 sts. and 21 rows = 10 cm. (4 in.) square over stocking stitch on 5½mm. needles. If your tension square does not correspond to these measurements see page 166 for adjustment instructions.

ABBREVIATIONS

k. = knit; p. = purl; st(s). = stitch(es); inc. = increas(ing) (see page 166); dec. = decreas-(ing) (see page 167); beg. = begin(ning); rem. = remain(ing); rep. = repeat; alt. = alternate; tog. = together; sl. = slip stitch (transfer one stitch *purlwise* from left to right hand needle.); cont. = continue; patt. = pattern; foll. = following; folls. = follows; mm. = millimetres; cm. = centimetre(s); in. = inch(es); p.s.s.o. = pass slipped st. over; k.1(2)b. = knit into back of st(s). st.st. = stocking stitch.

BACK

Cast on 59(63:67:71:75) sts. with 4½mm. needles.
1st row (right side facing): k.1 b., * p.1, k.1 b., rep. from * to end.
2nd row: p.1, * k.1 b., p.1, rep. from * to end.

Rep. last 2 rows 5 times more.
Change to 5½mm. needles and st.st., starting with a k. row, shaping sides by inc. 1 st. at each end of 5th and every foll. 10th row until there are 71(75:79:83:87) sts.
Work straight until back measures 36 cm. (14 in.) at centre from start, ending with a p. row.

Shape Raglans
Cast off 3(3:4:4:5) sts. at beg. of next 2 rows.
Next row: k.2, k.2 tog., k. to last 4 sts., sl.1, k.1, p.s.s.o., k.2.
Work 3(3:3:3:1) rows straight.
On 2nd size only: rep. last 4 rows once more. [63(65:69:73:75) sts.]
Cont. dec. as before, but on next and every alt. row until 19(21:21:23:23) sts. rem., ending with right side facing. Cast off.

LEFT FRONT

Cast on 29(31:33:35:37) sts. with 4½mm. needles, and starting with 1st row, work 12 rows in k.1, p.1 twisted rib, as for back.
Place pocket as folls.:
Next row: k.3 (4:5:6:7) sts., rib 23 sts., turn, placing rem. sts. on stich holder. Cont. straight in twisted rib on these 23 sts. for pocket for 13 cm. (5 in.). Cast off evenly in rib.
With right side facing, rejoin yarn to left-hand set of sts. on holder, cast on 23, k. across these sts., k.3(4:5:6:7) sts.
Change to 5½mm. needles and, starting with a p. row and incorporating rem. sts. on holder at end of row, work 3 rows straight, then shape side edge by inc. 1 st. at beg. of next and every foll. 10th row until there are 35(37:39:41:43) sts.
Work straight until front matches back at side edge, ending with right side facing.

Shape Raglan
Cast off 3(3:4:4:5) sts. at beg. of next row. Work 1 row straight.
Next row: k.2, k.2 tog., k. to end.
Work 3(3:3:3:1) rows straight.
On 2nd size only: rep. last 4 rows once more. [31(32:34:36:37) sts.]
Cont. dec. as before, but on next and every alt. row until 18(19:19:20:20) sts. rem.
With wrong side facing, shape neck by casting off 2(3:3:4:4) sts. at beg. of next

row. Cont. dec. at raglan edge on next and every alt. row as before, and *at the same time* dec. 1 st. at neck edge on every foll. alt. row until 6 sts. rem., (all sizes).
Now keep neck edge straight and cont. dec. at raglan edge on alt. rows as before until 3 sts. rem.
Next row: p.
Next row: k.1, k.2 tog.
Next row: p.2, turn. k.2 tog. and fasten off.

RIGHT FRONT

Work to correspond with left front, reversing all shapings and noting that 'sl.1, k.1, p.s.s.o.' will be worked when shaping raglan.

SLEEVES

Cast on 37(39:41:43:45) sts. with 4½mm. needles, and work 12 rows in k.1, p.1 twisted rib, as for back.
Change to 5½mm. needles and stocking stitch, starting with a k. row, shaping sides by inc. 1 st. at each end of 3rd and every foll. 4th row until there are 51(53:55:57:59) sts., then on every foll. 6th row until there are 59(61:63:65:67) sts.
Work straight until sleeve seam measures 36 cm. (14 in.), ending with a p. row.

Shape Raglans
Cast off 3(3:4:4:5) sts. at beg. of next 2 rows.
Next row: k.2, k.2 tog., k. to last 4 sts., sl.1, k.1, p.s.s.o., k.2.
Work 3 rows straight.
On 2nd, 3rd, 4th and 5th sizes only: rep. last 4 rows once more. [51(51:51:53:53) sts.]
Cont. dec. as before, but on next and every foll. alt. row until 7 sts. rem., all sizes, ending with right side facing. Cast off.

LEFT FRONT BAND

Cast on 13 sts. with 4½mm. needles.
1st row (right side facing): k.2 b., * p.1, k.1 b., rep. from * to last st., k.1 b.
2nd row: k.1 b., * p.1, k.1. b., rep. from * to end.
Rep. last 2 rows until border fits up left front to start of neck shaping, ending with right side facing. For a good fit, sew border in position as you go along, stretching slightly to prevent fluting and when it measures required length, cast off evenly in rib.

Mohair Cardigan with Rounded Collar

RIGHT FRONT BAND

Work to correspond with left border with the addition of 5 buttonholes, 1st to come 1 cm. (½ in.) above lower edge, 5th 1 cm. (½ in.) below start of neck shaping and remainder spaced evenly between.

First mark position of buttons on left border with pins to ensure even spacing, then work holes to correspond. To make a buttonhole: with right side facing rib 5 sts., cast off 3 sts., rib to end; work back in rib, casting on 3 sts. over those cast off.

COLLAR

Cast on 27 sts. with 4½ mm. needles, and work 2 rows in k.1, p.1 twisted rib as for front border.

3rd row: rib 18, turn.
4th row: sl. 1, rib to end.
Rep. last 4 rows until shorter edge measures 38(41:42:43:43) cm. (15(16: 16½:16¾:16¾) in.), ending with 4th row. Work 2 rows straight.
Cast off evenly in rib.

MAKING UP

Press work lightly on wrong side omitting ribbing.
Sew up raglan, side and sleeve seams. Sew sides of pockets to main work, then sew cast-on sts. lightly at back of pocket. Pin short edge of collar round neck, starting and ending in centre of front borders; sew in position. Press all seams. Sew on buttons.

Shawl-collared Mohair Cardigan   *1959*

Soft, loose-fitting mohair cardigan in twisted rib, with knitted-in front bands, shawl collar and doubled border mitred into fronts

** Suitable for knitters with some previous experience

MATERIALS

Yarn
Jaeger Mohair Spun
20(21:22:23:24) × 25g. balls

Needles
1 pair 3¼ mm.
1 pair 4½ mm.
1 pair 6mm.

Buttons
6

MEASUREMENTS

Bust
82(87:92:97:102) cm.
32(34:36:38:40) in.

Length
62(65:66:67:69) cm.
24¼(25½:26:26¼:27) in.

Sleeve Seam (with cuff turned back)
46 cm.
(18 in.)

TENSION

8 sts. and 11 rows = 5 cm. (2 in.) square over stocking stitch on 6mm. needles. If your tension square does not correspond to these measurements see page 166 for adjustment instructions.

ABBREVIATIONS

k. = knit; p. = purl; st(s). = stitch(es); inc. = increas(ing) (see page 166); dec. = decreas-(ing) (see page 167); beg. = begin(ning); rem. = remain(ing); rep. = repeat; alt. = alternate; tog. = together; sl. = slip stitch (transfer one stitch from left needle, purl-wise, to right hand needle); cont. = continue; patt. = pattern; foll. = following; folls. = follows; mm. = millimetres; cm. = centimetre(s); in. = inch(es); p.s.s.o. = pass slipped st. over; k.1b. = knit into back of st.

BACK

Cast on 77(81:85:89:93) sts. with 4½m. needles.
1st row (right side): k.1b., *p.1, k.1b., rep. from * to end.
2nd row: p.
These 2 rows form patt., rep. until work measures 5 cm. (2 in.), ending with 2nd row, then change to 6mm. needles and cont. in patt. until back measures 37(37:36: 36:34) cm. (14½:14½:14:14:13¼) in.) at centre from start, ending with right side facing.

Shape Raglans
Cast off 4 sts. at beg. of next 2 rows.
1st row: (k.1b., p.1) 3 times, sl.1, k.1, p.s.s.o., patt. to last 8 sts., k.2 tog., (p.1, k.1b.) 3 times.
2nd row: p.
3rd row: (k.1b., p.1) 3 times, k.1, patt. to last 7 sts., k.1, (p.1, k.1b.) 3 times.
4th row: p.
Rep. last 4 rows 2(4:6:8:10) times more. [63 sts.]

Now rep. 1st and 2nd rows until 21(23:25:27:29) sts. rem. ending with 2nd row.
Cast off.

LEFT FRONT

Cast on 51(53:55:57:59) sts. with 4½mm. needles.
1st row: * k.1 b., p.1, rep. from * to last 15 sts., k.1 b., k.14.
2nd row: p.
Rep. last 2 rows until work measures 5 cm. (2 in.), ending with 2nd row.
Change to 6mm. needles and, keeping 15 sts. at front edge in st.st., cont. in rib patt. until front matches back side edge, ending with right side facing.

Shape Raglan

Cast off 4 sts. at beg. of next row. Work 1 row straight.
1st row: (k.1 b., p.1) 3 times, sl.1, k.1, p.s.s.o., patt. to last 15 sts., k.1 b., k.14.
2nd row: p.
3rd row: (k.1 b., p.1) 3 times, k.1, patt. to last 15 sts., k.1 b., k.14.
4th row: p.
Work rows 1–3 inclusive again.
With wrong side facing, shape front edging as folls.:
1st row: p.7 sts., turn.
2nd row: k.2 tog., k.5.
Cont. on these 6 sts., dec. 1 st. at beg. of every foll. alt. row until all sts. are gone.
With wrong side facing, rejoin yarn to rem. 38(40:42:44:46) sts., p. to end.
Dec. 1 st. at front edge on next and every foll. alt. row and *at the same time* cont. dec. at raglan edge on next and every foll. 4th row until 33(29:25:24:28) sts. rem.
Work 1 (1:1:3:1) rows straight.
Cont. as folls.:
5th size only: cont. dec. at raglan edge as before on next and every foll. 4th row and *at the same time* dec. 1 st. at front edge on every foll. 4th row from last dec., until 22 sts. rem.
Work 1 row straight.
1st, 4th and 5th sizes only: cont. dec. at raglan edge as before but on next and every alt. row and *at the same time* dec. 1 st. at front edge on every foll. alt. 4th row from last dec., until 9 sts. rem.
2nd and 3rd sizes only: cont. dec. at raglan edge as before, but on next and every alt. row and *at the same time* dec. 1 st. at front edge on next and every alt. row until 17(19) sts. rem., then on every foll. 3rd(4th) row until 9 sts. rem.
All sizes:
Next row: p.
Next row: (k.1 b., p.1) 3 times, sl.1, k.2 tog., p.s.s.o.
Next row: p.
Next row: (k.1 b., p.1) twice, k.1 b., sl.1, k.1, p.s.s.o.
Next row: p.
Next row: (k.1 b., p.1) twice, sl.1, k.1, p.s.s.o.
Next row: p.

Cont. dec. at front edge on next and every alt. row until 2 sts. rem., p.2, turn.
k.2 tog. and fasten off.

RIGHT FRONT

Work to correspond with left front with the addition of 6 buttonholes.
Mark position of buttons on left front with pins to ensure even spacing, then work holes to correspond, 1st 2 cm. (1 in.) from lower edge, 6th level with start of raglan shaping and rest evenly spaced between.
To make a buttonhole (right side facing): k.2, cast off 3 sts., k.4, cast off 3 sts., k.2, patt. to end. Work back, casting on 3 sts. over those cast off.
NOTE: When shaping raglan work 'k.2 tog.' for 'sl.1, k.1, p.s.s.o.'.

LEFT SLEEVE

Cast on 43(45:47:49:51) sts. and work 7 cm. (2¾ in.) in st.st. ending with a p. row.
Change to 6mm. needles and starting with 1st row, work in rib patt. as for back, shaping sides by inc. 1 st. at each end of 5th and every foll. 8th row until there are 63(65:67:69:71) sts., taking inc. sts. into patt.
Work straight until sleeve seam measures 49 cm. (19¼ in.), ending with right side facing.

Shape Raglans

Cast off 4 sts. at beg. of next 2 rows, then dec. 1 st. as for back each end of next and every foll. 4th row until 49(47:45:43:41) sts. rem.
Work 3 rows straight, then dec. as before, but on next and every alt. row until 15 sts. rem., ending with right side facing.
Cont. as folls.:
1st row: (k.1 b., p.1) 3 times, sl.1, k.2 tog., p.s.s.o., (p.1, k.1 b.) 3 times.
2nd row: p.
3rd row: (k.1 b., p.1) twice, k.1 b., p.3 tog., (k.1 b., p.1) twice, k.1 b.
4th row: cast off 3 sts., p. to end.
5th row: (k.1 b., p.1) 3 times, sl.1, k.1, p.s.s.o.
6th row: as 4th.
7th row: (k.1 b., p.1) twice.
8th row: as 2nd.
Cast off.

RIGHT SLEEVE

Work to correspond with left sleeve, reversing top shaping.

COLLAR

Cast on 95(101:105:109:113) sts. with 6mm. needles, and starting with 1st row, work in rib patt. as for back, shaping collar as folls.:
1st row: patt. 57(61:65:69:73) sts., turn.
2nd row: sl.1, p.18(22:26:30:34), turn.
3rd row: sl.1, patt. 21(25:29:33:37) sts., turn.
4th row: sl.1, p.5, * (p. into front, back and front of next st.), p.5(7:9:11:13), rep. from

* once more, (p. into front, back and front of next st.), p.6, turn. [101(107:111:115:119) sts.]
5th row: sl.1, patt. 33(37:41:45:49) sts., turn.
6th row: sl.1, p.36(40:44:48:52), turn.
7th row: sl.1, patt. 39(43:47:51:55) sts., turn.
8th row: sl.1, p.5, * (p. into front, back and front of next st.), p.7(9:11:13:15), (p. into front, back and front of next st.) *, p.13, rep. from * to *, p.6. [109(115:119:123:127) sts.]
9th row: sl.1, patt. 56(60:64:68:72) sts., turn.
Cont. working 3 sts. more on every row until the row 'sl.1, patt. 98(102:106:110:114) sts., turn' has been worked. Now work 1 st. more on every row until all sts. are worked.
Cast off purlwise.

Border

Cast on 2 sts. with 4½mm. needles. Starting with a k. row, cont. in st.st., shaping mitre by inc. 1 st. at each end of next and every alt. row until there are 14 sts.
Work straight until border fits from last inc. round outer edge of collar, ending with a p. row. Now dec. 1 st. at each end of next and every alt. row until 2 sts. rem.
Cast off.

MAKING UP

Press work very lightly on wrong side, taking care not to spoil the patt.
Sew up raglan, side and sleeve seams.
Pin cast on edge of collar round neck, sew in position.
Pin border round collar, right side of collar to right side of border, sew in position, then fold borders to wrong side and slip-hem lightly in position all round.
Fold cuffs in half to wrong side and finish as for borders.
Oversew loosely round double buttonholes. Press all seams. Sew on buttons.

Yoked Jacket with Shaped Hem

Thigh length warm jacket with collar, shaped lower edge, squared yoke with pleated edges, all knitted in stocking stitch with doubled-over, ribbed welts

★★ For knitters with some previous experience

MATERIALS

Yarn
Pingouin Confort DK
16(17:18:19) × 50g. balls

Needles
1 pair 3¼mm.
2 pairs 3¾mm.

Buttons
6

MEASUREMENTS

Bust
84–87(89–92:94–97:99–102) cm.
33–34(35–36:37–38:39–40) in.

Length (at centre back)
66(67:68:69) cm.
26(26¼:26¾:27) in.

Sleeve Seam (excluding section set into main parts)
48(49:49:50) cm.
18¾(19¼:19¼:19½) in.

TENSION

23 sts. and 30 rows = 10 cm. (4 in.) square over stocking stitch on 3¾mm. needles. If your tension square does not correspond to these measurements see page 166 for adjustment instructions.

ABBREVIATIONS

k. = knit; p. = purl; st(s). = stitch(es); inc. = increas(ing) (see page 166); dec. = decreas-(ing) (see page 167); beg. = begin(ning); rem. = remain(ing); rep. = .repeat; alt. = alternate; tog. = together; sl. = slip stitch (transfer one stitch from left needle, knit-wise unless otherwise stated, to right hand needle.); cont. = continue; patt. = pattern; foll. = following; folls. = follows; mm. = millimetres; cm. = centimetre(s); in. = inch(es); st.st. = stocking stitch.

BACK

Cast on 113(119:125:131) sts. with 3¾mm. needles.
Work 10 cm. (4 in.) in st.st.
Now cast on 12 sts. at beg. of next 2 rows. [137(143:149:155) sts.]
Cont. without shaping until work measures 28(28:29:29) cm. (11(11:11¼: 11¼) in.) from beg.

Shape Armhole
Cast off 25(26:27:28) sts. at beg. of next 2 rows. [87(91:95:99) sts.]
Cont. without shaping until work measures 44(45:46:47) cm. (17¼(17¾:18: 18½) in.) from beg.
Cast off all sts.

RIGHT FRONT

Cast on 56(59:62:65) sts. with 3¾mm. needles.
Work in st.st. until work measures 10 cm. (4 in.), ending with a k. row.

Cast on 12 sts. at beg. of next row.
Cont. on these 68(71:74:77) sts. until work measures 13 cm. (5 in.) from beg., ending with a p. row.

Pocket Opening
Next row: k.16(18:20:22) sts., cast off next 42 sts., k.·to end.
Leave these sts.
With the spare pair of 3¾mm. needles, cast on 42 sts. for pocket lining.
Work same number of rows as on right front, in st.st., ending with a k. row.
Break off yarn.
Return to sts. of right front.
Next row: p.10(11:12:13) sts., now p. sts. of pocket lining, p. to end.
Cont. in st.st. until work measures 28(28:29:29) cm. (11(11:11¼:11¼) in.) from beg., ending at side edge, after a k. row.

Armhole Shaping
Cast off 25(26:27:28) sts. at beg. of next row.
Cont. on rem. 43(45:47:49) sts. until work measures 44(45:46:47) cm. (17¼(17¾:18: 18½) in.) from beg.
Cast off all sts.

LEFT FRONT

Work as for right front, reversing position of pocket opening, and working all shapings at opposite edges.

BACK YOKE

Cast on 87(91:95:99) sts. with 3¾mm. needles.
Work 12 rows in st.st.
Now inc. 1 st. at each end of next and every foll. 6th row until there are 97(101:105:109) sts.
Work 9 rows without shaping.

Shoulder Shaping
Cast off 6(6:7:7) sts. at beg. of next 8 rows and 8(10:7:9) sts. at beg. of foll. 2 rows.
Cast off rem. 33(33:35:35) sts. for back neck.

RIGHT FRONT YOKE

Cast on 43(45:47:49) sts. with 3¾mm. needles.
Beg. with a k. row, work 12 rows in st.st.
Inc. 1 st. at *end* of next row and every foll. 6th row, 5 times in all.
Work one row after these shapings are complete, thus ending on straight front edge.

Shape Neck and Shoulder
Cast off 4(4:5:5) sts. at beg. of next row.
Then cast off 2 sts. at same edge on next 4 alt. rows, thus ending at side edge.
1st row: cast off 6(6:7:7) sts., work to last 3 sts., dec. 1 st., work 1 st.
2nd row: work without shaping.
Rep. rows 1 and 2 three more times each.
Cast off rem. 8(10:7:9) sts. to complete shoulder edge.

LEFT FRONT YOKE

Work as right front yoke, reversing all shapings.

SLEEVES

Cast on 41(43:43:45) sts. with 3¼mm. needles.
1st row (right side): k.2, * p.1, k.1, rep. from * to last st., k.1.
2nd row: k.1, * p.1, k.1, rep. from * to end.
Rep. these 2 rows until work measures 13 cm. (5 in.), ending with 2nd row.
Change to 3¾mm. needles.
Next row: k.2, k. into front and back of each of next 37(39:39:41) sts., k.2. [78(82:82: 86) sts.]
Beg. with a p. row, work in st.st., inc. 1 st. at both ends of every foll. 12th row 7 times.
Cont. on these 92(96:96:100) sts. until work measures 48(49:49:50) cm. (18¾(19¼: 19¼:19½) in.) from beg.

Yoked Jacket with Shaped Hem

Cast on 24 sts. at beg. of next 2 rows, then cont. without shaping for further 14(14:15:16) cm. (5½(5½:5¾:6¼) in.). Cast off 20 sts. at beg. of next 6 rows. Cast off rem. 20(24:24:28) sts.

COLLAR

Cast on 33(33:35:35) sts. with 3¾mm. needles.
Cont. in st.st., k. 1 row, then cast on 7 sts. at beg. of next 4 rows, and 7(7:8:8) sts. at beg. of next 2 rows. [75(75:79:79) sts.] Cont. straight on these sts. until work measures 20 cm. (7¾ in.) along side edge, ending with a k. row.
Cast off 7(7:8:8) sts. at beg. of next 2 rows, and 7 sts. at beg. of next 4 rows.
Cast off rem. 33(33:35:35) sts.

POCKET EDGINGS

Cast on 47 sts. with 3¼mm. needles.
Work in rib as on sleeves for 10 cm. (4 in.) Cast off loosely ribwise.
Make another likewise.

FRONT EDGINGS

Cast on 215(223:231:239) sts. with 3¼mm.

needles and work as for pocket edgings. Make another likewise.

BACK EDGING

Cast on 151(159:167:175) sts. with 3¼mm. needles and work as for pocket edging.

MAKING UP

Yoke and Shoulders
Sew yokes to upper edges of fronts and back, oversewing the seam, then pinch up 2 cm. (¾ in.) of material to create a pleat 1 cm. (½ in.) deep, from yoke.
Backstitch shoulder seams, press lightly on wrong side with warm iron using a damp cloth.

Sleeves and Sides
Sew in sleeves, creating a pleat exactly as on yoke. Backstitch side seams above the 12 cast on sts.
Press, using a damp cloth.
Backstitch and press sleeve seams.

Edgings and Collar
Sew pocket edgings to pocket openings, with right side of ribbing to front of gar-

ment. Press seam with damp cloth and point of iron.
Fold edging in half, slipstitch edge of ribbing to seam just made.
Slipstitch pocket lining inside garment.
Sew cast on edges of collar to neck edges, press seam as above, fold collar in half to wrong side, slipstitch cast off edge to previous seam.
Pin front edging along ends of collar, down front edges, across lower edge and up sides of slits, easing them in around the corners and stretching slightly along front edges.
Mark position for 6 buttons on left front, when sewing edging onto left front, leave corresponding spaces for buttonholes between edging and the body of the garment (see detail).
Fold and slipstitch as for other edgings, except at buttonholes, where cast on and cast off edges should be slipstitched tog.; neatly slipstitch top ends of band tog.
Sew on back edging in same way.
Sew on buttons.
Press edging and seams lightly with damp cloth and point of iron, paying particular attention to front corners of edging.

Thick Twisted Rib Jacket

1960

Long, warm jacket with knitted-in front bands, raglan sleeves and simple collar, knitted throughout in twisted rib with double yarn

★★ Suitable for knitters with some previous experience

MATERIALS

Yarn
Emu Shetland DK
18(18:19:20) × 50g. balls

Needles
1 pair 6mm.

Buttons
6

MEASUREMENTS

Bust
82(87:92:97) cm.
32(34:36:38) in.

Length
64(64:66:66) cm.
25(25:26:26) in.

Sleeve Seam
44(44:44:46) cm.
17¼(17¼:17¼:18) in.

TENSION

8 sts. and 10 rows = 5 cm. (2 in.) square over pattern on 6mm. needles. If your tension square does not correspond to these measurements, see page 166 for adjustment instructions.

ABBREVIATIONS

k. = knit; p. = purl; st(s). = stitch(es); inc. = increas(ing) (see page 166); dec. = decreas-(ing) (see page 167); beg. = begin(ning); rem. = remain(ing); rep. = repeat; alt. = alternate; tog. = together; sl. = slip stitch (transfer one stitch from left needle, knit-wise unless otherwise stated, to right hand needle.); cont. = continue; patt. = pattern; foll. = following; folls. = follows; mm. = millimetres; cm. = centimetre(s); in. = inch(es); tw.2 = twist 2, (k.2 tog., leave sts. on the left hand needle, k. the 1st st. again and sl. both the sts. from needle tog.); g.st. = garter stitch.
NOTE: Work with double yarn throughout.

BACK

Cast on 67(73:79:85) sts. with 6mm. needles.
1st row (wrong side): k.1, * p.2, k.1, * rep. from * to * to end.
2nd row: p.1, * tw.2, p.1, * rep. from * to * to end.
Rep. these 2 rows throughout until work measures 41(41:43:43) cm. (16(16:16¾: 16¾) in.).

Shape Armholes
Cast off 2 sts. at beg. of next 2 rows, keeping patt. correct.
1st row: p.2, p.2 tog., patt. to last 4 sts., p.2 tog., p.2.
2nd row: p.3, patt. to last 3 sts., p.3.
Rep. these 2 rows until 23(27:29:29) sts. rem.
Cast off.

LEFT FRONT

Cast on 40(43:46:49) sts. with 6mm. needles, cont. as folls.:
1st row: k.7, * p.2, k.1, * rep. from * to * to end.
2nd row: * p.1, tw.2, * rep. from * to * to last 7 sts., k.7.
Rep. these 2 rows until work corresponds with back to armholes, ending at armhole edge.

Shape Armholes
Cast off 2 sts. at beg. of next row. Work 1 row.
1st row: p.2, p.2 tog., patt. to last 7 sts., k.7.
2nd row: k.7, patt. to last 3 sts., p.3.
Cont. in this manner until 23(25:27:27) sts. rem., ending at front edge.
Next row: cast off 10(12:12:12) sts., work to end. Cont. to dec. at armhole edge as before, at same time dec. 1 st. at front edge every row 6(6:7:7) times.
Cont. to dec. at armhole edge until 1 st. rem. Cast off this st.

RIGHT FRONT

Cast on 40(43:46:49) sts. with 6mm. needles.
1st row: * k.1, p.2, * rep. from * to * to last 7 sts., k.7.
2nd row: k.7, * tw.2, p.1, * rep from * to * to end.
3rd and 5th rows: as 1st row.

4th row: as 2nd row.
6th row: k.2, cast off 3 sts., k.1, patt. to end.
7th row: patt. to last 7 sts., (including the cast off sts.), k.2, cast on 3 sts., k.2.
Cont. to rep. the 6th and 7th rows every 18th(18th:20th:20th) row and 19th(19th: 21st:21st) rows to neck, meanwhile cont. to work as for left front, reversing all shapings.

SLEEVES

Cast on 37(40:43:46) sts. with 6mm. needles.
Work in patt. as before, at same time inc. 1 st. at each end of 6th row until there are 61(64:69:75) sts. Cont. straight on these sts. until work measures 44(44:44:46) cm. (17¼(17¼:17¼:18) in.).

Shape Top
Cast off 2 sts. at beg. of next 2 rows, working 1st dec. row as for back armholes, 8

times, then working 1st and 2nd dec. rows alternately until 10 sts. rem.
Cast off.

COLLAR

With right sides together, backstitch sleeves into armholes, then with 6mm. needles and right side facing, pick up and k.91(91:97:97) sts. evenly round neck.
Next row: p.1, * k.2, p.1, * rep. from * to * to the end of the row.
Now cont. in patt. as for back until work measures 18 cm. (7 in.).
Cast off.

MAKING UP

Press all pieces on reverse side, sew in all ends.
Backstitch side and sleeve seams. Button-hole stitch round each buttonhole, sew on buttons.

Finely Checked T-shirt Dress

Knee-length T-shirt dress with short sleeves and back opening, knitted in one piece in patterned check stitch with crochet sleeve and neck bands

★★ Suitable for knitters with some previous experience

MATERIALS

Yarn

Emu Superwash DK
8(8:9) × 50g. balls (Main Colour)
4(5:5) × 50g. balls (Contrast Colour)

Needles

1 pair 3¾mm.
1 pair 4½mm.
1 3.50 crochet hook

Buttons

2

MEASUREMENTS

Bust

82(87:92) cm.
32(34:36) in.

Hips

87(92:97) cm.
34(36:38) in.

Length

102(102:106) cm.
40(40:41½) in.

TENSION

11 sts. = 5 cm. (2 in.) over pattern on 4½mm. needles. If your tension square does not correspond to this measurement, see page 166 for adjustment instructions.

ABBREVIATIONS

k. = knit; p. = purl; st(s). = stitch(es); inc. = increas(ing) (see page 166); dec. = decreas-ing) (see page 167); beg. = begin(ning); rem. = remain(ing); rep. = repeat; alt. = alternate; tog. = together; sl. = slip stitch (transfer one stitch from left needle, knit-wise unless otherwise stated, to right hand needle.); cont. = continue; patt. = pattern; foll. = following; folls. = follows; mm. = millimetres; cm. = centimetre(s); in. = inch(es); y.bk. = yarn back; g.st. = garter stitch (every row k.); d.c. = double crochet; C = contrast colour; M = main colour; ch. = chain; y.fwd. = yarn forward.

COMMENCING AT BACK HEM

Cast on 97(103:109) sts. with 3¾mm. needles and M. Work in g.st. for 22 rows. Change to 4½mm. needles and cont. in patt. as folls.:

1st row: k. in M.
2nd row: k. in M.
3rd row: in C, * k.1, sl.1 purlwise, rep. from * to last st., k.1.
4th row: in C, * k.1., y.fwd., sl.1 purlwise, y.bk., rep. from * to last st., k.1.
Rep. these 4 rows until work measures 83(83:85) cm. (32½(32½:33¼) in.)

Shape Sleeves

Cast on 4 sts. at beg. of next 6 rows. [121(127:133) sts.]
Work straight until sleeve edge measures 6(6:7) cm. (2¼(2¼:2¾) in.)

** Shape Back Neck Opening

Work 60(63:66) sts., turn.
Keep patt. correct on these sts. until work measures 18(18:20) cm. (7(7:7¾) in.) along sleeve edge, ending at neck edge.
Cast off 13 sts., work to end.
Cont. straight on these sts. until work measures 6 cm. (2¼ in.) along straight edge of neck.
Inc. 1 st. at neck edge every row 4 times.**
Now rejoin yarn to neck edge of rem. sts., and work from ** to **, dec. 1 st. at beg. of 1st row, and ending section of patt. at neck edge.
Cast on 19 sts. at end of last row.
Next row: beg. at sleeve edge of 1st. side, work these 51(54:57) sts. in patt., cont. across rem. sts. of 2nd piece. [121(127:133) sts.]
Cont. straight on these sts. until sleeve edge measures 33(33:37) cm. (13(13:14½) in.)
Cast off 4 sts. at beg. of next 6 rows.
Cont. straight on these sts. until work corresponds with back to g.st. border.
Change to 3¾mm. needles and work 22 rows in g.st.
Cast off these sts. loosely.

SLEEVE BANDS

With 3.50 crochet hook and right side of work facing, work 4 rows d.c. along each sleeve edge, fasten off.

NECKBAND

With 3.50 crochet hook and right side of work facing, working from lower edge of centre back opening, work in d.c. to cor-ner, 1 ch., cont. in d.c. round neck to 2nd corner, 1 ch., work in d.c. along 2nd side, turn.
2nd row: work in d.c., working 1 d.c., 1 ch., into the 1 ch. space at each corner.
3rd row: work 6 d.c., 2 ch., miss 2 sts.,

work 1 d.c. into each st. to last 4 sts. from corner, 2 ch., miss 2 sts.
Cont. to work round neck, dec. 1 st. in line with shoulder back, and at side centre front on each side.
4th row: as 2nd, working 1 d.c. into each ch.st. of the buttonholes.

MAKING UP

Press work, sew in all ends.
Backstitch seams and sew on buttons.

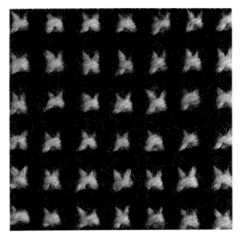

Thick, Ribbed Sweater Dress

Chunky, knee-length, body-hugging simple dress with long, cuffed sleeves, polo collar and set-in sleeves, in single rib

★ Suitable for beginners

MATERIALS

Yarn
Robin Aran
19(20:22:23) × 50g. balls

Needles
1 pair 4mm.
1 pair 4½mm.

MEASUREMENTS

Bust
82(87:92:97) cm.
32(34:36:38) in.

Side Seam
84 cm.
33 in.

Length
104(105:105.5:106:5) cm.
40¾(41:41¼:41¾) in.

Sleeve Seam (excluding cuff)
43 cm.
16¼ in.

TENSION

22 sts. and 12 rows = 5 cm. (2 in.) square over single rib on 4½mm. needles. If your tension square does not correspond to these measurements see page 166 for adjustment instructions.

ABBREVIATIONS

k. = knit; p. = purl; st(s). = stitch(es); inc. = increas(ing) (see page 166); dec. = decreas-(ing) (see page 167); beg. = begin(ning); rem. = remain(ing); rep. = repeat; alt. = alternate; tog. = together; sl. = slip stitch (transfer one stitch from left needle, knit-wise unless otherwise stated, to right hand needle.); cont. = continue; patt. = pattern; foll. = following; folls. = follows; mm. = millimetres; cm. = centimetre(s); in. = inch(es); single rib = k.1, p.1 alternately.

BACK

Cast on 105(111:117:123) sts. with 4½mm. needles and work in single rib, beg. odd-numbered rows with k.1, and even-numbered rows with p.1 until work measures 37 cm. (14½ in.) i.e. 88 rows, or 25 cm. (9¾ in.) less than required skirt length.
Cont. in rib, dec. 1 st. at each end of next and foll. 12th rows 6 times in all. [93 (99:105:111) sts.]

Mark each end of the last row with a thread to denote waist. ** Rib 49 rows, (adjust here if a different length from that above is required).

Shape Armholes
Cast off 3(4:5:6) sts. at the beg. of the next 2 rows, then dec. 1 st. at both ends of the next and 6 foll. right-side rows. [73(77: 81:85) sts.]
Work 28 rows straight.
Next row: rib 27(28:29:30) sts. and leave on a spare needle for left shoulder, rib 19(21:23:25) sts. and leave on a stitch holder for polo collar, rib to end and work on these 27(28:29:30) sts.

Shape Right Shoulder
1st row: cast off 8 sts. rib to last 2 sts., work 2 tog.
2nd row: work 2 tog., rib to end.
Rep. these 2 rows once. Cast off the rem. 7(8:9:10) sts.

Shape Left Shoulder
Rejoin yarn to right side of 27(28:29:30) sts. and rib to end, then work as given for the right shoulder.

FRONT
Work as given for back as far as ** then rib a further 43 rows, (or 6 rows less than those worked on back from waist to armholes if length has been adjusted). Work bust darts:
1st row: rib until 24 sts. rem., turn.
2nd row: s1.1, rib until 24 sts. rem., turn.
3rd and 4th rows: s1.1, rib until 16 sts. rem., turn.
5th and 6th rows: s1.1, rib until 8 sts. rem., turn.

7th row: s1.1, rib to end. Rib 5 rows more.

Shape Armholes
Follow instructions given for the armhole shaping for back, then on 73(77:81:85) sts. which rem. after dec., rib 14(16:18:20) rows.

Shape Neck
Next row: rib 31(32:33:34) and leave these sts. on a spare needle for right shoulder, rib 11(13:15:17) sts. and leave these sts. on a stitch-holder for polo collar, rib to end and work on these 31(32:33:34) sts.

Shape Left Shoulder
Dec. 1 st. at neck edge on next 8 rows, [23(24:25:26) sts.]
Work 4 rows straight. Cast off 8 sts. at beg. of the next and foll. alt. row. Work 1 row, then cast off rem. 7(8:9:10) sts.

Shape Right Shoulder
With right side facing, rejoin yarn to neck edge of 31(32:33:34) sts. and rib to end, then work as given for left shoulder.

SLEEVES
Cast on 41(43:45:47) sts. with 4mm. needles and work 27 rows in single rib as given for back. Change to 4½mm. needles. Cont. in rib, inc. 1 st. at both ends of the next and every foll. 6th row 12(13:14:14) more times. [67(71:75:77) sts.]
Work 15(9:3:3) rows straight.

Shape Sleeve Top
Cast off 3(4:5:6) sts. at beg. of the next 2 rows, then dec. 1 st. at the beg. only of the next 18(20:22:22) rows. Cast off 2 sts. at the beg. of the next 4 rows, and 3 sts. at the beg. of the foll. 6 rows. Cast off rem. 17 sts.

POLO COLLAR
Sew up right shoulder seam. With right side of work facing, using 4mm. needles, pick up and k.21 sts. from left front neck edge, rib across 11(13:15:17) centre front sts. pick up and k.21 sts. from right front neck edge, 8 sts. from right back neck edge, rib across 19(21:23:25) centre back sts., pick up and k.8 sts. from left back neck edge. [88(92:96:100) sts.]
Beg. each row with k.1, work 17 rows in single rib. Change to 4½mm. needles and rib a further 18 rows. Cast off in rib.

MAKING UP
DO NOT PRESS.
Sew up left shoulder seam, cont. seam along ends of polo collar rows, reversing the top half for collar turn-back.
Sew sleeves into armholes then join side and sleeve seams.
Fold polo collar over to right side. Turn up sleeve cuffs for 5 cm. (2 in.).

Knee-length Bobble Pattern Dress 1967

Straight, hemmed dress with three-quarter length set-in sleeves, round neck and shoulder fastening, in bobble pattern with ribbed belt, neck and sleeve bands

★★ Suitable for knitters with some previous experience

MATERIALS

Yarn
Hayfield Grampian DK
18(20) × 50g. balls

Needles
1 pair 3¼mm.
1 pair 4mm.
3.5 crochet hook

Buttons
2

MEASUREMENTS

Bust
82–87(92–97) cm.
32–34(36–38) in.

Length
100(102) cm.
39¼(40) in.

Sleeve Seam (including cuffs)
37 cm.
14½ in.

TENSION
22 sts. and 30 rows = 10 cm. (4 in.) square over stocking stitch on 4mm. needles. If your tension square does not correspond to these measurements see page 166 for adjustment instructions.

ABBREVIATIONS
k. = knit; p. = purl; st(s). = stitch(es); inc. = increas(ing) (see page 166); dec. = decreas-(ing) (see page 167); beg. = begin(ning); rem. = remain(ing); rep. = repeat; alt. = alternate; tog. = together; sl. = slip stitch (transfer one stitch from left needle, knit-wise unless otherwise stated, to right hand needle.); cont. = continue; patt. = pattern; foll. = following; folls. = follows;

Knee-length Bobble Pattern Dress

mm. = millimetres; cm. = centimetre(s); in. = inch(es); d.c. = double crochet; reqd. = required; sl. = slip; t.b.l. = through back of loops; y.fwd. = yarn forward; B.1 (make bobble) = (k.1, y.fwd., k.1, y.fwd., k.1) all into next st., turn, p.5, turn, k.5, turn, p.5, turn, k.2 tog. t.b.l., k.3 tog., pass first st. over 2nd; rev.st.st. = reverse stocking stitch, wrong side knit, right side purl.

BACK

Cast on 103 sts. with 3¼mm. needles and beg. with a p. row work 8 rows in rev.st.st. Change to 4mm. needles and cont. in patt. as folls.:
** Work 2 rows in rev.st.st.
3rd row: p.11, * B.1, p.19, rep. from * 3 times more, B.1, p.11.
Work 3 rows in rev.st.st.
7th row: p.9, * B.1, p.3, B.1, p.15, rep. from * 3 times more, B.1, p.3, B.1, p.9.
Work 3 rows.
11th row: p.7, * B.1, p.7, B.1, p.11, rep. from * 3 times more, (B.1, p.7) twice.
Work 3 rows.
15th row: p.5, * B.1, p.11, B.1, p.7, rep. from * 3 times more, B.1, p.11, B.1, p.5.
Work 3 rows.
19th row: p.3, * B.1, p.15, B.1, p.3, rep. from * 3 times more, B.1, p.15, B.1, p.3.
Work 3 rows.
23rd row: p.1, * B.1, p.19, rep. from * 4 times more, B.1, p.1.
Work 3 rows.
27th row: As 19th.
31st row: As 15th.
35th row: As 11th.

39th row: As 7th.
Work 3 rows.
The 3rd–42nd rows form the patt. and are rep. throughout.
Cont. until work measures 80 cm. (31¼ in.) from hemline (beg. of bobble patt.) ending with a wrong side row. Adjust length here if reqd.

Shape Armholes
Cast off 5(0) sts. at beg. of next 2 rows, then dec. one st. at each end of every alt. row until 79(85) sts. rem. Cont. without shaping until armholes measure 20(22) cm. (7¾(8½) in.), ending with a wrong side row.

Shape Shoulders
Cast off 6(7) sts. at beg. of next 6 rows, then 5 sts. at beg of next 2 rows.
Cast off rem. 33 sts.

FRONT

Cast on 103(123) sts. with 3¼mm. needles and work as given for back to armholes, ending with a wrong side row, noting that on 2nd size every patt. row will have one more rep. i.e. rows 3, 7, 11, 15 and 23 will read 'rep. from * 4 times more'.

Shape Armholes
Cast off 5(10) sts. at beg. of next 2 rows, then dec. 1 st. at each end of every alt. row until 79(85) sts. rem. Cont. without shaping until armholes measure 16(18) cm. (6¼(7) in.) ending with a wrong side row.

Shape Neck
Next row: patt. 34(37) sts., cast off 11 sts.,

patt. to end. Cont. on last 34(37) sts., work 1 row.
Cast off 3 sts. at beg. of next row, then 2 sts. at beg. of foll. 3 alt. rows. Dec. 1 st. at beg. of foll. 2 alt. rows, ending at armhole edge.

Shape Shoulders
Cast off 6(7) sts. at beg. of next and foll. 2 alt. rows. Work 1 row, then cast off rem. 5 sts.
Return to the other 34(37) sts. and work to match, starting at neck edge.

SLEEVES

Cast on 63(63) sts. with 4mm. needles and work in patt. as for back from ** inc. 1 st. at each end of 9th and every foll. 10th(8th) row until there are 79(85) sts., incorporating inc. sts. into patt. Then cont. without shaping until sleeve measures 33 cm. (13 in.) from beg., ending with a wrong side row.

Shape Top
Cast off 5 sts. at beg. of next 2 rows.
Dec. 1 st. at each end of next and every alt. row until 47(49) sts. rem., ending with a wrong side row.
Cast off 2 sts. at beg. of next 8 rows, 3 sts. at beg. of next 4 rows, then 4 sts. at beg. of next 2 rows.
Cast off rem. 11(13) sts.

NECKBAND

Cast on 11 sts. with 3¼mm. needles.
1st row: k.2, * p.1, k.1, rep. from * to last st., k.1.
2nd row: k.1, * p.1, k.1, rep. from * to end.
Rep. these 2 rows until work measures approx. 40 cm. (15¾ in.).
Cast off.

CUFFS

Work as for neckband, making each piece about 20 cm. (7¾ in.) long.
Cast off.

BELT

Work as for neckband for 160 cm. (62¾ in.).
Cast off.

MAKING UP

Press work, if necessary, according to instructions on ball band.
Sew right shoulder seam, then sew left shoulder seam for 2 cm. (¾ in.) from armhole edge.
Sew in sleeves. Sew up side and sleeve seams. Turn up hem at lower edge and slipstitch.
Sew neckband to neck edge. Sew cuffs into a round and sew to sleeve edge, easing sleeve in to fit.
With 3.50 crochet hook work a row of d.c. along both edges of left shoulder, making 2 buttonhole loops on front edge.
Sew on buttons. Press seams.

Gathered Wool and Mohair Skirt

Simple skirt with hem, gathered into a waistband faced with ribbon and fastened with side zip, in twisted stocking stitch

★ Suitable for beginners

MATERIALS

Yarn
Pingouin Laine et Mohair
9(9:10:10) × 50g. balls

Needles
1 pair 5mm.
1 pair 5½mm.
3mm. crochet hook

Notions
18 cm. (7 in.) zip fastener
ribbon for facing, 2.5 cm. (1 in.) longer than your waist measurement

MEASUREMENT

Hip
87(92:97:102) cm.
34(36:38:40) in.

Length (completed including waistband)
69 cm.
27 in.

TENSION

17 sts. and 20 rows = 10 cm. (4 in.) square over twisted stocking stitch on 5½mm. needles. If your tension square does not correspond to these measurements see page 166 for adjustment instructions.

ABBREVIATIONS

k. = knit; p. = purl; st(s). = stitch(es); inc. = increas(ing) (see page 166); dec. = decreas-(ing) (see page 167); beg. = begin(ning); rem. = remain(ing); rep. = repeat; alt. = alternate; tog. = together; sl. = slip stitch (transfer one stitch from left needle, knit-wise unless otherwise stated, to right-hand needle.); cont. = continue; patt. = pattern; foll. = following; folls. = follows; mm. = millimetres; cm. = centimetre(s); in. = inch(es); t.b.l. = through back of loops.
NOTE: For twisted st.st. all sts. are wor-ked through the back on the right side. Where instructions state 'k.' on the dec. rows, this means k. t.b.l.

BACK

Cast on 158(162:168:172) sts. with 5mm. needles.

Beg. with k. row, work 5 rows in st.st. for hem.
k. next row (wrong side) to make hemline ridge.
Change to 5½mm. needles and patt.
1st row: k. every st. t.b.l.
2nd row: k.1, p. to last st., k.1.
These 2 rows form patt.
Cont. until work measures 37 cm. (14½ in.) from hemline, ending with wrong side row.
1st dec. row: k.16(16:17:17), k.2 tog. t.b.l., (k.29(30:31:32), k.2 tog. t.b.l.) 4 times, k.16(16:17:17).
Cont. on rem. 153(157:163:167) sts. in patt. until work measures 45 cm. (17¾ in.) from hemline, ending with wrong side row.
2nd dec. row: k.15 (15:16:16), k.2 tog. t.b.l., (k.28(29:30:31), k.2 tog. t.b.l.) 4 times, k.16(16:17:17).
Cont. on rem. 148(152:158:162) sts. in patt. until work measures 53 cm. (20¾ in.) from hemline, ending with a wrong side row.
3rd dec. row: k.15(15:16:16) sts., k.2 tog. t.b.l., (k.27(28:29:30). k.2 tog., t.b.l.) 4 times, k.15(15:16:16) sts.
Cont. on rem. 143(147:153:157) sts. in patt. until work measures 61 cm. (24 in.) from hemline, ending with a wrong side row.
4th dec. row: k.14(14:15:15) sts., k.2 tog. t.b.l., (k.26(27:28:29), k.2 tog. t.b.l.) 4 times, k.15(15:16:16) sts.
Cont. on rem. 138(142:148:152) sts. in patt. until work measures 66 cm. (26 in.) from beg., ending with a wrong side row.
5th dec. row: k.1, * k.2 tog. t.b.l., rep. from * to last st., k.1. Now p. 1 row on rem. 70(72:75:77) sts., then cast off loosely.

FRONT

Work as for back.

MAKING UP

Backstitch the side seams, leaving left side open at top for 15 cm. (5¾ in.).
Fold up hem all around lower edge and slipstitch in place on wrong side.
Using crochet hook work double crochet around top of skirt for 2.5 cm. (1 in.). Fasten off.
Work 1 row of double crochet along both sides of opening. Cut ribbon to your waist measurement + 2.5 cm. (1 in.), and pin to inside of waist edge, easing in skirt to fit and folding under 1.25 cm. (½ in.) at each end.
Sew in place along upper edge and ends.
Sew zip into opening.
This garment can be brushed, very lightly, for a still softer effect.

Long, Bloused Mohair Waistcoat

Loose, hip-length waistcoat in lacy pattern, with drop shoulders, knitted-up ribbed sleeve and front button bands

★★ Suitable for knitters with some previous experience

MATERIALS

Yarn
Lister-Lee Tahiti Mohair
or Lister-Lee Giselle
11(12:13) × 25g. balls

Needles
1 pair 4mm.
1 pair 5mm.

Buttons
4

MEASUREMENTS

Bust
87(92:97) cm.
34(36:38) in.

Length
58 cm.
22¾ in.

TENSION

10 sts. and 10 rows = 5 cm. (2 in.) square over pattern on 5mm. needles. If your tension square does not correspond to these measurements see page 166 for adjustment instructions.

ABBREVIATIONS

k. = knit; p. = purl; st(s). = stitch(es); inc. = increas(ing) (see page 166); dec. = decreas-(ing) (see page 167); beg. = begin(ning); rem. = remain(ing); rep. = repeat; alt. =

alternate; tog. = together; sl. = slip stitch (transfer one stitch from left needle, knit-wise unless otherwise stated, to right hand needle.); cont. = continue; patt. = pattern; foll. = following; folls. = follows; mm. = millimetres; cm. = centimetre(s); in. = inch(es); m.2 = wind yarn twice round needle to make 2 sts.; k.m. = knit into front of first 'made st.', knit into back of 2nd 'made st.'; p.s.s.o. = pass the slipped stitch over.

BACK

Cast on 81(85:89) sts. using 4mm. needles.
1st row: * k.1, p.1, rep. from * to last st., k.1.
2nd row: * p.1, k.1, rep. from * to last st., p.1.
These two rows form the k.1, p.1 rib.
Cont. in rib until work measures 8 cm. (3¼ in.) inc. 11 sts. evenly across last row. [92(96:100) sts.]
Now work in patt. as folls., using 5mm. needles.
1st row: k.3, * sl.1, k.1, p.s.s.o., m.2, k.2 tog., rep. from * to last st., k.1.
2nd row: p.1, * p.1, k.m., p.1, rep. from * to last 3 sts., p.3.
3rd row: k.1, *sl.1, k.1, p.s.s.o., m.2, k.2 tog., rep. from * to last 3 sts., k.3.
4th row: p.3, * p.1, k.m., p.1, rep. from * to last st., p.1.
These 4 rows form the patt.
Rep. until work measures 36 cm. (14 in.), ending with a wrong side row.

Shape Sleeves

Keeping patt. correct, inc. 1 st. at each end of next and foll. 3 alt. rows. [100(104:108) sts.] Cont. in patt. until work measures 58 cm. (22¾ in.)

Shape Shoulders

Cast off 8(9:9) sts. at beg. of next 2 rows.
Cast off 9(9:10) sts. at beg. of next 4 rows.
Cast off 9(10:10) sts. at beg. of next 2 rows.
Cast off 30 sts.

RIGHT FRONT

Cast on 37(41:45) sts. using 4mm. needles and work 8 cm. (3¼ in.) in k.1, p.1 rib as given for back, inc. 7(7:7) sts., evenly across last row. [44(48:52) sts.]
Using 5mm. needles, cont. in patt. until work measures 25 cm. (9¾ in.), ending with a wrong side row.

Shape Front Edge

Dec. 1 st. at beg. of next and every foll. 4th row until work measures same as back to sleeve shaping.

Shape Sleeve

Still dec. at front edge as before, inc. 1 st. at end of next and foll. 3 alt. rows. Cont. to dec. at front edge as before until 35(37:39) sts. rem. Cont. in patt. until work measures same as back to shoulder, ending with a right side row.

Shape Shoulder

Cast off 8(9:9) sts. at beg. of next row. Work one row. Cast off 9(9:10) sts. at beg. of next and foll. alt. row. Work one row. Cast off rem. 9(10:10) sts.

LEFT FRONT

Work to correspond with right front, reversing all shapings, starting front edge dec. on wrong side, shoulder dec. on right side.

LEFT FRONT BAND

Sew shoulder seams. Using 4mm. needles, pick up and knit 117 sts. evenly from centre back of neck to lower edge of left front. Work 7 rows in k.1, p.1 rib. Cast off loosely in rib.

RIGHT FRONT BAND

Using 4mm. needles, pick up and knit 117 sts. evenly from lower edge of right front to centre back of neck, Work 3 rows in k.1, p.1 rib.
Next row (to make buttonholes): rib 4, (cast off 2 sts., rib 10 including st. already on needle) 4 times, rib to end.
Next row: work in rib, casting on 2 sts. over cast off sts.
Work 2 rows more in rib. Cast off loosely in rib.

Armhole Edging

Using 4mm. needles, pick up and knit 85 sts. evenly around armhole edge. Work 5 rows in k.1, p.1 rib. Cast off in rib.

MAKING UP

Sew side seams. Sew on buttons to correspond with buttonholes.
Sew neckband seam at centre back. Press as instructions on ball band.

Four-colour Lacy Mohair Waistcoat *1978*

Hip-length, V-neck buttoned waistcoat in four-coloured point dentelle pattern with garter stitch separating bars

★★★ Suitable for experienced knitters only

MATERIALS

Yarn
Laines Anny Blatt Kid Anny
1 × 50g. ball Col. A (Vieux Rose/Deep pink)
1 × 50g. ball Col. B (Chair/Pale peach)
1 × 50g. ball Col. C (Biche/Pale camel)
2 × 50g. balls Col. D (Roseraie/Pale pink)

Needles
1 pair 5mm.
1 pair 7mm.

Buttons
4

MEASUREMENTS

Bust
87–97 cm.
34–38 in.

Length
63 cm.

TENSION
10 sts. and 14 rows = 10 cm. (4 in.) square over stocking stitch on 7mm. needles. If your tension square does not correspond to these measurements, see page 166 for adjustment instructions.

ABBREVIATIONS
k. = knit; p. = purl; st(s). = stitch(es); inc. = increas(ing) (see page 166); dec. = decreas-(ing) (see page 167); beg. = begin(ning); rem. = remain(ing); rep. = repeat; alt. = alternate; tog. = together; sl. = slip stitch (transfer one stitch from left needle, knit-wise unless otherwise stated, to right hand needle.); cont. = continue; patt. = pattern; foll. = following; folls. = follows; mm. = millimetres; cm. = centimetre(s); in. = inch(es); p.s.s.o. = pass the slip stitch over; y.r.n. = yarn round needle; g.st. = garter stitch (every row knit).

BACK
Cast on 60 sts. with 5mm. needles and colour D.
Work 8 cm. (3¼ in.) in k.1, p.1 rib.
Change to 7mm. needles and colour C.
Work one purl row, increasing 9 sts. *evenly* across the row (wrong side).
Now work in point dentelle patt.:
1st row: k.1, y.r.n., k.4, * sl.1, k.2 tog.,

p.s.s.o., k.4, y.r.n., k.3, y.r.n., k.4, * rep. from * to * 4 times (to last 8 sts.), sl.1, k.2 tog., p.s.s.o., k.4, y.r.n., k.1.
2nd row: p.
3rd row: k.2, y.r.n., k.3, * sl.1, k.2 tog., p.s.s.o., k.3, y.r.n., k.5, y.r.n., k.3, * rep. from * to * 4 times (to last 8 sts.), sl.1, k.2 tog., p.s.s.o., k.3, y.r.n., k.2.
4th row: p.
5th row: k.3, y.r.n., k.2, * sl.1, k.2 tog., p.s.s.o., k.2, y.r.n., k.7, y.r.n., k.2, * rep. from * to * 4 times (to last 8 sts.), sl.1, k.2 tog., p.s.s.o., k.2, y.r.n., k.3.
6th row: p.
7th row: k.4, y.r.n., k.1, * sl.1, k.2 tog., p.s.s.o., k.1, y.r.n., k.9, y.r.n., k.1, * rep. from * to * 4 times (to last 8 sts.), sl.1, k.2 tog., p.s.s.o., k.1, y.r.n., k.4.
8th row: p.
9th row: k.5, y.r.n., * sl.1, k.2 tog., p.s.s.o., y.r.n., k.11, y.r.n., * rep. from * to * 4 times (to last 8 sts.), sl.1, k.2 tog., p.s.s.o., y.r.n., k.5.
10th row: k.
Rep. rows 1 to 10 inclusive once.
Change to colour B.
Work 2 rows in g.st.
Work rows 1 to 10 inclusive twice.
Change to colour D.
Work 2 rows in g.st.
Work rows 1 to 10 inclusive twice.
Change to colour A.
Work 2 rows in g.st.
Work rows 1 to 7.

Shape Neck
Next row: p.23, cast off 23 sts., p.23, keeping patt. correct.
Finish right shoulder:
k.5, y.r.n., sl.1, k.2 tog., p.s.s.o., y.r.n., k.11, y.r.n., sl.1, k.2 tog., p.s.s.o., k.1.
Next row: cast off knitwise.

Finish Left Shoulder
Rejoin yarn, having right side facing.
Next row: k.1, sl.1, k.2 tog., p.s.s.o., y.r.n., k.11, y.r.n., sl.1, k.2 tog., p.s.s.o., y.r.n., k.5.
Next row: cast off knitwise.

LEFT FRONT
Cast on 26 sts. using 5mm. needles and colour D.
Work 8 cm. (3¼ in.) in k.1, p.1 rib.
Change to 7mm. needles and colour C.
Next row: inc. 1 st., p. to last st., inc. 1 st. (wrong side).
Now work in patt. as for back, *knitting one extra st.* at beg. of each odd numbered

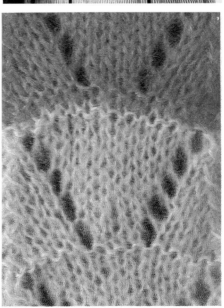

row, and *purling one extra st.* at the end of each even numbered row.
The section of patt. between * and * on each odd numbered row should be worked only ONCE.
Work rows 1 to 10 of patt. twice in colour C.
Change to colour B.
Work 2 rows in g.st.
Work rows 1 to 8 of patt.
9th row: patt. to last 2 sts., dec. 1 st.
Now work 10th row and rep. rows 1 to 3.
4th row: dec. 1st., patt. to end.
Now work rows 5 to 8.
9th row: patt. to last 2 sts., dec. 1 st.
Work 10th row of patt.
Change to colour D.
Work 2 rows in g.st.
Work 1st row of patt.

2nd row: dec. 1st., patt. to end.
Work rows 3 to 6 of patt.
7th row: patt. to last 2 sts., dec. 1 st.
Now work rows 8 to 10, and rep. rows 1 to 10 inclusive.
Change to colour A.
Work 2 rows in g.st.
Work rows 1 to 10 of patt. once.
Cast off.

RIGHT FRONT

Work as for left front, reversing *all* shapings, and *knitting the extra st. at the end* of each odd numbered row, *purling the st. at beg.* of each even numbered row.

MAKING UP AND BAND

Sew up shoulder seams.

Sew up side seams leaving 22 cm. (8½ in.) open either side for the armhole.

Front Band
Cast on 7 sts. using 5mm. needles and colour D. Work approx. 1.35 metres (53 in.) in k.1, p.1 rib, making 4 buttonholes (see page 170) 5 cm. (2 in.) apart, the first one three rows from the end of the band. Join edging to front of waistcoat using a flat seam (see page 171).

Armhole Edging
Cast on 7 sts. using 5mm. needles and colour D.
Work 45 cm. (17¾ in.) in k.1 p.1 rib. Sew onto armhole, using flat seam.
Sew on buttons.
DO NOT PRESS.

Light, Ribbed Mohair Coat 1960

Long coat in slipped stitch rib pattern, with pockets, cuffed set-in sleeves, knitted-in front bands, patterned collar and belt

★★ Suitable for knitters with some previous experience

MATERIALS

Yarn
Wendy Mohair
28(30:32:34) × 25g. balls

Needles
1 pair 5mm.
1 pair 6½mm.

Buttons
4

MEASUREMENTS

Bust
82(87:92:97) cm.
32(34:36:38) in.

Length
108(108:111:111) cm.
42¼(42¼:43½:43½) in.

Sleeve Seam
34 cm.
13¼ in.

TENSION

9 sts. and 12 rows = 5 cm. (2 in.) square over pattern on 6½mm. needles. If your tension square does not correspond to these measurements, see page 166 for adjustment instructions.

ABBREVIATIONS

k. = knit; p. = purl; st(s). = stitch(es); inc. = increas(ing) (see page 166); dec. = decreas-(ing) (see page 167); beg. = begin(ning); rem. = remain(ing); rep. = repeat; alt. = alternate; tog. = together; sl. = slip stitch (transfer one stitch from left needle, knit-wise unless otherwise stated, to right hand needle.); cont. = continue; patt. = pattern; foll. = following; folls. = follows; mm. = millimetres; cm. = centimetre(s); in. = inch(es); sl.2p. = slip 2 sts. purlwise; st. st. = stocking stitch.

LEFT FRONT

** Pocket lining
Cast on 30 sts. with 5mm. needles.
Work 15 cm. (5¾ in.) in st.st., ending with a k. row.
Break yarn and leave sts. on spare needle.
Now cast on 58(62:62:66) sts. with 6½mm needles.
1st row: (wrong side): k.2, * p.2, k.2, rep. from * to end.
2nd row: k.2, sl.2p. with yarn at back, * p.2, sl.2p. with yarn at back, rep. from * to the last 2 sts., k.2.
These 2 rows form patt.
Work until front measures 13(10:13:10) cm. (5(4:5:4) in.) from beg., ending with a wrong side row.
Dec. 1 st. at side edge on the next row, and

then every 21st (17th:21st:17th) row until 53(55:57:59) sts. rem.
Work 17(5:17:5) rows, ending with a wrong side row. **

Make Pocket

Next row: patt. 9(9:11:11) sts., cast off 30 sts., patt. to end.
Foll. row: patt. to end, working pocket lining sts. in place of those cast off.
Work 1(9:1:9) rows.
Dec. 1 st. at side edge on the next row, and then the 2 foll. 21st(17th:21st:17th) rows.
Work until front measures 86(86:87:87) cm. (33¾(33¾:34:34) in.) from beg., ending at side edge.

Shape Armhole

Next row: cast off 5 sts., work to end.
Work 1 row.
Now dec. 1 st. at armhole edge on the next 3(5:5:5) rows, and then the 2(2:2:4) foll. alt. rows. [40(40:42:42) sts.]
Work until armhole measures 18(18:19:20) cm. (7(7:7½:7¾) in.) measured straight, ending at centre front edge.

Shape Neck

Next row: cast off 12(12:13:13) sts., work to end.
Work 1 row.
Dec. 1 st. at neck edge on next and foll. alt. rows until 24(24:25:25) sts. rem., ending at armhole edge.

Shape Shoulder

Dec. at neck edge on foll. alt. rows twice more, and at the same time cast off 6(6:5:5) sts. at beg. of next row, and 5(5:6:6) sts. at beg. of 2 foll. alt. rows.
Work 1 row.
Cast off 6 rem. sts.
Pin the positions of 4 buttons on front, the first 37 cm. (14½ in.) from cast on edge, the 4th 2.5 cm (1 in.) below start of neck shaping, and the other 2 equally spaced between.

RIGHT FRONT

Follow instructions for left front from ** to **, having side shapings at opposite edge, and making buttonholes to correspond with marked positions as folls.:
From centre front edge work 4 sts., cast off 3 sts., work to end.
In the next row, cast on 3 sts. over those cast off.

Make Pocket

Next row: patt. 14(16:16:18) sts., cast off 30 sts., patt. to end.
Foll. row: patt. to end, working pocket lining sts. in place of those cast off.
Work 1(9:1:9) rows.
Dec. 1 st. at side edge on the next row, and then the 2 foll. 21st(17th:21st:17th) rows.
Work until front measures same as left front to armhole, working 1 row more to end at side edge.

Shape Armhole

Next row: cast off 5 sts., work to end.
Now dec. 1 st. at armhole edge on the next 3(5:5:5) rows, and then the 2(2:2:4) foll. alt. rows.

Light, Ribbed Mohair Coat

Work until armhole measures same as left front to neck, ending at armhole edge.

Shape Neck
Next row: patt. to last 12(12:13:13) sts., cast off these sts.
Break yarn.
Turn and rejoin yarn to rem. sts. at neck edge and complete to match left front, working 1 row more before shaping shoulder.

BACK
Cast on 102(110:110:118) sts. with 6½ mm. needles and work 13(10:13:10) cm. (5(4:5:4) in.) in patt., ending with a wrong side row.
Dec. 1 st. at each end of next row, and then every 21st(17th:21st:17th) row until 86(90:94:98) sts. rem.
Work until back measures same as fronts to armholes, ending with a wrong side row.

Shape Armholes
Cast off 5 sts. at beg. of next 2 rows.
Now dec. 1 st. at each end of every row until 70(70:74:78) sts. rem. and then every alt. row until 66(66:70:70) sts. rem.
Work until armholes measure same as fronts, ending with a wrong side row.

Shape Shoulders and Back of Neck
Cast off 6(6:5:5) sts. at beg. of next 2 rows.
Next row: cast off 5(5:6:6) sts., patt. 11(11:12:12) sts. including st. on needle, cast off 22(22:24:24) sts., patt. to end.

Cont. on last set of sts.
Cast off 5(5:6:6) sts. at beg. of next and foll. alt. row.
Work 1 row.
Cast off 6 rem. sts.
Rejoin yarn to rem. sts. at neck edge.
Work 1 row.
Cast off 5(5:6:6) sts. at beg. of next row.
Work 1 row.
Cast off 6 rem. sts.

SLEEVES
Cast on 54(54:58:58) sts. with 6½ mm. needles and work in patt.
Work 10 rows.
Inc. 1 st. at each end of next row, and then every 12th (10th:12th:10th) row until there are 66(68:70:72) sts.
Work until sleeve measures 34 cm. (13¼ in.) from beg., ending with a wrong side row.

Shape Top
Cast off 5 sts. at beg of next 2 rows.
Now dec. 1 st. at each end of next row, and then every alt. row until 24 sts. rem., and then every row until 14 sts. rem. Cast off.

COLLAR
Cast on 114(114:118:118) sts. with 6½ mm. needles.
Work in patt. for 14 cm. (5½ in.), ending with a wrong side row.
Next row: k.2, sl.2p., * p.2 tog., sl 2p., rep. from * to the last 2 sts., k.2.

Work 5 rows with 1 st. less in p. ribs.
Cast off.

POCKET TOPS (make 2)
Cast on 10 sts. with 6½ mm. needles.
Work 16 cm. (6¼ in.) in patt., ending with a wrong side row.
Cast off.

CUFFS (make 2)
Cast on 10 sts. with 6½ mm. needles.
Work 29(29:31:31) cm. (11¼(11¼:12¼:12¼) in.) in patt., ending with a wrong side row.
Cast off.

BELT
Cast on 10 sts. with 6½ mm. needles.
Work 127(132:137:142) cm. (49¾(51¾:53¾:55¾) in.) in patt., ending with a wrong side row.
Cast off.

MAKING UP
Press each piece lightly with warm iron and damp cloth.
Sew up shoulder, side and sleeve seams.
Sew sleeves into armholes. Sew collar to neck edge to within 2.5 cm. (1 in.) of centre front edges. Sew pocket linings, pocket tops and cuffs in position.
Buttonhole stitch round buttonholes.
Press seams lightly.
Sew on buttons.

Chunky Wool Double-breasted Coat 1965

Double-breasted short coat with saddle sleeves, collar, pockets in side seams, knitted in stocking stitch with ribbed details

★ Suitable for beginners

MATERIALS

Yarn
Jaeger Naturgarn
16(17:18) × 100g. hanks

Needles
1 pair 5½ mm.
1 6mm. crochet hook

Buttons
10 (large)
1 (small)

MEASUREMENTS

Bust
87(92:97) cm.
34(36:38) in.

Length (from top of shoulders)
102(104:104) cm.
40(41:41) in.

Sleeve Seam
36 cm.
14 in.

TENSION
16 sts. and 20 rows = 10 cm. (4 in.) square over stocking stitch on 5½ mm. needles. If your tension square does not correspond to these measurements see page 166 for adjustment instructions.

ABBREVIATIONS
k. = knit; p. = purl; st(s). = stitch(es); inc. = increas(ing) (see page 166); dec. = decreas-(ing) (see page 167); beg. = begin(ning); rem. = remain(ing); rep. = repeat; alt. =

Chunky Wool Double-breasted Coat

alternate; tog. = together; sl. = slip stitch (transfer one stitch from left needle, purl-wise unless otherwise stated, to right hand needle.); cont. = continue; patt. = pattern; foll. = following; folls. = follows; mm. = millimetres; cm. = centimetre(s); in. = inch(es); p.s.s.o. = pass the slipped st. over; t.b.l. = through back of loops; st. st. = stocking stitch; ch. = chain.
NOTE: Coat will drop approx 4 cm. (1½ in.) in wear.

BACK

Cast on 95(99:103) sts.
1st row (right side): k.1, * p.1, k.1, rep. from * to end.
2nd row: p.1, * k.1, p.1, rep. from * to end.
Rep. last 2 rows until work measures 18 cm. (7 in.) at centre from start, ending with right side facing.
Change to st.st., starting with a k. row, and work straight until back measures 76(77:77) cm. (29¾:30¼:30¼ in.) at centre from start, ending with a p. row.

Shape Armholes

Cast off 6 sts. at beg. of next 2 rows.
Next row: k.2 tog., k. to last 2 sts., sl.1, k.1, p.s.s.o.
Next row: p.2 tog. t.b.l., p. to last 2 sts., p.2 tog.
Rep. last 2 rows 3 times more. [67(71:75) sts.]
Next row: k.2 tog., k. to last 2 sts., sl.1, k.1, p.s.s.o.
Next row: p.
Rep. last 2 rows until 59(61:63) sts. rem.
Work straight until back measures 94(97:97) cm. (37:38:38 in.) at centre from beg., ending with a p. row.

Shape Shoulders

Cast off 7(7:6) sts. at beg. of next 2 rows, then 6(6:7) sts. at beg. of next 4 rows. Cast off rem. 21(23:23) sts.

LEFT FRONT

Cast on 66(68:70) sts.
1st row (right side): * k.1, p.1, rep. from * to end.
Rep. 1st row until work measures 18 cm. (7 in.) at centre from start, ending with right side facing.
Next row: k.37(39:41), rib to end.
Next row: rib 29, p.37(39:41).
Rep. last 2 rows until front side edge matches back to armhole, ending with right side facing.

Shape Armhole

Cast off 6 sts. at beg. of next row. Work 1 row straight, then dec. 1 st. at armhole edge on every row until 52(54:56) sts. rem. Now dec. 1 st. at beg. of next and every alt. row until 48(49:50) sts. rem.
Work straight until front matches back armhole edge, ending with wrong side facing.

Shape Neck and Shoulder

1st row: cast off 23(24:24) sts., work to end.
2nd row: cast off 7(7:6) sts., work to end.
3rd row: cast off 3 sts., work to end.
4th row: cast off 6(6:7) sts., work to end.
5th row: as 3rd.
Cast off rem. 6(6:7) sts.

RIGHT FRONT

Cast on 66(68:70) sts.
1st row (right side): * p.1, k.1, rep. from * to end.
Rep. 1st row until work measures 18 cm. (7 in.) at centre from start, ending with right side facing.
Next row: rib 29, k. to end.
Next row: p.37(39:41), rib to end.
Finish to correspond with left front, working 5 pairs of buttonholes, 1st pair to come 29 cm. (11¼ in.) from beg., 5th pair in 5th and 6th rows below neck shaping and rest spaced evenly between. Mark position of buttons on left front with pins, then work holes to correspond.
To make a pair of buttonholes (right side facing): rib 3, cast off 3, rib 17, cast off 3, work to end. Work back, casting on 3 sts. over those cast off.

RIGHT SLEEVE

** Cast on 51(53:55) sts. and, starting with 1st row, work 10 rows in k.1, p.1 rib as for back.
Cont. in rib, shaping sides by inc. 1 st. at each end of next and every foll. 8th row until there are 65(67:69) sts., taking inc. sts. into rib.
Work straight until sleeve seam measures 36 cm. (14 in.), ending with right side facing.

Shape Top

Cast off 6 sts. at beg. of next 2 rows, then dec. 1 st. at each end of next and every alt. row until 33(35:39) sts. rem.
Work 1 row straight, then dec. 1 st. at each end of every row until 15 sts. rem., all sizes.

Continue straight on these 15 sts. for saddle until strip fits along shoulder edge when slightly stretched, ** ending with right side facing (front edge).

Shape Top

Cast off 5 sts. at beg. of next and foll. 2 alt. rows.

LEFT SLEEVE

Work as for right sleeve from ** to ** but ending with wrong side facing (front edge).
Shape top as for right sleeve.

COLLAR

Cast on 85 sts. and work in k.1, p.1 rib as for back until work measures 14 cm. (5½ in.) at centre from start, ending with 1st row.

Shape Top

Next 2 rows: rib to last 12 sts., turn, sl.1.
Next 2 rows: rib to last 24 sts., turn, sl.1.
Next 2 rows: rib to last 36 sts., turn, sl.1.
Next 2 rows: rib all sts., picking up a loop at each point where work was turned and working it tog. with next st. to avoid a hole. Cast off very firmly in rib.

POCKET LININGS

Right: cast on 11 sts. and p.1 row. Cont. in st.st., inc. 1st. at beg. of every k. row until there are 25 sts.
Work straight until lining measures 14 cm. (5½ in.) at centre from start, ending with a p. row.
Now dec. 1 st. at beg. of next row, then at this edge on every row until 9 sts. rem. Cast off.
Left: work to correspond with right lining, working shapings at other end of row.

MAKING UP

Following instructions on the ball band, press work lightly on wrong side, omitting ribbing.
Join side seams leaving a 17 cm. (6½ in.) opening on each side for pockets, top of opening to come 18 cm. (7 in.) below arm-hole.
Pin lining in position, right side of lining to wrong side of work, longer straight edge towards back; sew in position all round. With crochet hook work slip stitch along front edge of pocket and short edges of collar. Join sleeve seams; insert sleeves, with saddle strips along shoulders on back and front, with longer edge towards back. Work slip stitch up right front edge, make 2 ch. for buttonloop at corner, then along 16(17:17) cast off sts. for neck, then cont. round neck edge to left corner, then work down left front edge.
Sew shaped edge of collar round neck, starting and ending at beg. of neck shaping. Press all seams. Sew on buttons, sewing small button on left front opposite buttonloop.

Thick Check Pattern Coat

Thigh-length raised check pattern coat with doubled collar, hemmed cuffs and lower edge, button bands backed with binding tape

★★ Suitable for knitters with some previous experience

MATERIALS

Yarn
Emu Shetland DK (used double)
24(24:26) × 50g. balls

Needles
1 pair 4½mm.
1 pair 5½mm.

Buttons
5

Binding Tape
1.50 metres
1½ yards

MEASUREMENTS

Bust
82–87(87–92:92–97) cm.
32–34(34–36:36–38) in.

Length
74(74:76) cm.
29(29:29¾) in.

Sleeve Seam
41(41:43) cm.
16(16:16¾) in.

TENSION

7½ sts. and 10 rows = 5 cm. (2 in.) square over pattern on 5½mm. needles. If your tension square does not correspond to these measurements, see page 166 for adjustment instructions.

ABBREVIATIONS

k. = knit; p. = purl; st(s). = stitch(es); inc. = increas(ing) (see page 166); dec. = decreas(ing) (see page 167); beg. = begin(ning); rem. = remain(ing); rep. = repeat; alt. = alternate; tog. = together; sl. = slip stitch (transfer one stitch from left needle, knitwise unless otherwise stated, to right hand needle.); cont. = continue; patt. = pattern; foll. = following; folls. = follows; mm. = millimetres; cm. = centimetre(s); in. = inch(es); y.bk. = yarn back; y.fwd. = yarn forward; st.st. = stocking stitch.
NOTE: Yarn is used double throughout.

BACK

Cast on 74(78:82) sts. using double yarn and 4½mm. needles. Work 9 rows in st. st., beg. with k. row.
10th row: k., to mark hemline. Change to 5½mm. needles and cont. in patt. thus:
1st row: k.6(8:10) sts., p.2, * (leave wool at front of work, sl.1, y.bk., y.fwd., sl.1,

y.bk., k.1, p.2) twice, k.10, p. 2*, rep. from * to * to last 6(8:10) sts., k.6(8:10).
2nd and 4th rows: p.6(8:10) sts., *(k.2, p.4) twice, k.2, p.10,* rep. from * to * to last 6(8:10) sts., p.6(8:10) sts.
3rd row: k.6(8:10)sts., p.2, *(k.1, y.fwd., sl.1, y.bk., k.1, y.fwd., sl.1, leave yarn at front of work, p.2) twice, k.10, p.2*, rep. from * to * to last 6(8:10) sts., k.6(8:10).
Rep. 1st–4th rows inclusive twice more.
13th row: as 1st.
14th row: as 2nd.
15th row: p.
16th row: k.
17th row:
1st size: p.2, leave yarn at front of work, sl.1, y.bk., k.1, y.fwd., sl.1, y.bk., k.1, y.fwd., p.2, k.10, p.2, *(sl.1, y.bk.,k.1, y.fwd., sl.1, y.bk., k.1, y.fwd., p.2) twice, k.10, p.2,* rep. from * to * to end of row.
2nd size: leave yarn at front, sl.1, y.bk., k.1, y.fwd., p.2, sl.1, y.bk., k.1, y.fwd., sl.1, y.bk., k.1, y.fwd., p.2, k.10, p.2, *(sl.1, y.bk., k.1, y.fwd., sl.1, y.bk., k.1, p.2) twice, k.10, p.2*, rep. from * to * to end of row.
3rd size: leave yarn at front, *(sl.1, y.bk., k.1, y.fwd., sl.1, y.bk., k.1, p.2) twice, k.10, p.2*, rep. from * to * to last 10 sts., sl.1, y.bk., k.1, y.fwd., sl.1, y.bk., k.1, p.2, sl.1, y.bk., k.1, y.fwd., sl.1, y.bk., k.1.
18th and 20th rows: p.0(2:4), k.2, p.4, *k.2, p.10, (k.2, p.4) twice,* rep. from * to *, but ending p.0(2:4).
19th row:
1st size: p.2, k.1, y.fwd., sl.1, y.bk., k.1, y.fwd., sl.1, leave yarn at front of work, p.2, k.10, p.2, *(k.1, y.fwd., sl.1, y.bk., k.1, y.fwd., sl.1, leave yarn at front of work, p.2) twice, k.10, p.2*, rep. from * to end of row.
2nd size: k.1, y.fwd., sl.1, y.bk., p.2, k.1, y.fwd., sl.1, y.bk., k.1, y.fwd., sl.1, leave yarn at front, p.2, k.10, p.2, *(k.1, y.fwd., sl.1, y.bk., k.1, y.fwd., sl.1, y.bk., p.2) twice, k.10, p.2*, rep. from * to * to end of row.
3rd size: *(k.1, y.fwd., sl.1, y.bk., k.1, y.fwd., sl.1, p.2) twice, k.10, p.2*, rep. from * to * to end of row.
Rep. 17th–20th rows inclusive twice more.
29th row: as 17th.
30th row: as 18th.
31st row: p.
32nd row: k.
Cont. to rep. these 32 rows until work measures 53(53:54) cm. (20¾(20¾:21¼) in.) from beg. of patt.

Shape Armholes
Cast off 2 sts. at beg. of next 2 rows.

Dec. 1 st. at each end of every row until 60(62:66) sts. rem.
Cont. straight on these sts. until work measures 21(21:22) cm. (8¼(8¼:8½) in.) from beg. of armholes.

Shape Shoulders
Cast off 7 sts. at beg. of next 4 rows, then cast off 6(6:7) sts.
Cast off rem. sts.

POCKET LINING

Cast on 22 sts. with 5½mm. needles.
Work 34 rows in st.st.
Leave sts. on stitch holder.

LEFT FRONT

Cast on 44(46:48) sts. with 4½mm. needles.
Work 9 rows in st.st.
10th row: k.
Change to 5½mm. needles, cont. in patt.:
1st row (1st size: k.6, p.2; 2nd size: k.8, p.2;

Thick Check Pattern Coat

3rd size: p.2): ** (leave yarn at front, sl.1, y.bk., k.1, y.fwd., sl.1, y.bk., k.1, p.2) twice, ** k.10, p.2, rep. from ** to ** once more, (1st size: p.2; 2nd size: p.2; 3rd size: k.10).
This row sets patt.
Cont. in patt. as for back until 48 rows have been worked.
49th row: patt. 2, sl. 22 sts. onto stitch holder, patt. 22 sts. of pocket lining, patt. to end.
Cont. until work corresponds with back to armholes, ending with a p. row.

Shape Armholes
Cast off 2 sts. at beg. of next row. Work 1 row.
Dec. 1 st. at armhole edge every row until 39(40:41) sts. rem.
Cont. straight on these sts. until work measures 16(16:17) cm. (6¼(6¼:6½) in.) from beg. of the armholes, ending at centre front edge. Cast off 6(8:9) sts. at beg. of next row, dec. 1 st. at neck edge every row until 20(20:21) sts. rem.
Cont. straight until work corresponds with back to shoulders, ending at armhole edge.
Cast off 7 sts. at beg. of next 2 alt. rows.
Cast off 6(6:7) rem. sts.
With 4½mm. needles and right side facing, slip pocket sts. left on holder onto needle and work 1 row k., 1 row p., for 8 rows.
Cast off these sts.
Slipstitch pocket edging on inside of pocket top. Sew facing in position.

RIGHT FRONT

Work pocket lining as before with 5½mm. needles.
Cast on 44(46:48) sts. with 4½mm. needles.
Work 9 rows in st.st.
10th row: k.
Change to 5½mm. needles.
1st row: (1st and 2nd sizes: p.2; 3rd size: k.10, p.2): ** (leave yarn at front, sl.1, y.bk., k.1, y.fwd., sl.1, y.bk., k.1, p.2) twice, ** k.10, p.2, rep. from ** to ** twice, k.6(8:0). This row sets patt.
Cont. in patt. and work buttonholes every 27th and 28th rows thus: work 3 sts., cast off 4 sts., work to end.
Next row: work along row and cast on 4 sts. above the sts. cast off in previous row.
Cont. to work in pattern as for left front, reversing all shaping instructions.

SLEEVES

Cast on 40(42:44) sts. with 4½mm. needles.
Work 9 rows in st.st.
10th row: k.
Change to 5½mm. needles.
1st row: k.1(2:3), p.2, * (leave yarn at front, sl.1, y.bk., k.1) twice, p.2, * rep. from * to * once, k.10, p.2, rep. from * to * twice, k.1(2:3). This row sets patt. Cont. in patt. and inc. 1 st. at each end 9th and every foll. 8th row until 54(68:62) sts. rem.

Thick Check Pattern Coat

Cont. straight on these sts. until work measures 41(41:43) cm. (16(16:16¾) in.) or length required.

Shape Top

Cast off 2 sts. at beg. of next 2 rows, dec. 2 sts. at each end of every alt. row until 40(42:44) sts. rem., then dec. 1 st. at each end of every alt. row, until 28(30:32) sts. rem.
Dec. 1 st. at each end of every row until 16(18:18) sts. rem.
Cast off rem. sts.

COLLAR

Cast on 26 sts. with 4½ mm. needles.
Work in st.st., beg. with a k. row.
Cast on 5 sts. at beg. of next 8 rows.
Inc. 1 st. at each end of next 2 rows. [70 sts.]
Work 5 rows straight. Inc. 1 st. at each end of next and every foll. 5th row until 80 sts. rem.
Work 4 rows straight, ending with a k. row.
Next row: k. Change to 5½ mm. needles.
1st row: k.9, * p.2, (leave yarn at front, sl.1, y.bk., k.1, y.fwd., sl.1, y.bk., k.1, p.2) twice, k.10, * rep. from * to *, but ending last rep. k.9. This row sets patt.
Dec. 1 st. at each end of every 5th row until 70 sts. rem.

Work 5 rows straight. Dec. 1 st. at each end of next 2 rows. Cast off 5 sts. at beg. of next 8 rows.
Cast off rem. sts.

MAKING UP

Press all pieces lightly on reverse side. Sew in all ends. Backstitch shoulder, side and sleeve seams, turn up hem and cuffs and stitch.
With right sides together, stitch collar sides. Turn, then stitch collar into position.
Sew binding tape down each front, sew round buttonholes, sew on buttons.

Long, Slim, Cabled Waistcoat   1979

Hip-length waistcoat with front and back cable pattern on reversed stocking stitch ground, and horizontally ribbed armhole and front bands

★★ Suitable for knitters with some previous experience

MATERIALS

Yarn
3 Suisses Aubretia
7(8:8:8) × 50g. balls

Needles
1 pair 3¼ mm.
1 pair 4mm.
1 cable needle
1 circular needle, med. length, 3¼ mm.

Buttons
6

MEASUREMENTS

Bust
87(92:97:102) cm.
34(36:38:40) in.

Length
72(73:73:74) cm.
28¼(28½:28½:29) in.

TENSION

18 sts. and 26 rows = 10 cm.(4 in.) square over reversed stocking stitch on 4mm. needles. If your tension square does not correspond to these measurements, see page 166 for adjustment instructions.

ABBREVIATIONS

k. = knit; p. = purl; st(s). = stitch(es); inc. = increas(ing) (see page 166); dec. = decreas-(ing) (see page 167); beg. = begin(ning); rem. = remain(ing); rep. = repeat; alt. = alternate; tog. = together; sl. = slip stitch (transfer one stitch from left needle, knit-wise unless otherwise stated, to right hand needle.); cont. = continue; patt. = pattern; foll. = following; folls. = follows; mm. = millimetres; cm. = centimetre(s); in. = inch(es); rev. st.st. = reversed stocking stitch (right side purl); p. loop = pick up loop lying between needles and p. it through the back; t.b.l. = through back loops.

BACK

Cast on 85(89:95:99) sts. with 3¼ mm. needles and work in rib:

1st row (right side): k.2, * p.1, k.1, rep. from * to last st., k.1.
2nd row: k.1, * p.1, k.1, rep. from * to end.
Rep. these 2 rows until work measures 12 cm. (4¾ in.), ending with a 1st rib row.
Inc. row (wrong side): k.17(19:21:23), p.2, (p. loop, p.1) 3 times, k.41(41:43:43), p.2 (p. loop, p.1) 3 times, k.17(19:21:23). [91(95:101:105) sts.]
Change to 4mm. needles and patt.
1st row: p.17(19:21:23), k.8, p.41(41:43:43), k.8, p.17(19:21:23).
2nd row: k.17(19:21:23), p.8, k.41(41:43:43), p.8, k.17(19:21:23). Rep. these 2 rows 3 times more.
9th row: p.17(19:21:23), * slip next 4 sts. onto cable needle, leave at front, k.4, then k.4 from cable needle, * p.41(41:43:43), rep. from * to * , p.17(19:21:23).
Rep. 2nd row once then 1st and 2nd rows again.
These 12 rows form one patt.
Cont. in patt. without shaping until work measures 52 cm. (20½ in.) from beg., ending with a wrong side row.

Shape Armhole

Cast off 4 sts. at beg. of next 2 rows, 2 sts. at beg. of next 2(2:4:4) rows and 1 st. at beg. of next 8(10:10:12) rows. Cont. on rem. 71(73:75:77) sts. until work measures 72(73:73:74) cm. (28¼(28½:28½:29) in.) from beg., ending with a wrong side row.

Shape Shoulders and Neck

Cast off 6 sts. at beg. of next 2 rows.
Next row: cast off 6 sts., work until there are 18(19:19:20) sts. on right hand needle, now cast off next 11(11:13:13) sts., patt. to end.

Cont. on 24(25:25:26) sts. now rem. at end of needle for left back.
Cast off 6 sts. at beg. of next row and 10 sts. at neck edge on foll. row.
Cast off rem. 8(9:9:10) sts.
With wrong side facing, rejoin yarn to neck edge of rem. sts. of right back.
Cast off 10 sts., work to end.
Cast off rem. 8(9:9:10) sts.

RIGHT FRONT

Cast on 43(45:47:49) sts. with 3¼mm. needles, and work in rib as for back.
Inc. row (wrong side): k.17(19:21:23) sts., p.2, (p. loop, p.1) 3 times, then k.21 for sizes 87 cm. (34 in.) and 92 cm. (36 in.), but for sizes 97 cm. (38 in.) and 102 cm. (40 in.) k.10, inc. 1 st. in next st., k.10. [46(48:51:53) sts.]
Change to 4mm. needles and patt.
1st row: p.21(21:22:22) sts., k.8, p.17(19: 21:23) sts.
Cont. in patt. as now set, working one cable panel on same rows as patt. for back without shaping until work measures 45 cm. (17¾ in.) from beg., ending with a right side row.

Shape Front
Next row: patt. to last 3 sts., k.2 tog., k.1.
Cont. to dec. in this position on every foll. 4th row 15(15:16:16) times more. AT THE SAME TIME keep side edge straight until work measures 52 cm. (20½ in.) from beg., ending at side.

Shape Armhole
Cast off 4 sts. at beg. of next row, 2 sts. at same edge on next 1(1:2:2) alt. rows, and 1 st. on next 4(5:5:6) alt. rows.
Now, keeping this edge straight, cont. with front decs. until all are completed, then cont. on rem. 20(21:21:22) sts. until work measures 72(73:73:74) cm. (28¼ (28½:28½:29) in.) from beg., ending at armhole edge.

Shape Shoulder
Cast off 6 sts. at beg. of next row and next alt. row.
Work 1 row then cast off rem. 8(9:9:10) sts.

LEFT FRONT

Work as for right front until welt is completed.
Inc. row: (wrong side): k.21 sts. for sizes 87 cm. (34 in.) and 92 cm. (36 in.), but for sizes 97 cm. (38 in.) and 102 cm. (40 in.) k.10, inc. 1.st. in next st., k.10, then for all sizes p.2, (p. loop, p.1) 3 times, k.17(19:21:23). [46(48:51:53) sts.]
Change to 4mm. needles and patt.
1st row: p.17(19:21:23), k.8, p.21(21:22:22).
Cont. in patt. as now set and complete as for right front, working shapings at opposite edges. For front shaping, work k.1, k.2 tog. t.b.l., at beg. of corresponding rows.

FRONT AND NECK BANDS

Join shoulder seams matching patt., with backstitch seam.
Press all seams lightly on wrong side with warm iron and damp cloth.
With right side of work facing and using smaller needles, pick up and knit 109(113:115:121) sts. all round one armhole edge.
Beg. with 2nd row, work 7 rows in rib as on welt.
Cast off loosely ribwise.
Work other armhole band in same way.
With right side of work facing and using circular needle, pick up and knit 93 sts. along straight front edge of right front, 71(73:73:75) sts. along sloping edge to shoulder, 35(35:37:37) sts. across back neck, 71(73:73:75) sts. down left front slope and 93 sts. along straight left front edge.

Beg. with a 2nd row, work in rib as on welt. Work 2 rows, now make buttonholes:
1st row (wrong side): rib to last 92 sts., cast off 3 sts., (rib until there are 14 sts. on the right hand needle after previous buttonhole, cast off 3 sts.) 5 times, rib to end.
2nd row: cast on 3 sts. over each buttonhole, working in rib. Work 3 more rows in rib, cast off loosely ribwise.

MAKING UP

Sew up side seams and ends of armhole bands.
Sew on buttons to correspond with buttonholes.

Shaped Man-style Waistcoat

Short, buttoned waistcoat in reversed stocking stitch, with shaped hemline, two crochet mock pockets and crochet borders

★ Suitable for beginners

MATERIALS

Yarn
3 Suisses Suizasport
7(7:8:8) × 50g. balls

Needles
1 pair 5mm.
1 7mm. crochet hook

Buttons
4

MEASUREMENTS

Bust
82(87:92:97) cm.
32(34:36:38) in.

Length (including crochet border)
45(45:46:46) cm.
17¾(17¾:18:18) in.

TENSION

15 sts. and 21 rows = 10 cm. (4 in.) square over stocking stitch on 5mm. needles. If your tension square does not correspond to these measurements, see page 166 for adjustment instructions.

ABBREVIATIONS

k. = knit; p. = purl; st(s). = stitch(es); inc. = increas(ing) (see page 166); dec. = decreas-(ing) (see page 167); beg. = begin(ning); rem. = remain(ing); rep. = repeat; alt. = alternate; tog. = together; sl. = slip stitch (transfer one stitch from left needle, knit-wise unless otherwise stated, to right hand needle.); cont. = continue; patt. = pattern; foll. = following; folls. = follows; mm. = millimetres; cm. = centimetre(s); in. = inch(es); ch. = chain; d.c. = double crochet; rev.st.st. = reversed stocking stitch (right side p., wrong side k.).

BACK

Cast on 60(64:68:72) sts. and beg. with a p. row, work in rev. st.st.
Inc. 1 st. at both ends of row when work measures 4 cm. (1½ in.), 8 cm. (3¼ in.), 12 cm. (4¾ in.) and 16 cm. (6¼ in.) from beg., then cont. on 68(72:76:80) sts. until work measures 21 cm. (8¼ in.) from beg., ending with a k. row.

Shape Armhole

Cast off 4 sts. at beg. of next 2 rows, 2 sts. at beg. of next 2(2:4:4) rows and 1 st. at beg. of next 8(10:8:10) rows.
Cont. on rem. 48(50:52:54) sts. until work

measures 43(43:44:44) cm. (16¾(16¾:17¼:17¼) in.) from beg., ending with a k. row.

Shape Neck and Shoulders

1st row: cast off 4 sts., p. until there are 11(12:12:13) sts. on right needle, leave these for right back. Now cast off next 18(18:20:20) sts., p. to end.
Cont. on 15(16:16:17) sts. now rem. on needle for left back.
2nd row: cast off 4 sts., k. to last 2 sts. at neck edge, k.2 tog.
3rd row: cast off 1 st., p. to end.
4th row: as 2nd.
p. 1 row, then cast off rem. 4(5:5:6) sts.
With wrong side facing rejoin yarn to neck edge of right back sts., cast off 1 st., k. to end.
Next row: cast off 4 sts., p. to last 2 sts., p.2 tog. Cast off 1 st. at beg. of foll. row.
Cast off rem. 4(5:5:6) sts.

RIGHT FRONT

Cast on 2 sts.
Beg. with a p. row., work in rev. st.st. shaping both edges.
For front shaping, inc. 1 st. at front edge (end of wrong side rows), on 2nd row, then every foll. 4th row 6 times in all.
AT SAME TIME, for side shaping, cast on at beg. of wrong side rows 2 sts. 8 times, 2(3:3:4) sts. once and 3(4:6:7) sts. once.
When all incs. have been completed, cont. on these 29(31:33:35) sts. until work measures 4 cm. (1½ in.) from the last cast-ing on at side.
Inc. 1 st. at side edge on next row then at same edge at 4 cm. (1½ in.) intervals 3 times more.
Cont. on 33(35:37:39) sts. until work measures 21 cm. (8¼ in.) at side edge, ending at this edge.

Shape Armhole and Front

Next row: cast off 4 sts., k. to last 2 sts., k.2 tog.
Cast off at armhole edge 2 sts. on next 1(1:2:2) alt. rows and 1 st. on next 4(5:4:5) alt. rows.
AT THE SAME TIME dec. 1 st. at front edge at 3 row intervals twice more, then at same edge on every foll. 4th row 8(8:9:9) times more.
Cont. on rem. 12(13:13:14) sts. until arm-hole matches back to shoulder, ending at armhole edge.

Shape Shoulder

Cast off 4 sts. at beg. of next row and next alt. row.
Work 1 row then cast off rem. 4(5:5:6) sts.

LEFT FRONT

Work as for right front, working all shap-ings at opposite edges.

MAKING UP AND MOCK POCKETS

Backstitch shoulder and side seams and press seams lightly on wrong side with warm iron and damp cloth.
With right side of work facing join on yarn at lower edge of right side seam, work 1 ch., then work in d.c. all round entire front, neck and lower edges, join with a slip st. to 1st ch., turn.
On 2nd row work in back loops only, of the d.c. in first row, working 2 d.c. into each of 2 adjacent sts. at lower points and making 4 loops for buttonholes on right front, the top one just below 1st dec. and the bottom one just above last inc. with rem. 2 evenly spaced between.
For each buttonhole work 2 ch. and miss 2 d.c.
Work 2 more rows of d.c. always into back loops and working inc. as before; join at end of last row and fasten off.
Similarly work 4 rows of d.c. round each armhole edge.
For the mock pockets work 15 ch., miss 1st ch. and work 1 d.c. in each rem. ch. Work 4 more rows of d.c., working in back loops only, and always turning with 1 ch. Fasten off.
Press rev. st.st. and crochet borders.
Sew flaps to fronts as shown in photograph.
Sew on buttons.

'Sampler' Slipover Waistcoat

Sleeveless slipover with moss, diagonal, striped rib, garter and oblique stitch bands, and separating bar between each

★ Suitable for beginners

MATERIALS

Yarn
A.N.I. Scottish Homespun
5(5:6) × 50g. hanks

Needles
1 pair 3¼mm.
1 pair 5mm.
1 set of double pointed, or one circular needle 3¼mm.

MEASUREMENTS

Bust
87(92:97) cm.
34(36:38) in.

Length
57.5 cm.
22½ in.

TENSION

20 sts. and 32 rows = 10 cm. (4 in.) square over garter stitch on 5mm. needles. If your tension square does not correspond to these measurements see page 166 for adjustment instructions.

ABBREVIATIONS

k. = knit; p. = purl; st(s). = stitch(es); inc. = increas(ing) (see page 166); dec. = decreas-(ing) (see page 167); beg. = begin(ning); rem. = remain(ing); rep. = repeat; alt. = alternate; tog. = together; sl. = slip stitch (transfer one stitch from left needle, knit-wise unless otherwise stated, to right hand needle.); cont. = continue; patt. = pattern; foll. = following; folls. = follows; mm. = millimetres; cm. = centimetre(s); in. = inch(es); p.s.s.o = pass slipped stitch over; m.st. = moss stitch; g.st. = garter stitch.

BACK

**Cast on 92(100:108) sts. with 3¼mm. needles.
Work in k.1, p.1 rib for 8 cm. (3¼ in.)
Change to 5mm. needles.
Work 6 rows raised separating bar patt.:
1st row (right side), *4th and 5th rows:* k.
2nd, 3rd and 6th rows: p.
Work m. st. band:
1st row: k.1, p.1, rep. to end.
2nd row: p.1, k.1, rep. to end.
Cont. until band measures
8cm. (3¼ in.), ending with a wrong side row.

Now work 6 rows raised separating bar patt.
Work diagonal st. band:
1st row: k.2, p.2, rep. to end.
2nd, 4th, 6th and 8th rows: k. all k. sts., p. all p. sts.
3rd row: k.1, * p.2, k.2, rep. from * to last 3 sts., p.2, k.1.
5th row: p.2, k.2 to end.
7th row: p.1, * k.2, p.2, rep. from * to last 3 sts., k.2, p.1.
Cont. until band measures 8 cm. (3¼ in.), ending with a wrong side row.
Now work 6 row raised separating bar patt.
Work g.st. band:
k. every row until band measures 8 cm. (3¼ in.) deep, ending with a wrong side row.
Now work 6 row raised separating bar patt.
Work striped ribbing band and armhole:
1st row: cast off 5(6:7) sts., (k.1, p.1) to end.
2nd row: cast off 5(6:7) sts., p. to end.
3rd row: cast off 5(6:7) sts., (p.1, k.1) to end.
4th row: as 2nd row. [72(76:80) sts.]
5th row: k.1, p.1 to end.
6th row: p. **
Rep. 5th and 6th rows until the band measures 8 cm. (3¼ in.).
Now work 6 row raised separating bar patt.
Work oblique stitch band and shoulder shaping:
*1st row: k.3, p.1, rep. to end.
2nd, 4th, 6th and 8th rows: k. all the k. sts., p. all the p. sts.
3rd row: p.1, k.3, rep. to end.
5th row: k.1, p.1, k.2, rep. to end.
7th row: k.2, p.1, k.1, rep. to end.
Rep. these 8 rows once more, then rows 1 and 2.*
Keeping patt. correct, cast off 4 (5:6) sts. at beg. of next 4 rows.
Cast off 4 sts. at beg. of next 6 rows. [32 sts.]
Cast off rem. sts. loosely.

FRONT

Work as for back from ** to **.
Rep. rows 5 and 6 of striped ribbing band once more, then row 5 again.
Next row: p. 28(30:32) sts., cast off 16 sts., p. to end.
Finish this side first:
1st row: k.1, p.1 to end.
2nd row: dec. 1 st., p. to end.
Rep. these 2 rows 7 times more. [20(22:24) sts.]

Now work 6 row raised separating bar patt., dec. 1 st. at neck edge on 2nd and 4th rows.
Work oblique st. patt. from * to * as back.
** Cast off 4(5:6) sts. at beg. of next and foll. alt. row.
Work 1 row.
Cast off 4 sts. twice, 2 sts. once on next and foll. 2 alt. rows.
Fasten off. **
Finish right side:
Rejoin yarn.
1st row: k.1, sl.1, p.s.s.o, * k.1, p.1 rep. from, * to end.
2nd row: p.
Rep. these 2 rows 7 times more. [20(22:24) sts.]
Now work 6 row raised separating bar patt., dec. 1 st. at neck edge on 2nd and 4th rows.
Work oblique st. patt. from * to * as back.
Work 1 row.
Work as for other side of front from ** to **.

NECKBAND

Sew shoulder seams using backstitch to create a gently sloping shoulder. Starting at right-hand end of back neck, using set of double pointed or circular 3¼mm. needles, pick up and knit 32 sts. across back neck, 50 sts. down left side of opening, 16 sts. across cast off lower section of neck opening, and 50 sts. up right side of opening. [148 sts.]
Work 8 rows of g.st. Cast off loosely.
Now pick up and knit 70 sts. evenly around armhole edge, beg. at armhole edge.
Work 8 rows of g.st. Cast off loosely.

MAKING UP

Sew up side seams including bands. Press lightly with damp cloth and warm iron.

Thigh-length Silk Coolie Coat

1934

Straight coat in linen stitch, with wide, cuffed, set-in sleeves, straight collar in moss stitch, and patch pockets

★ Suitable for beginners

MATERIALS

Yarn
Sunbeam Shantung
26(28:30:32) × 25g. balls

Needles
1 pair 4mm.
1 pair 5½mm.

Buttons
1

MEASUREMENTS

Bust
82(87:92:97) cm.
32(34:36:38) in.

Length
72(74:75:76) cm.
28¼(29:29½:29¾) in.

Sleeve Seam (with cuff turned up)
45 cm.
17¾ in.

TENSION

11½ sts. and 15 rows = 5 cm. (2 in.) square over pattern on 5½mm. needles, using DOUBLE yarn. If your tension square does not correspond to these measurements, see page 166 for adjustment instructions.

ABBREVIATIONS

k. = knit; p. = purl; st(s). = stitch(es); inc. = increas(ing) (see page 166); dec. = decreas-(ing) (see page 167); beg. = begin(ning); rem. = remain(ing); rep. = repeat; alt. = alternate; tog. = together; sl. = slip stitch (transfer one stitch from left needle, knit-wise unless otherwise stated, to right hand needle.); cont. = continue; patt. = pattern; foll. = following; folls. = follows; mm. = millimetres; cm. = centimetre(s); in. = inch(es); sl.1 p. = slip one st. purl-wise.
NOTE: Use two strands of yarn throughout.

BACK

Cast on 115(121:127:133) sts. with 4mm. needles.
Change to 5½mm. needles and patt.
1st row (wrong side): * k.1, sl.1p. with yarn at front, rep. from * to the last st., k.1.
2nd row: k.1, * p.1, sl.1p. with yarn at back, rep. from * to the last 2 sts., p.1, k.1.
These 2 rows form patt.
Work 21 more rows.
Dec. 1 st. at each end of next row, and

then every 22nd row until 103(109:115:121) sts. rem.
Work until back measures 51(51:52:52) cm. (20(20:20½:20½) in.) from beg., ending with a wrong side row (mark each end of last row to indicate start of armholes).

Shape Raglans

Dec. 1 st. at each end of every row until 89(95:97:103) sts. rem., and then every alt. row until 33(35:35:37) sts. rem., ending with a wrong side row.
Cast off.

LEFT FRONT.

** Cast on 61(63:67:69) sts. with 4mm. needles.
Change to 5½mm. needles and patt.
Work 23 rows.
Dec. 1 st. at side edge on next row, and then every 22nd row until 55(57:61:63) sts. rem.
Work until front measures same as back to armholes, ending with a wrong side row.
** (Mark end of last row to indicate start of armhole).

Shape Raglan

Dec.1 st. at armhole edge on every row until 48(50:52:54) sts. rem., and then every alt. row until 27(27:28:28) sts. rem., ending at front edge.

Shape Neck

Next row: cast off 8(8:9:9) sts., work to end.
Cont. to dec. for raglan on next and foll. alt. rows, and at the same time dec. 1 st. at neck edge on the next 6 rows, and then the 4 foll. alt. rows.
k.2 tog. and fasten off.

RIGHT FRONT

Follow instructions for left front from ** to ** having decreasings at opposite edge. (Mark beg. of last row to indicate start of armhole).

Shape Raglan

Dec. 1 st. at armhole edge on every row until 48(50:52:54) sts. rem., and then every alt. row until 27(27:28:28) sts. rem., ending at armhole edge.

Shape Neck

Next row: work to last 8(8:9:9) sts., cast off these sts. Break yarn.
Turn and rejoin yarn to rem. sts. at neck edge and complete to match left front.

SLEEVES

Cast on 51(53:55:57) sts. with 4mm. needles.
Change to 5½mm. needles and patt. as back.
Work 11 rows.
Inc. 1 st. at each end of next row, and then every 10th(9th:8th:8th) row until there are 75(79:83:87) sts.
Work until sleeve measures 44 cm. (17¼ in.) from beg., ending with a wrong side row. (Mark each end of last row to indicate start of sleeve top).
Work 2(2:4:4) more rows.

Shape Top

Dec. 1 st. at each end of next row, and then every alt. row until 11 sts. rem.
Work 1 row. Cast off.

COLLAR

Cast on 93(93:97:97) sts. with 4mm. needles.
1st row: k.2, * p.1, k.1, rep. from * to the last st., k.1.
2nd row: * k.1, p.1, rep. from * to the last st., k.1.
Rep. 1st and 2nd rows until collar measures 6.5 cm. (2½ in.) from beg., ending with 2nd row.

Change to 5½mm. needles and work 6.5 cm. (2½ in.) in patt., ending with 2nd row.
Cast off.

POCKETS (2)

Cast on 33 sts. with 4mm. needles.
Change to 5½mm. needles.
Work 15 cm. (5¾ in.) in patt. ending with 2nd row.
Cast off.

CUFFS (2)

Cast on 51(53:55:57) sts. with 4mm. needles.
Change to 5½mm. needles.
Work 11 cm. (4¼ in.) in patt., ending with 2nd row.
Cast off.

MAKING UP

Press each piece lightly on the wrong side with warm iron and damp cloth.

Sew cast off edge of cuffs to cast on edge of sleeves so that patt. is reversed.
Sew up raglan seams. Sew up side and sleeve seams, reversing the seam at cuffs.
Turn up cuff.
Sew pockets in position.
Sew cast on edge of collar to neck edge, leaving 1 cm. (½ in.) open for buttonhole at right side, starting 1 cm. (½ in.) from front edge.
Press seams lightly.
Sew on button.

Collarless Checked Mohair Coat

1963

Thigh-length, borderless coat with three-quarter length sleeves and neck facing, in checked stocking stitch pattern worked from chart

★★★ Suitable for experienced knitters

MATERIALS

Yarn
Hayfield Aspen Mohair
10(11) × 25g. balls in colour A
9(10) × 25g. balls in colour B

Needles
1 pair 10mm.

MEASUREMENTS

Bust
82–87(92–97) cm.
32–34(36–38) in.

Length (at centre back)
82(83) cm.
32¼(32½) in.

Sleeve Seam
36 cm.
14 in.

TENSION

13 sts. and 11 rows = 10 cm. (4 in.) square over pattern on 10mm. needles. If your tension square does not correspond to these measurements see page 166 for adjustment instructions.

ABBREVIATIONS

k. = knit; p. = purl; st(s). = stitch(es); inc. = increas(ing) (see page 166); dec. = decreas-(ing) (see page 167); beg. = begin(ning); rem. = remain(ing); rep. = repeat; alt. = alternate; tog. = together; sl. = slip stitch (transfer one stitch from left needle, knit-wise unless otherwise stated, to right hand needle.); cont. = continue; patt. = pattern; foll. = following; folls. = follows; mm. = millimetres; cm. = centimetre(s); in. = inch(es); reqd. = required; st.st. = stocking stitch.
NOTE: Entire coat is in st.st. with check pattern worked from chart. (Carry yarn LOOSELY at back of work. When working more than 3 sts. weave yarn every 3rd or 4th st. to prevent long strands, see page 168).

BACK

Beg. at lower side of left sleeve.
With A cast on 3 sts. Join in B.
1st row: k.1A, 1B, (1A, 1B) into last st.
2nd row: p.1A, 1B, 2A, cast on 6 sts.
3rd row: k.(1A, 1B) 3 times, 1A, 2B, k. twice into last st. with B.
4th row: p.5B, (1A, 1B) 3 times, cast on 6 sts.
5th row: k.6B, (1A, 1B) 3 times, 1A, 3B, k. twice into last st. with B.
6th row: p.6B, (1A, 1B) twice, 1A, 7B, cast on 6 sts.
7th row: k.(1A, 1B) twice, 1A, 7B, (1A, 1B) 3 times, 1A, 4B, k. twice into last st. with B.

Collarless Checked Mohair Coat

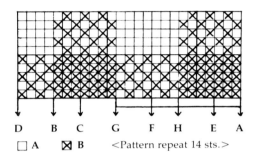

D B C G F H E A

□ A   ☒ B   <Pattern repeat 14 sts.>

8th row: p.(1B, 1A) twice, 1B, 9A, (1B, 1A) twice, 1B, 6A, cast on 4 sts.
9th row: k.1A, 1B, 7A, (1B, 1A) 3 times, 1B, 7A, (1B, 1A) twice, 1B, (1A, 1B) into last st.
10th row: p.(1A, 1B) 3 times, 9A, (1B, 1A), twice, 1B, 9A, 1B, cast on 4 sts.
11th row: * k.(1A, 1B) 3 times, 7A, 1B, rep. from * once more, (1A, 1B) twice, 1A, (1B, 1A) into last st.
12th row: p.2A, * (1B, 1A) twice, 1B, 9A, rep. from * once more, (1B, 1A) twice, 1B, cast on 4 sts.
13th row: k.1A, 1B, 1A, * 7B, (1A, 1B) 3 times, 1A, rep. from * once more, 7B, (1A, 1B) into last st.
14th row: * p.1A, 9B, (1A, 1B) twice, rep. from * once more, 1A, 9B, 1A, 1B, cast on 4 sts.
15th row: k. * (1A, 1B) 3 times, 1A, 7B, rep. from * twice more, 1A, (1B, 1A) into last st.
16th row: p.1B, 1A, * 9B, (1A, 1B) twice, 1A, rep. from * twice more, 1B, cast on 3 sts. [48 sts.] ***
Break yarn and leave sts. on spare needle.

Work Lower Back
Cast on 77(91) sts. with A.
p. 1 row. k. 1 row. p. 1 row.
Join in B and beg. working patt. from chart, working k. rows from point A and p. rows from point B. Work 20 rows.
Keeping patt. correct dec. 1 st. each end of next and every 10th row until 71(85) sts. rem.
Work 13 rows, ending with 4th row of patt.
Break yarn and leave sts. on spare needle.

Right Sleeve
Cast on 3 sts. with A.
1st row: k.(1B, 1A) into first st., 1B, 1A, cast on 6 sts.
2nd row: p.8A, 1B, 1A.

3rd row: k.2B into first st., 2B, (1A, 1B) 3 times, 1A, cast on 6 sts with B.
4th row: p.7B, (1A, 1B) twice, 1A, 5B.
5th row: k.2B into first st., 3B, (1A, 1B) 3 times, 1A, 6B, cast on 6 sts. with A, weaving B.
6th row: p.(1B, 1A) twice, 9B, (1A, 1B) twice, 1A, 6B.
7th row: k.2B into first st., 4B, (1A, 1B) 3 times, 1A, 7B, (1A, 1B) twice, 1A, cast on 4 sts.
8th row: p.1B, 9A, (1B, 1A) twice, 1B, 9A, (1B, 1A) twice, 1B.
9th row: k.(1B, 1A) into first st, (1B, 1A) twice, 1B, 7A, (1B, 1A) 3 times, 1B, 7A, 1B, 1A, cast on 4 sts.
10th row: p.(1B, 1A) twice, 1B, 9A, (1B, 1A) twice, 1B, 9A, (1B, 1A) 3 times.
11th row: k.(1A, 1B) into first st., (1A, 1B) 3 times, 7A, (1B, 1A) 3 times, 1B, 7A, (1B, 1A) 3 times, cast on 4 sts.
12th row: p.4A, (1B, 1A) twice, 1B, 9A, (1B, 1A) twice, 1B, 9A, (1B, 1A) 3 times, 1B.
13th row: k.(1B, 1A) into first st., * 7B, (1A, 1B) 3 times, 1A, rep. from * once more, 7B, 1A, 1B, 1A, cast on 4 sts.
14th row: p.(1B, 1A) 3 times, * 9B, (1A, 1B) twice, 1A, rep. from * once more, 9B, 1A.
15th row: k.(1A, 1B) into first st., 1A, * 7B, (1A, 1B) 3 times, 1A, rep. from * twice more, cast on 3 sts. [48 sts.]
16th row: p.4B, * (1A, 1B) twice, 1A, 9B, rep. from * twice more, 1A, 1B.
17th row: k.(1B, 1A) into first st., work in patt. to end, ** then across sts. of back and left sleeve to last st., (1A, 1B) into last st. [169(183) sts.]
Working from chart and keeping patt. correct, inc. 1 st. each end of every k. row twice more. [173(187) sts.]
Work 1 row.

Shape Upper Sleeves and Shoulders
Cast off at beg. of next and foll. rows 3 sts. 18 times, 5 sts. 6 times and 7 sts. 10(12) times. [154(168) sts.]
Cast off rem. 19 sts. for neck.

LEFT FRONT
Cast on 46(53) sts. with A.
p. 1 row. k. 1 row. p. 1 row.
Join in B and beg. working patt. from chart, working k. rows from points (A to G) 3 times, then G to C(D) once, and p. rows from point C(D) to A once, then (G to A) twice.
Work 20 rows.
Dec. 1 st. at beg. of next and every 10th row until 43(50) sts. rem.

Work 13 rows, ending with 4th row of patt. Break off yarn.
Work lower sleeve as for right sleeve of back to **.
Work across sts. of front. [92(99) sts.]
Inc. 1 st. at beg. of next 2 k. rows.
Work 1 row.

**** Shape Upper Sleeve and Shoulder
Cast off at beg. of next and foll. k. rows 3 sts. 9 times, 5 sts. 3 times, and 7 sts. once, ending at front edge. [45(52) sts.]

Shape Neck
1st row: cast off 12(10) sts., p. to end.
2nd row: cast off 7 sts., k. to last 2 sts., k.2 tog.
3rd row: p.2 tog., p. to end.
Rep. last 2 rows once (twice) more.
Next row: as 2nd. [7 sts.]
p. 1 row.
Cast off.

RIGHT FRONT
Follow instructions for left front, working k. rows from points E(F) to B once, then (H to B) 2(3) times and p. rows from (B to H) 2(3) times and B to E(F) once. Work dec. at end of rows instead of beg.
Work 12 rows after last dec., ending with a 3rd row.
For sleeve work as for left sleeve back to ***.
Now work across sts. of front. [91(98) sts.]
Inc. 1 st. at end of next 3 k. rows.
Now finish as for left front from ****, reading p. for k. and k. for p.

NECK FACING
Cast on 10 sts. with A.
1st row: k. twice into first st., k.7, k.2 tog.
2nd row: p. to end.
Rep. last 2 rows until band measures 38 cm.(15 in.) from cast on sts., ending with a p. row.
Next row: k.2 tog., k. to last 2 sts. k.2 tog.
Next row: p. to last 2 sts. p.2 tog.
Rep. last 2 rows until 2 sts. rem.
Cast off.

MAKING UP
Do not press.
Sew up shoulders. Sew up sleeve seams. Sew up side seams. Turn up 4 cm.(1½ in.) hems on sleeves and 4 rows at lower edge, slipstitch. Turn back 4 sts. down front edges and slipstitch. Sew facing to neck, right sides together, turn to wrong side and slipstitch.

KNITTING KNOW-HOW

Here are all the knitting basics which you will need to know in order to make full use of 'Knitting in Vogue'. Whether you're a beginner, or need a refresher course, it's a good idea to familiarize yourself with the techniques drawn and described on the following pages before you begin to knit. There are sections covering all the knitting basics: casting on, knitting and purling, notes on simple stitch patterns, tension, increasing and decreasing, the finishing touches, casting off and making up. And if a disaster occurs, there is a problem section with diagrams to show you how, for example, to pick up dropped stitches, how to unpick your work. Finally, there is a section covering care of knitted garments, with notes on cleaning, and explanations of the international code symbols used on yarn ball bands.

Starting to Knit from a Pattern

Yarn: Use the yarn specified in the pattern (or the equivalents detailed on page 174) to achieve perfect results. The weight and type of yarn used for each pattern has been chosen for two reasons: firstly, because it can be knitted at a tension which produces standard sizings, and secondly, because it corresponds as closely as possible in character to the yarn originally used. Buy all your yarn at once, checking that dye lots are identical. Colour differences between lots are often marked and you will not achieve satisfactory results from a mixture.

Tension: Always check by knitting a sample square (see page 166 for more tension details) and, if necessary, change your needle size. The needle size given in the pattern will, in many cases, produce the correct tension but, since every knitter's tension varies slightly, there can be no one yarn/needle combination to suit everyone.

Sizes: The smallest size is always printed first, larger sizes following in brackets. This system applies throughout the pattern wherever instructions differ according to size, and wherever one instruction is given, it applies to all sizes. It is a good idea to mark the size you are knitting, in pencil, throughout the pattern (which can, of course be rubbed out later) to prevent mistakes.

Abbreviations: These are used to save space in knitting instructions and are explained at the head of each pattern. It is advisable to familiarize yourself with these before starting to knit. Asterisks (*) are used where a section of the pattern is to be repeated, in order to save space. The asterisk will appear beside a pattern section. Where the pattern is to be repeated the wording reads 'repeat from *'. Where more than one section is to be repeated, two or three asterisks may be used for differentiation.

Charts: These are used for multi-coloured patterns. Each square of the graph paper denotes one stitch and one row. Colours are indicated by symbols. When working in stocking stitch row 1 (at the bottom of the chart) and all odd-numbered rows are knit rows, worked from right to left. Even numbered rows are purl, and worked from left to right. For further details on multicoloured knitting see page 168.

Keeping your place: Mark your pattern at each stage. The easiest way to make a mistake is to lose your place. Use a ruler to underline the row which you have reached, or a card marker. Where you have to count rows, for example when increasing, use a stitch counter (available from knitting departments and shops) on your needle, or make a note of each row you knit.

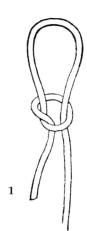

1

Casting On

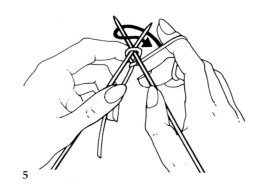

5

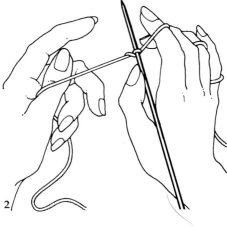

2

There are several methods of casting on stitches, each of which creates a slightly different first row of loops on the needle. The simplest method to learn is the thumb method, which is therefore a good starting point for beginners. All the methods begin with a slip loop (fig 1), which is made as follows:

1. Make an X twist of wool around your thumb.
2. Pull lower right half of this X through upper right half using needle point, and pull yarn end to tighten.

Thumb method

1. Make a slip loop as above, leaving an end of yarn about a metre (yard) long. Put loop on needle.
2. Draw up both ends of yarn to tighten the loop. Take the needle in your right hand (fig 2), holding the yarn end in your left hand, main yarn in your right hand, as shown.
3. Wind the yarn around your left hand in an X shape and put the needle through the loop (fig 3). Wind the main yarn around the needle and draw this loop through (fig 4).
4. Leave this stitch on the needle and repeat the process from step 3. until the required number of stitches have been made. For an extra strong edge, you can double the loose end of yarn.
This method of casting on produces an elastic, hard-wearing edge.

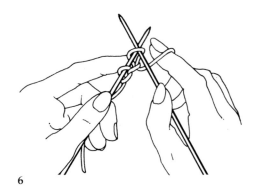

6

3

Cable method with 2 needles

1. Make a slip loop on the left-hand needle.
2. Put the right-hand needle into the loop and wind the yarn round it (fig 5).
3. Draw the yarn through the loop on the left-hand needle with right needle and transfer loop to the left-hand needle (fig 6).
4. Put the right-hand needle between the last two stitches on the left-hand needle (fig 7), and wind the yarn around the right-hand needle as before. Draw the loop through and transfer the stitch onto the left-hand needle (fig 8).
5. Repeat step 4. until the required number of stitches have been made.
This method of casting on produces a firm edge, and can be used where casting on is necessary within the garment as well as to begin the work. For a slightly less firm finish, put the needle into the stitch *knitwise* in step 4. instead of between stitches.

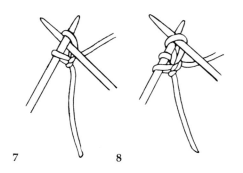

7   8

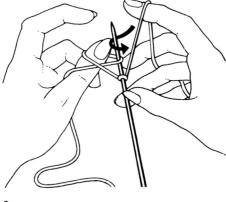

4

Cable method with 4 needles

Use four needles with points at both ends for this method.

1. With two needles, cast on the number of stitches for one needle on first needle.
2. With the third and second needles cast on the required number of stitches for the second needle, likewise with the following needle.
3. Ensure that the stitches are not twisted, draw the last stitch on the third needle up close to the first stitch on the first needle, for the next row, forming a triangle (fig 9). The right side of the work will always be on the outside of the triangle.
This method of casting on produces a firm edge.

Knitting and Purling

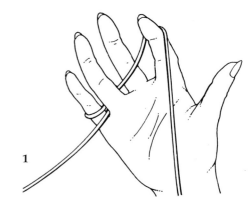

Casting on with a circular needle

1. Cast on the required number of stitches using the cable method for two needles.
2. Draw the last stitch on the needle up close to the first to prevent a loose stitch. The right side of the work is always on the outside of the circle.

Looped method with 1 needle

1. Make a slip loop on the needle, which should be held in the right hand.
2. Loop the yarn around the left thumb, and put the loop on the needle (fig 10).
3. Repeat step **2.** until the required number of stitches have been made.
This method of casting on produces a very loose cast on edge, which is suitable for lacy patterns and for hems which are to be knitted up.

Once you have created your first row of loops, or stitches, (see preceding pages) you can begin to knit. Use long, firm needles, for they are the easiest to manipulate, and the right needle can be held under your right arm to give your right hand complete freedom to knit. In order to achieve firm, even tension, it is essential to have complete control of the yarn, one simple method of achieving this is shown below.

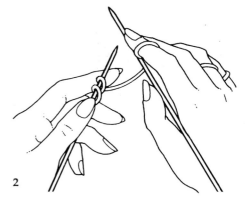

How to hold the yarn and prepare to knit

1. Wind the yarn around the little finger of your right hand, over your third finger, under the second and over the index finger (fig 1).
2. Rest the right-hand needle between thumb and the palm of the hand. Allow the needle to slide between thumb and hand, using only the index finger to manipulate the yarn (fig 2).

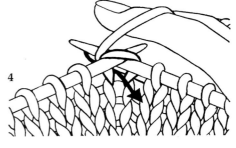

Knit stitch

1. With the needle containing the cast on stitches in your left hand and the wool at the back of the work, put the right-hand needle through the front of the first stitch from right to left (fig 3).
2. Wind the yarn around the right-hand needle between the two needle points with the index finger (fig 4), and turn the right needle slightly to pull the new loop of wool through the old loop and onto the right-hand needle. Slip the old stitch off the left-hand needle.
Repeat this process until all the stitches are knitted. *Abbreviation: 'k.'*. The side of the work facing you while knitting is known as the 'knit' side.

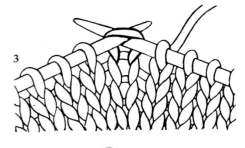

Purl stitch

1. With the needle containing the cast on stitches in your left hand and the wool at the front of the work, put the right-hand needle through the front of the first stitch, from right to left (fig 5).
2. Wind the yarn around the right-hand needle from above with the index finger (fig 6), and turn the right-hand needle slightly to pull the new loop of yarn through the old loop and onto the right-hand needle. Slip the old stitch off the left-hand needle.
Repeat this process until all the stitches are purled. *Abbreviation: 'p.'*. The side of

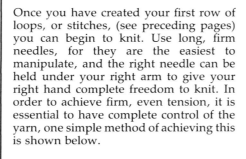
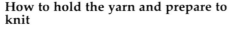

9

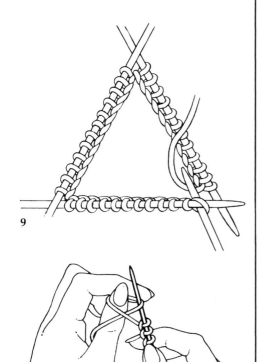

10

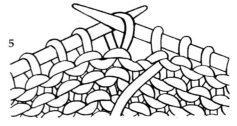

the work facing you while purling is called the 'purl' side.

Stitch notes

Some knitters find that slipping the first stitch in every row and knitting the last gives an extra firm and even selvedge to the work.

Garter stitch

This is one of the simplest for beginners, achieved by knitting every row. Purling every row would achieve a similar effect. *Abbreviation: 'g.st.'.*

Stocking stitch

One row purl, one row knit. *Abbreviation: 'st.st.'.* The knit side of the fabric is usually treated as the 'right' side, but some patterns are worked in 'reversed stocking stitch' (*abbreviated as rev.st.st.*), when the purl side is treated as the right side.

Ribbing

Ribbing can be worked in various widths, the most usual being one stitch knit, one stitch purl. This is worked as follows: k.1, *bring the yarn forward, p.1, bring the yarn back, k.1, rep. from * to end. On the following row all the knit sts. (which appear as purl sts. on the opposite side) will be purled, and all the purl sts. (which appear as knit sts. on the opposite side) will be knitted. For a chunkier rib, the stitch combination might be k.2, p.3, or k.2, p.2, instead of k.1, p.1, but the pattern will be worked in exactly the same way, reversing the type of stitch on the following row. Ribbing is usually referred to in patterns as 'rib'.

Moss stitch

This stitch is derived from ribbing. On the first row the stitches are alternated as for ribbing, and as for ribbing the number of stitches worked in each block vary. On the second row all the knit stitches are knitted, and all the purl stitches are purled. A 'single' moss stitch pattern, i.e. one stitch purl, one stitch plain, will work thus on an even number of stitches: k.1, p.1 to end; the second row will work thus: p.1, k.1 to end. *Abbreviation: 'm.st.'.*

Tension

'Tension' means the number of rows and stitches in a given measurement over the knitted fabric. Since every knitting pattern is based on a particular ratio of these, it is essential to check your tension before beginning to knit a new pattern. Personal tension is very variable and adjustments in needle sizes are often necessary. In particular, when the yarn suggested in the pattern is unavailable and an equivalent has to be used, great care in checking tension is necessary. There are tremendous variations in thickness between yarns of the same 'ply': the importance of checking tension cannot be overstressed.

How to check your tension

1. Work a small square, measuring at least 10 cm. (4 in.), in the pattern stitch or that mentioned in tension section.
2. Put the work on a flat surface, and, using a rigid ruler, measure 5 cm. (2 in.), (or the measurement suggested in the pattern) across stitches and rows. Carefully mark this square with pins.
3. If there are more rows or stitches in the pinned area than there should be, your tension is too tight and you should work a new sample using larger needles.
4. If there are too few stitches or rows in the pinned area, your tension is too loose and you should work a new sample using smaller needles.
Continue in this way until you have achieved the correct tension for the pattern. A variation from that suggested in the pattern by even as much as ½ stitch or row could mean that the garments will be a size smaller or larger, and the effect of the stitch too loose or tight for the design. Where a substitute yarn has been used it is sometimes impossible to obtain the correct width and depth tension. In this case the width tension should be obtained and the depth adjusted by working more or less rows as required.

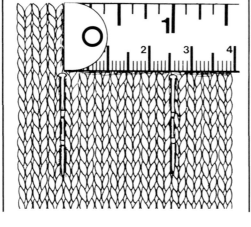

Shaping: Increasing

Knitting is shaped by the addition and subtraction of stitches. There are many different ways of doing this, some purely functional, some decorative too. Single stitches can be increased or decreased at any point in the row, groups of stitches are increased or decreased by casting on and casting off at the end of rows.

Casting on

This method is used where blocks of stitches are to be added. Cast on the required number of stitches at the beginning of a row using the cable method (see page 164), or at the end of a row by the looped method (see page 165).

Simple increasing

1. On a knit row: increase one stitch by knitting first into the front and then into the back of the same stitch. Slip stitch off left-hand needle, (fig 1).
On a purl row: increase one stitch by purling first into the front and then into the back of the same stitch. *Abbreviation: 'inc. 1 st.'.*

2. On a knit or a purl row: increase one stitch by knitting (or purling) the stitch below the next stitch on the left-hand needle, and then knitting (or purling) the next stitch on the left-hand needle, (fig 2). *Abbreviation: 'k.1 up'.*

3. On a knit or a purl row: increase one stitch by picking up the loop lying between the needles, knitwise or purlwise, using the right-hand needle. Put the loop onto the left-hand needle and knit or purl into the back of it, (fig 3). *Abbreviation: 'm. 1'.*

Decorative increasing

These methods produce a series of holes in the fabric which can be used to create lacy patterns.
1. On a knit row: increase one stitch by bringing the yarn forward between needles (as for a purl stitch), then carrying the yarn over the needle to knit the stitch in the usual way, (fig 4). *Abbreviation: 'y.fwd.'.*

2. On a purl row: increase one stitch by bringing the yarn over and round the right-hand needle, then purling the stitch in the usual way, (fig 5). *Abbreviation: 'y.r.n.'.*

3. Between a purl and a knit stitch: increase one stitch by taking the yarn from the front of the work over the needle, then knitting the next stitch in the usual way, (fig 6). *Abbreviation: 'y.o.n.'.*

Shaping: Decreasing

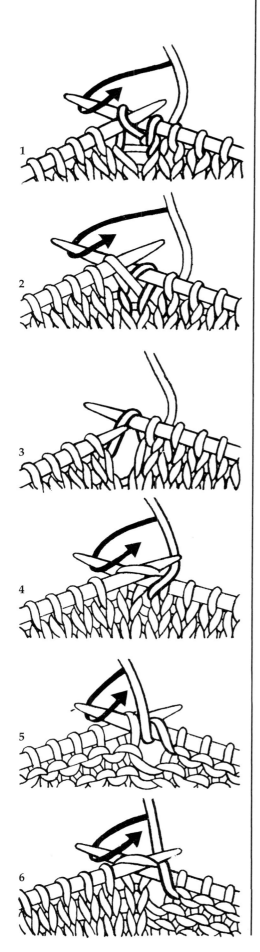

Casting off

This method is used where blocks of stitches are to be removed, for example at shoulder or neck. Casting off should be worked loosely, particularly at the neck (to allow for stretch in wear), and it is often helpful to use a size larger needle.

Simple decreasing

1a. On a knit row: decrease one stitch by putting the right-hand needle knit-wise into second and then first stitch, then knitting them together in the usual manner (fig 1). *Abbreviation: 'k.2 tog.'.*

b. On a purl row: decrease one stitch by putting the right-hand needle purl-wise through the first and then second stitches and purling them together in the usual manner (fig 2). *Abbreviation: 'p.2 tog.'*

c. On a purl row: decrease one stitch by putting the right-hand needle through the back of the first and then second stitches on the left-hand needle and purling them together in the usual manner (fig 3). *Abbreviation: 'p.2 tog. t.b.l'.*

2. On a knit row: decrease one stitch by slipping the next stitch purlwise on to the right-hand needle. Knit the next stitch, put the point of the left-hand needle purl-wise into the slipped stitch and slip it over the knitted stitch and off the needle (fig 4). *Abbreviation: 'sl. 1, k. 1, p.s.s.o.'.*

3. On a knit row: decrease two stitches by putting the right-hand needle through the next three stitches and knitting them together in the usual manner (fig 5). *Abbreviation: 'k.3 tog.'.*

4. On a knit row: decrease two stitches by slipping the next stitch purlwise. Knit the next two stitches together, then put the point of the left-hand needle purlwise into the slipped stitch and slip it over the stitches knitted together and off the needle (fig 6). *Abbreviation: 'sl. 1, k. 2 tog., p.s.s.o.'.*

Decorative decreasing

Decreased stitches lean either to left or right. Different methods of decreasing, *see above*, can thus be used to create patterns. For example, 'sl. 1, k. 1, p.s.s.o.' is used on the decreased edge of raglan sleeves.
Of the methods above:
1a., **1b.** and **4.** lean to the right;
1c., **2.** and **3.** lean to the left.

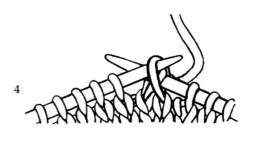

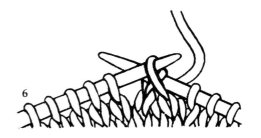

Problems

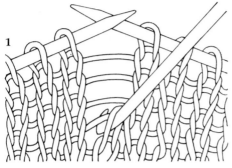

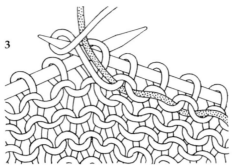

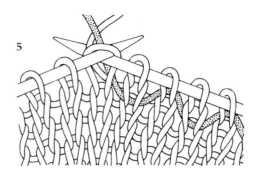

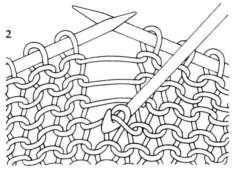

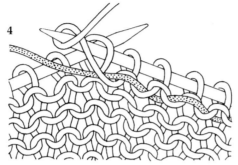

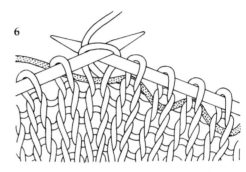

Keeping work clean and evenly knitted

Never leave your knitting in the middle of a row, or an uneven stitch will result. Don't stick your needles into the ball of wool, because this splits the yarn. When knitting very furry or pale yarns, it may be helpful to pin a polythene bag or linen cloth over the finished work to keep it clean.

Dropped stitches

Even if the stitch has dropped several rows, it is usually very simple to pick it up again using a crochet hook.

1. On a knit row (fig 1), with right side facing:
a. Insert crochet hook from the front into the dropped stitch.
b. Put hook under the thread above the stitch and pull it through the stitch.
c. Continue in this way until the dropped stitch is level with the rest of the work.

2. On a purl row (fig 2), with wrong side facing:
a. Insert the crochet hook between the bottom and second threads lying above the dropped stitch, then into the stitch from back to front.
b. Draw the thread through the stitch.
c. Put the new stitch onto a spare needle. Insert hook between the next two threads as in step a. pick up stitch from needle and draw thread through.

If you are knitting in pattern, it may be impossible to pick up dropped stitches in this manner. Unpicking will then be necessary.

Unpicking mistakes

If you make a mistake don't tear your work off the needles. Unpicking may be time-consuming, but it is simple and, when worked as below, will prevent your dropping any stitches in the process.

1. On a knit row:
a. With the knit side facing you, put the right-hand needle into the stitch below the first stitch on your left-hand needle.
b. Gently pull the first stitch off the left-hand needle and pull the yarn out of the stitch on your left-hand needle, leaving it at the back of the work.
c. Continue in this way until you have unpicked the required number of stitches.

2. On a purl row:
With the purl side of the work facing you, proceed as above, remembering that the yarn will unravel at the front of the work instead of the back.

Running out of yarn

Yarn should always be joined in at the end of a row, for best results, with a loose knot which can later be untied, and the yarn ends darned in. Splicing, an invisible method of joining yarn, is sometimes used by experienced knitters in mid-row, but it creates a weak join. If you inadvertently run out of yarn in mid-row, unpick to the beginning of the row and join there.

Snagging

If you catch your work and pull a thread, you can rectify this by easing the stitches on the same row gently with a crochet

hook or a knitting needle until the loop disappears. If the snag is really bad, you can either unpick, or pull the loop through to the back of the work and ease the stitches around it.

Working with several colours:

There are two methods of dealing with the spare colours running behind the work. Over small pattern repeats, up to four or five stitches, the stranding method is used, over large pattern repeats the weaving method is used. Some patterns combine the two.

Weaving method

Carry the yarn not in use over the yarn in use for one stitch (fig 3, purl row; fig 5, knit row), and under it for the next stitch (fig 4, purl row; fig 6, knit row), on the wrong side of the work. As with the stranding method, the yarns should be carried loosely to prevent pulling of the work.

Stranding method

Carry the yarn not in use loosely along the back of the work, being careful not to pull it too tightly when picking it up to use again (fig. 7).
See page 163 for notes on working from pattern charts.

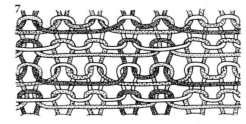

Casting Off

Casting off is used both at the end of a piece of work, to fasten off all the stitches, and also to decrease blocks of stitches within the work, such as at shoulder and underarm. Casting off should be worked loosely, often a larger size needle makes this easier. Where a block of stitches is cast off at the end of a row, the yarn must be broken off and rejoined at the beginning of the following row.

Simple casting off

On a knit row
1. Knit the first two stitches.
2. Lift the first stitch over the second with the point of the left-hand needle (fig 1).
3. Drop the first stitch off the needle leaving the second on the right-hand needle.
4. Knit one stitch.
5. Repeat steps 2. to 4. inclusive until the required number of stitches have been cast off. If block decreasing, cast off number of stitches required and knit to end of row (fig 2). If finishing off work, continue until one stitch remains. Break off yarn leaving an end of 15 cm. (5¾ in.). Draw end through remaining stitch and pull tight.

On a purl row
1. Purl the first two stitches. Keep yarn forward.
2. As above (fig 3).
3. As above.
4. Purl one stitch.
5. Repeat steps 2. to 4. inclusive until the required number of stitches have been cast off. If block decreasing, cast off the number of stitches required and purl to end of row (fig 4). If finishing off work, continue until one stitch remains. Break off yarn leaving an end of 15 cm. (5¾ in.). Draw end through remaining stitch and pull tight.

Casting off in pattern

Cast off each stitch by knitting or purling it according to the pattern being knitted. Where casting off a block, cast off in pattern and continue to work in pattern to end of row.

Casting off on 4 needles

This is done exactly as on two needles, except for the adjoining stitches at each end of needles, worked as follows each time:
1. Cast off to last stitch on needle.
2. Knit (or purl) first stitch on next needle.
3. Cast off last stitch on needle by lifting it over the first on the next needle.

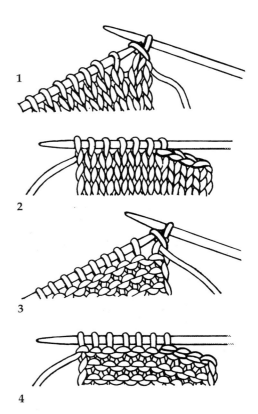

1

2

3

4

Finishing Touches

Knitting with sequins
Thread sequins onto yarn as follows:
1. Fold a 25 cm. (9¾ in.) length of sewing cotton in half, thread a needle with the cut ends.
2. Pass 20 cm. (7¾ in.) of the knitting yarn through the cotton loop, and thread the sequins onto the needle, over the cotton and onto the yarn.

When a sequin is required
1. Knit to position of sequin, slide sequin down yarn and position close to work.
2. Knit the next stitch through the back of the loop in the usual manner, pushing the sequin through the stitch to the front of the work (fig 1).

Swiss darning

Swiss darning is a type of embroidery used on knitted fabric to create a pattern which appears knitted-in. It is worked on stocking stitch, using a yarn of similar weight to that of the piece of work.

1. Thread a blunt darning needle with the yarn. Insert needle from back to front of the work at the centre of the first stitch to be embroidered over.
2. Following fig 2, insert the needle behind both strands of the stitch above.
3. Then thread the needle through the two next strands below, as marked by the arrow in fig 2. Be careful to ensure that the tension of the embroidery matches that of

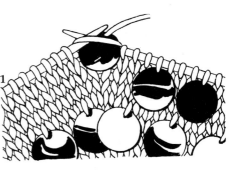

1

2

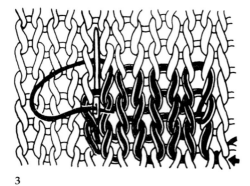

3

the original work, to prevent the fabric pulling.

4. Where the embroidery is to cover several rows, complete one row as above and insert the needle under the upper loop of the last stitch (fig 3). Turn the work upside down and continue with steps **1.** to **3.** and reverse again for following row.

Buttonholes

The patterns detail how and when buttonholes are to be made. You can alter their size by adding or taking away stitches to be cast off (on the armhole edge) on a horizontal buttonhole, or by increasing or decreasing the number of rows worked for a vertical buttonhole.

Horizontal buttonholes

1. Loosely cast off required number of stitches. The stitch remaining after casting off is counted as part of the row, NOT of the buttonhole.
2. In the next row, cast on the same number of stitches as were cast off in the previous row (figs 4 and 5).

Vertical buttonholes

1. Divide stitches to form the sides of the buttonhole.

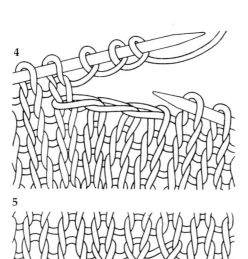

4

5

6

7

2. Work individually to required height, rejoin the two sides.
3. Later, work buttonhole stitch with the end of yarn left when the two sides were joined together, to strengthen the buttonhole.

Working separate front bands

When separate front bands have to be worked, as for a cardigan, it is a good idea to knit both bands simultaneously to ensure that they are exactly the same length. As you knit the buttonholes mark the button position on the other band.

When measuring the band length ensure that the band is *very* slightly stretched against the main work, otherwise the band will sag in wear.

Knitting up stitches

Always ensure that stitches are picked up evenly, thus count rows or stitches and compare with the number of stitches to be picked up before starting.

Knitting up vertically, used for knitted-on front bands

1. Compare number of stitches to be picked up with number of rows.
2. To pick up each stitch: having yarn at back of work, put needle from front to back of work, pick up a loop of yarn and bring it through to front (fig 6).

Knitting up along straight or curved edges

1. Compare number of stitches to be picked up with the number of stitches along the edge to be worked on.
2. To pick up each stitch: having yarn at back of work, put needle from front to back of work, pick up a loop of yarn and bring it through to front (fig 7).

Making Up

Careful making up is essential to the success of your work. There are pressing and making up instructions on each pattern, which you should follow. Below there are further details on how to block, press, and how to sew up seams to achieve a professional finish.

Blocking and pressing

Only press where this is specifically mentioned in the pattern.

Where the pattern instructs you to press the finished pieces of your garment, proceed as follows (fig 6):
1. Pin each piece, right side downwards, onto a well-padded surface. Do NOT stretch any part of the fabric, be careful to keep rows and stitches in straight lines.
2. Press the fabric, excluding any ribbing, under a damp cloth if specified.
3. Allow fabric to cool and remove pins.
4. Push ribbing together so that only the knit stitches show, pin out carefully and press lightly, again under a damp cloth if specified.

Sewing up seams

Use your knitting yarn to sew up seams wherever possible. If the yarn is very heavy, or very textured, substitute a similar-coloured 4 ply yarn. Your pattern will tell you the order in which to sew up the pieces you have knitted. There are several methods of sewing up seams, of which the backstitch and flat seam methods, below, are the most popular. Backstitch can be used for most seams except ribbing, where flat seaming is used. Flat seaming is also used on fabrics knitted in very fine yarns.

Flat Seam (fig 2)

1. Put the right sides of the two pieces together, matching rows if working on a straight edge.
2. Put your left forefinger between the two pieces of work. Join in yarn with several

1

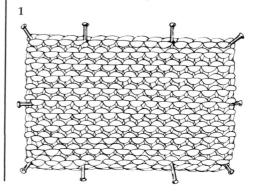

running stitches one over the other at the beginning of the seam.

3. Bring the needle from front to back close to the edge of the fabric, pull yarn through, create a small running stitch by putting needle through the fabric again from back to front, one stitch further on along the fabric.

4. Continue to end, ensuring that the stitches are not drawn too tightly, thus pulling the work. Press (if pressing is recommended for the yarn) under a damp cloth.

Backstitch Seam (fig 3)

1. Put the right sides of the two pieces together, matching rows if working on a straight edge.

2. Join in yarn with several running stitches one over the other at the beginning of the seam.

3. Put needle into right-hand end of the running stitches and bring out at front of work one stitch from the edge of the fabric, and one stitch beyond the left-hand end of the running stitches.

4. Put needle back into work at left-hand end of the running stitches, and bring out to front of work one stitch beyond the stitch created in step 3. Continue in this way taking care not to split stitches. Use running stitches as in step 2. to finish the end of the seam. Press (if pressing is recommended for the yarn) under a damp cloth.

Special seam notes

Shoulder seams: match shapings on both pieces. When stitching, work in a straight line across these shaping steps, in firm backstitch. Press seams on the wrong side. Reinforce with tape, in the case of very heavy garments.

Sleeve and side seams: join with backstitch, using flat seaming for ribbing (and throughout for jumpers in very fine yarns).

Set-in sleeves: mark the centre top of the sleeve and pin to shoulder seam, match cast off stitches in sleeve and armhole and pin together. Pin remaining sloping sides of sleeve evenly into the armhole. Backstitch as near the edge as possible, using fine stitches.

Raglan sleeves: match raglan seams row for row, and stitch using a flat seam, with very small stitches.

Sewn on collars: with right side of collar facing wrong side of the work, pin centre of collar to centre of neckline, and each end of the collar to neckline edges, or position marked in the pattern. Stitch, taking care not to stretch the neckline, as close to the edge as possible.

Hems: where the hem has been marked by a line of knit stitches, or where a length of fabric is to be turned up as hem, this should be pressed, and slipstitched in place.

Lapped seams: place parts to be joined right sides together, with the underneath fabric extending 12mm. (½ in.) beyond the upper part. Backstitch close to the edge, turn to the right side and backstitch again through both layers of fabric 12mm. (½ in.) from the original seam, using small, neat stitches.

Front Bands: sew on using a flat seam.

Zips (fig 4): nylon zips are normally the best type for knitwear. Reinforce the edges of the knitting with a row of double crochet, if necessary, and pin zip in place, taking care not to stretch the knitting. With right side facing, using small backstitches, sew in with fine thread (to match yarn) and needle, as close to the edge of the knitting as possible. Stitch from top to bottom on both sides of the zip. Later, slipstitch the zip edges on the inside.

Yarn ends

Thread each end in turn into a blunt-ended darning needle. Darn neatly into the back of the work, including a couple of back stitches to hold it firmly. Trim end close to work.

Where more than one colour has been used, darn the ends of each into its own colour area.

Ribbon facing

Choose ribbon in a colour to match your yarn. You should allow at least a 6 mm. (¼ in.) hem on either side of the button bands, and a 12mm. (½ in.) hem at top and bottom of both bands.

1. Press the work lightly. Cut the button and buttonhole band facings together so that their length is identical.

2. Fold in all the turnings and press lightly.

3. Pin to the bands on the wrong side, checking that buttonholes are evenly spaced: ease work to adjust this. Slipstitch around the ribbon with matching fine cotton, using tiny stitches.

4. Mitre corners: slipstitch outer seam, fold ribbon at corner and stitch.

5. Cut buttonholes along grain, oversew ribbon and knitting together with sewing cotton, then work buttonhole stitch on top using the original yarn.

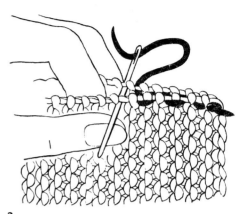

2

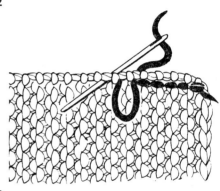

3

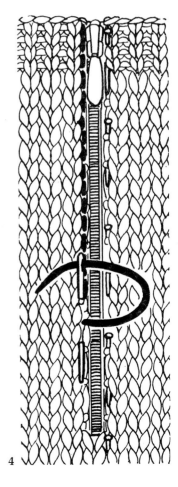

4

Care of Knitwear

Pilling

Many yarns are prone to pilling: this means that loose balls of fibre appear on the surface of the garment. These can be removed very simply with a strip of sticky tape, or with gentle brushing.

Snagging

This, too, can usually be remedied, see description of the process on page 168.

Cleaning knitted garments

The great variety of yarns now on the market has meant that washing instructions need to be individually described for each type: thus ball bands carry cleaning and pressing instructions in the International Textile Care Labelling Code. The symbols are explained briefly opposite.

General guidelines
1. Where the garment should be hand-washed, ensure that soap flakes are thoroughly dissolved before immersing the knitwear, or use Woolite cold water wash. Never use very hot water to wash wool, follow the temperature suggested on the ball band.
2. Rinse thoroughly in tepid water.
3. NEVER wring knitwear roughly by hand, spin briefly in a machine, or squeeze gently, to remove moisture.
4. Unless otherwise stated in the pattern, knitwear should be gently pulled into shape and dried on a clean flat surface.

60°C = Hot, hotter than the hand can bear, the temperature of water from a domestic hot tap.
50°C = Hand-hot, as hot as the hand can bear.
40°C = Warm, pleasantly warm to the hand.
30°C = Cool to the touch.

Can safely be washed by hand or machine. Number above line denotes washing process for machines, figure below it denotes water temperature in °C, see above for temperature details.

Wash *only* by hand.

Must *not* be washed.

Dry cleanable in all solvents.

Dry cleanable in perchloroethylene, white spirit, Solvent 113 and Solvent 11.

Goods sensitive to dry cleaning which may be cleaned with solvents shown for **P**, but with strict limitation on the addition of water during cleaning and/or restrictions concerning mechanical action or drying temperature or both.

Dry cleanable in white spirit and Solvent 113.

Goods sensitive to dry cleaning which may be cleaned with solvents shown for **F** but with a strict limitation on the addition of water during cleaning and/or certain restrictions concerning mechanical action or drying temperature or both.

Do *not* dry clean.

Tumble drying beneficial.

Do *not* tumble dry.

Where a triangle contains the letters **CL** the article can be treated with chlorine bleach. Where the triangle is crossed out chlorine bleach may *not* be used.

Hot iron up to 210°C.

Warm iron up to 160°C.

Cool iron up to 120°C.

Do not iron.

Addresses

If you have any difficulty in obtaining yarns, you can write to the address given below for the head office or agent of the yarn spinner for stockist information. Where there is no agent the address of sole or main stockists are given. Where the yarn is available only by mail order, this address is given.

A.N.I.

Head office and mail orders
A.N.I.
7 St Michael's Mansions
Ship Street
OXFORD OX1 3DG
U.K.

U.S.A. sole stockist
Textile Museum
2320 S Street
WASHINGTON D.C.
U.S.A.

CHAT BOTTE

U.K. agent
Groves of Thame Ltd.
Lupton Road
Industrial Estate
THAME
Oxon.
U.K.

U.S.A. agent
Armen Corporation
P.O. Box 8348
ASHEVILLE
NC 28814
U.S.A.

Canada agent
Districan III
Rue du Port
MONTREAL
Quebec
CANADA

CLECKHEATON

Australia
Cleckheaton
4 Croft Street
HUNTINGDALE
VIC 3166
AUSTRALIA

W. DILTHEY & CO.

U.S.A. agent
Fibercraft
Division of Fiberfolio
37 West 39 Street
NEW YORK N.Y. 10018
U.S.A.

ELLE

S. Africa
Mr J Norris
Consolidated Woolwashing
 and Processing mills Ltd.
P.O. Box 12017
JACOBS 4026
S. AFRICA

EMU

U.K.
Customer Service
Emu Wools
Leeds Road
Greengates
BRADFORD

W. Yorks.
U.K.

U.S.A. agent
Marino Wool Inc.
20th Floor
230 5th av.
NY 10001
U.S.A.

Australia agent and mail orders
Mrs R. Mallett
The Needlewoman
308 Centrepoint
Murray Street
Hobart
TASMANIA 7000

Canada agent
S R Kertzer Ltd.
257 Adelaide Street West
TORONTO N5H M1
Ontario
CANADA

S. Africa agent
Intexma Cape (Pty) Ltd.
P.O. Box 27
Observatory
CAPE 7935
S. AFRICA

HAYFIELD

U.K.
Hayfield Textiles Ltd.
Hayfield Mills
GLUSBURN
Nr. KEIGHLEY
W. Yorks. BD20 8QP
U.K.

U.S.A. and Canada agent
Craftsmen Distributors Inc.
4166 Halifax Street
BURNABY
British Columbia
CANADA

Australia agent
E C Birch Pty. Ltd.
153 Bridge Road
RICHMOND 3121
Victoria
AUSTRALIA

S. Africa
A & H Agencies
392 Commissioners Street
Fair View
JOHANNESBURG 2094
S. AFRICA

JAEGER see PATONS

LAINES ANNY BLATT

U.K. and mail orders
Priory Yarns
48 Station Road
OSSETT
W. Yorks.
U.K.

Head office
Laines Anny Blatt
2 Rue Blanc de Seau
TOURCOING 59200
FRANCE

U.S.A. agent
Irma Markus
29775 North Western Highway
SOUTHFIELD
Michigan 48034
U.S.A.

Canada agent
Diamond Yarn Corporation
9697 St Lawrence Boulevard
MONTREAL
CANADA

LAINES PLASSARD

U.K. and mail orders
Rebecca and David Elliot
Laines Couture
20 Bedford Street
London WC2
U.K.

Head office
Laines Plassard
VARENNES SOUS DUN
La Clayette
FRANCE 71800

U.S.A. agent
Joseph Geller
153 5th Avenue
NEW YORK
U.S.A.

LAINES TIBER

U.K. and mail orders
Rebecca and David Elliot
Laines Couture
20 Bedford Street
London WC2
U.K.

Head office
BP43
59051 ROUBAIX
Cedex 1
FRANCE

LISTER-LEE

U.K.
George Lee & Sons Ltd.
Whiteoak Mills
P.O. Box 37
WAKEFIELD
W. Yorks.

Canada (major stockist)
Mrs Hurtig
Anita Hurtig Imports Ltd.
P.O. Box 6124
Postal Station A

CALGARY
Alberta T2H 2L4
CANADA

Australia
Mrs Pat Coop
Woolcraft, 16 The Mall
WEST HEIDELBERG
3081 AUSTRALIA

Mrs R Mallet
The Needlewoman
308 Centrepoint
Murray Street
Hobart
TASMANIA 7000

U.S.A., S. Africa agent details
Fransha Wools
PO Box 99
Parkside Mills
BRADFORD
Yorks.
U.K.

PATONS and JAEGER

U.K.
Jaeger Handknitting *or*
Patons & Baldwins Ltd.
ALLOA
Clackmannanshire
SCOTLAND
U.K.

Mail orders
Woolfayre Ltd.
120 High Street
Northallerton
W. Yorks.
U.K.

U.S.A.
C J Bates and Sons Ltd.
Route 9a
CHESTER
Connecticut 06412
U.S.A.

Australia agent
Coats & Patons Aust. Ltd.
321–355 Fern Tree Gully Road
P.O. Box 110
MOUNT WAVERLEY
Victoria 3149
AUSTRALIA

Canada agent
Patons & Baldwins (Canada) Ltd.
1001 Roselawn Avenue
TORONTO
CANADA

S. Africa
Mr Bob Theis
Marketing Manager
Patons & Baldwins (S. Africa) Pty.
Ltd.
P.O. Box 33
RANDFONTEIN 1760
S. AFRICA

Continued on page 176

Yarn Conversion Chart

U.K.	U.S.A.	Australia
A.N.I. Scottish Homespun D K	A.N.I. Scottish Homespun D K	Mail order
Chat Botte Acrylique and Alpaga	Chat Botte Acrylique and Alpaga or Chat Botte Dolcevita	Patons Caressa, Scarf: 1 × 50g. ball Sweater: 8(8:9) × 50g. balls
Emu Scotch Superwash Wool 4 ply	Emu Scotch Superwash Wool 4 ply	Emu Scotch Superwash Wool 4 ply
Emu Scotch Superwash Wool D K	Emu Scotch Superwash Wool D K	Emu Scotch Superwash Wool D K
Emu Shetland D K	Emu Shetland D K	Emu Shetland D K
Hayfield Aspen Mohair	Hayfield Aspen Mohair	Hayfield Aspen Mohair or any mohair
Hayfield Beaulon 4 ply	Hayfield Beaulon 4 ply	Hayfield Beaulon 4 ply or any 4 ply
Hayfield Brig D K	Hayfield Brig D K	Hayfield Brig D K or any Hayfield D K
Hayfield Falkland D K	Hayfield Falkland D K	Hayfield Falkland D K or any Hayfield D K
Jaeger Botany Wool 3 ply	York Fingering 3 ply (Patons)	Jaeger Botany Wool 3 ply
Jaeger Langora	Jaeger Langora	Jaeger Langora
Jaeger MatchMaker 4 ply	Lady Galt Kroy 4 ply (Patons)	Jaeger MatchMaker 4 ply
Jaeger Mohair Spun	Molaine Vanessa (Patons)	Jaeger Mohair Spun
Jaeger Naturgarn	Jaeger Naturgarn	Jaeger Naturgarn
Laines Anny Blatt Kid Anny	Laines Anny Blatt Kid Anny	Cleckheaton Country Craft or mail order
Laines Plassard Harmonieuse	Laines Plassard Harmonieuse	Mail order
Laines Tiber Coton Velour	Jaeger Super Chenille, sweater 15(17:18), cardigan 15(17) × 50g. balls, 4½mm. needles	Jaeger Super Chenille, details as U.S.A. column or mail order
Laines Tiber Le Doux Mohair, Superkid	Any mohair used double on 4mm. needles or mail order	Any mohair used double on 4mm. needles or mail order
Lister-Lee Giselle	Lister-Lee Giselle	Lister-Lee Giselle
Lister-Lee Motoravia 4 ply	Lister-Lee Motoravia 4 ply	Lister-Lee Motoravia 4 ply
Lister-Lee Motoravia D K	Lister-Lee Motoravia D K	Lister-Lee Motoravia D K
Lister-Lee Tahiti Mohair	Lister-Lee Tahiti Mohair	Lister-Lee Tahiti Mohair
Patons Beehive Shetland Style Chunky Knitting	Patons Beehive Shetland Style Chunky Knitting	Patons Husky
Patons Capstan	Patons Canadiana Superwash	Patons Wayfarer
Patons Clansman D K	Patons Beehive D K or Patons Matchmaker D K	Patons Husky D K or Patons Hurdwick D K
Pingouin Confort D K	Pingouin Confort D K	Pingouin Confort D K or mail order
Pingouin Coton Naturel 4 ply	Pingouin Coton Naturel 4 ply	Pingouin Coton Naturel 4 ply or mail order
Pingouin Coton Naturel 8 fils	Pingouin Coton Naturel 8 fils	Pingouin Coton Naturel 8 fils or mail order
Pingouin Fil d'Ecosse	Pingouin Fil d'Ecosse	Pingouin Fil d'Ecosse or mail order
Pingouin Iceberg or Pingouin Pingoland	Pingouin Iceberg or Pingoland	Pingouin Iceberg, Pingoland or mail order
Pingouin Laine et Mohair	Pingouin Laine et Mohair	Pingouin Laine et Mohair or mail order
Pingouin Pingolaine 4 ply	Pingouin Pingolaine 4 ply	Pingouin Pingolaine 4 ply or mail order
Pingouin Pingorina	Pingouin Pingorina	Pingouin Pingorina or mail order
Pingouin Type Shetland	Pingouin Type Shetland	Pingouin Type Shetland or mail order
Poppleton Bijou Chunky	Poppleton Bijou Chunky	Mail order or any 12 ply yarn
Poppleton Pica or Poppleton Emmerdale Chunky	Poppleton Pica or Poppleton Emmerdale Chunky	Poppleton Pica or Poppleton Emmerdale Chunky
Robin Aran	Emu Aran	Robin Aran or Emu Aran
Sirdar Country Style 4 ply	Sirdar Country Style 4 ply	Any 4 ply
Sirdar Country Style D K	Sirdar Country Style D K	Any D K
Sirdar Majestic 4 ply	Sirdar Majestic 4 ply	Any 4 ply
Sirdar Sportswool	Sirdar Sportswool	Patons Wayfarer
Sunbeam Aran 4 ply	Mail order or any 4 ply	Mail order or any 4 ply
Sunbeam St. Ives 3 ply	Mail order or any 3 ply	Mail order or any 3 ply
Sunbeam Shantung	Sunbeam Shantung	Sunbeam Shantung or mail order
Templeton's H & O Shetland Fleece	Templeton's H & O Shetland Fleece	Mail order
3 Suisses Aubretia	3 Suisses Aubretia	Villawool Mimosa 11(12:12:12) × 50g. balls 5mm. needles
3 Suisses Barbara	3 Suisses Barbara	Mail order
3 Suisses Suizasport	3 Suisses Suizasport	Patons Husky 7(7:8:9) × 50g. balls 6mm. needles
Twilleys Goldfingering	W. Dilthey London Style 8(8:9) × 20g. balls	Twilleys Goldfingering
Twilleys Lyscordet	Pingouin Fil d'Ecosse 7(8:8:9:9:10) × 50g. balls	Twilleys Lyscordet
Wendy Mohair	Wendy Mohair	Jaeger Mohair Spun on 5½mm. needles
Wendy Shetland 4 ply	Wendy Shetland 4 ply	Any 4 ply
Wendy Pure Wool D K	Wendy Pure Wool D K	Wendy Shetland D K or any D K

Canada	S. Africa
Mail order	Mail order
Chat Botte Acrylique and Alpaga or Chat Botte Dolcevita	Patons Gemstone D K, scarf 1, sweater 8(8:9) × 50g. balls (but without fluffy effect)
Emu Scotch Superwash Wool 4 ply	Any 4 ply
Emu Scotch Superwash Wool D K	Any D K
Emu Shetland D K	Elle Shetland D K
Hayfield Aspen Mohair	Hayfield Aspen Mohair
Hayfield Beaulon 4 ply	Hayfield Beaulon 4 ply
Hayfield Brig D K	Hayfield Brig D K
Hayfield Falkland D K	Hayfield Falkland D K
York Fingering 3 ply (Patons)	Silver Sheen 3 ply (Patons)
Jaeger Langora	Red Heart Carmen Brushed 1(1:1) × 250g. cone
Lady Galt Kroy 4 ply (Patons)	Jaeger Matchmaker 4 ply
Molaine Vanessa (Patons)	Jaeger Mohair Spun
Jaeger Naturgarn	Patons Nomad 27(28:30) × 50g. balls
Laines Anny Blatt Kid Anny	Mail order
Mail order	Mail order
Jaeger Super Chenille, sweater 15(17:18), cardigan 15(17) × 50g. balls, 4½mm. needles	Jaeger Super Chenille, sweater 15(17:18), cardigan 15(17) × 50g. balls, 4½mm. needles
Any mohair used double on 4mm. needles or mail order	Any mohair used double on 4mm. needles or mail order
Lister-Lee Giselle	Lister-Lee Giselle
Lister-Lee Motoravia 4 ply	Lister-Lee Motoravia 4 ply
Lister-Lee Motoravia D K	Lister-Lee Motoravia D K
Lister-Lee Tahiti Mohair	Lister-Lee Tahiti Mohair
Patons Beehive Shetland Style Chunky Knitting	Patons Beehive Shetland Style Chunky Knitting
Patons Canadiana Superwash	Patons Capstan
Patons Beehive D K or Patons Matchmaker D K	Patons Beehive D K
Pingouin Confort D K	Pingouin Confort D K
Pingouin Coton Naturel 4 ply	Pingouin Coton Naturel 4 ply
Pingouin Coton Naturel 8 fils	Pingouin Coton Naturel 8 fils
Pingouin Fil d'Ecosse	Pingouin Fil d'Ecosse
Pingouin Iceberg or Pingouin Pingoland	Pingouin Iceberg or Pingouin Pingoland
Pingouin Laine et Mohair	Pingouin Laine et Mohair
Pingouin Pingolaine 4 ply	Pingouin Pingolaine 4 ply
Pingouin Pingorina	Pingouin Pingorina
Pingouin Type Shetland	Pingouin Type Shetland
Poppleton Bijou Chunky	Poppleton Bijou Chunky
Poppleton Pica or Poppleton Emmerdale Chunky	Poppleton Pica or Poppleton Emmerdale Chunky
Robin Aran or Emu Aran	Robin Aran or Emu Aran
Sirdar Country Style 4 ply	Any 4 ply
Sirdar Country Style D K	Any D K
Sirdar Majestic 4 ply	Any 4 ply
Sirdar Sportswool	Patons Capstan
Mail order or any 4 ply	Mail order or any 4 ply
Mail order or any 3 ply	Mail order or any 3 ply
Mail order	Mail order
Templeton's H & O Shetland Fleece	Elle Shetland D K (50g. balls but requires same no. as pattern)
3 Suisses Aubretia	Mail order
3 Suisses Barbara	Mail order
3 Suisses Suizasport	Mail order
Twilleys Goldfingering	Twilleys Goldfingering
Twilleys Lyscordet	Twilleys Lyscordet
Wendy Mohair	Wendy Mohair
Wendy Shetland 4 ply	Wendy Shetland 4 ply
Wendy Pure Wool D K	Wendy Pure Wool D K

USING THE CHART

Tension: all the patterns were knitted up and checked in the yarns listed in the first column. In many cases these are widely available, but where they are not, the nearest equivalent in both weight, character and appearance has been quoted. When using an equivalent yarn, it is *doubly* important to check your tension, in order to achieve perfect results.

Needles: unless otherwise stated in the chart, use the needle sizes quoted in the pattern.

Yarn: unless otherwise stated in the chart, yarn requirements are as given in the pattern. Individual tension variations may cause fluctuations in amount used.

Addresses: should you have difficulty in acquiring yarn, or want to order by post, the addresses to write to are listed on pages 173 and 176.

NEEDLE CONVERSIONS

U.K. and Australia metric	U.K. and Australia original, Canada, S. Africa	U.S.A
2mm.	14	00
2¼mm.	13	0
2¾mm.	12	1
3mm.	11	2
3¼mm.	10	3
3¾mm.	9	4
4mm.	8	5
4½mm.	7	6
5mm.	6	7
5½mm.	5	8
6mm.	4	9
6½mm.	3	10
7mm.	2	10½
7½mm.	1	11
8mm.	0	12
9mm.	00	13
10mm.	000	15

AMERICAN TERMINOLOGY

Most knitting and crochet terms are identical in English and American usage. The exceptions to this are listed below, with the English term used in the book given first, followed by the American term.

Double crochet (d.c.) = single crochet (s.c.); stocking stitch (st. st.) = stockinette stitch (st. st.); yarn round needle (y.r.n.) = yarn over needle (y.o.n.); cast off = bind off.

Addresses

Continued

PINGOUIN

U.K.
French Wools Ltd.
7–11 Lexington Street
LONDON W1R 4BU
U.K.

Head office and mail orders
Mr R Mesdagh
BP 9110
59061 ROUBAIX
Cedex 1
FRANCE

U.S.A. agent
Promafil Corp. (U.S.A.)
9179 Red Branch Road
COLUMBIA
Maryland 21045
U.S.A.

Australia stockist
The Needlewoman
308 Centrepoint
Murray Street
Hobart
TASMANIA 7000

Canada agent
Promafil (Canada) Ltd.
1500 Rue Jules Poitras
379 ST LAURENT
Quebec H4N 1X7
CANADA

S. Africa agent
Romatex/Yarns and Wools
P.O. Box 12
JACOBS 4026
Natal
S. AFRICA

POPPLETON

U.K.
Richard Poppleton & Sons Ltd.
Albert Mills
Horbury
WAKEFIELD
W. Yorks.
U.K.

U.S.A. agents
Mr D J Brawn
Kendex Corporation
31316 Via Colinas
Apt. No 107
WESTLAKE
California
U.S.A.

Mr Poodt
United Notions
55560 Faulton Industrial Blvd.
ATLANTA
Georgia 30336
U.S.A.

Mr & Mrs F Gordy
4483 North Ardmore
P.O. 11672
MILWAUKEE
Wisconsin 53211
U.S.A.

Australia agent and mail orders
The Craft Warehouse
13 Guess Avenue
ARNCLIFFE
N.S.W. 2205
AUSTRALIA

Canada agent
Mr R Frazer
Milne & Middleton Ltd.
1280 Homer Street
VANCOUVER V6B 2YB
British Columbia
CANADA

S. Africa agent
A & H Agencies
P.O. Box 33454
JEPPESTOWN
Transvaal 2043
S. AFRICA

RED HEART

S. Africa
Mr Bob Theis
Marketing Manager
Patons and Baldwins (S. Africa)
Pty. Ltd.
P.O. Box 33
RANDFONTEIN 1760
S. AFRICA

ROBIN

U.K.
Robin
Robin Mills
IDLE
BRADFORD
W. Yorks.
U.K.

U.S.A. and Canada agent
S R Kertzer Ltd.
257 Adelaide Street West
TORONTO
Ontario M5H 1Y1
CANADA

Australia agent
Mrs Rosemary Mallett
The Needlewoman
308 Centrepoint
Murray Street
Hobart
TASMANIA 7000

S. Africa agent
Intexma Cape (Pty.) Ltd.
P.O. Box 27
OBSERVATORY
Cape 7935
S. AFRICA

SIRDAR

U.K.
Sirdar Ltd.
Flanshaw Lane
Alverthorpe
WAKEFIELD WF2 9ND
W. Yorks.
U.K.

U.S.A. and Canada agent/ distributor
Diamond Yarn (Canada)
Corporation

153 Bridgeland Avenue
Unit 11
TORONTO M6A 2Y6
CANADA

SUNBEAM

U.K.
Sunbeam
Richard Ingham & Co. Ltd.
Crawshaw Mills
PUDSEY LS28 7BS
W. Yorks.
U.K.

U.S.A. agent, for Shantung only
Grandor Industries Ltd.
4031 Knob Hill Drive
SHERMAN OAKS
California 91403
U.S.A.

Australia (stockists for Shantung only)
David Jones
all stores in N.S.W.,
Adelaide, Brisbane

Mail orders, all yarns
Woolfayre Ltd.
120 High Street
NORTHALLERTON
W. Yorks.
U.K.

TEMPLETON'S

U.K. and mail orders
James Templeton & Son Ltd.
Mill Street
AYR KA7 1TL
Scotland
U.K.

U.S.A. stockists
The Little Mermaid
At the Castle
205 East Lawrence Street
APPLETON
Wisconsin 54911
U.S.A.

The Wool Gatherer Inc.
1502 21st Street
WASHINGTON D.C. 20036
U.S.A.

The Wool Shop
250 Birch Hill Road
LOCUST VALLEY
N.Y.
U.S.A.

Canada stockist
House of Heather
Lord Elgin Hotel
OTTAWA KIP 5K8
CANADA

3 SUISSES

U.K.
3 Suisses
Marlborough House
38 Welford Road
LEICESTER LE2 7AA
U.K.

U.S.A. and Canada agent
Bucilla
230 Fifth Avenue

NEW YORK
U.S.A.

Head office and mail orders
Filature de L'Espierres (3 Suisses)
Blvd. des Canadiens
7760 DOTTIGNIES
BELGIUM

TWILLEYS

U.K.
H G Twilley Ltd.
Roman Mill
STAMFORD
Lincs. PE9 1BG
U.K.

Australia agent
Panda Yarns International Ltd.
48–56 Western Street
BRUNSWICK 3056
Victoria
AUSTRALIA

Canada agent
S R Kertzer Ltd.
257 Adelaide Street W.
TORONTO N5H MI
Ontario
CANADA

S. Africa agents
S W Nyman Ltd.
P.O. Box 292
DURBAN 4000
S. AFRICA

Chester Mortonson Ltd.
P.O. Box 1179
JOHANNESBURG 2000
S. AFRICA

VILLAWOOL see PATONS AUSTRALIA

WENDY

U.K.
Wendy International
P.O. Box 3
GUISELEY
W. Yorks.
U.K.

U.S.A.
Wendy Yarns U.S.A.
P.O. Box 11672
MILWAULKEE
Wisconsin 53211
U.S.A.

Australia agent
The Craft Warehouse
13 Guess Avenue
ARNCLIFFE
N.S.W. 2205
AUSTRALIA

Canada agent
Milne & Middleton
1280 Homer Street
VANCOUVER V6B 2YH
CANADA

S. Africa agent
A & H Agents
P.O. Box 33454
JEPPESTOWN
Transvaal 2043
S. AFRICA